Gift of the

Bobby Roberts

Maritime Fund

GIRL
AT SEA

GIRL
AT SEA

*A Story of Courage, Strength, and Growth from One
of the First Women to Serve on US Warships*

JOANNA SPRTEL WALTERS

Skyhorse Publishing

10 9 8 7 6 5 4 3 2 1

Library of Congress Cataloging-in-Publication Data is available on file.

Cover design by Rain Saukus

Print ISBN: 978-1-63450-486-7
Ebook ISBN: 978-1-5107-0162-5

Printed in the United States of America

Dedication

I dedicate this book to my children, Ella Aspen Tree and Ali Bird: may you continue to grow into strong, independent, and gracious young women who have the courage to find the beauty in vulnerability.

To my wonderful parents who have made everything possible and better!

To my best friend, Jen Mendel Pascua, who is part of the family I choose.

And to mi amor, Esteban Acuña Arancibia.

Contents

Preface

As I begin this journey with you, I am in the year of my 20th reunion from the US Naval Academy, 2014. After twenty years, I finally decided that I was ready to dust off my memories, smooth out their edges, and share my story. You will find excerpts from my journals and many other pieces that I have written—these are true snapshots of exactly how I felt as I was living these moments. Most names have been changed to protect people's identities, but the story is true.

Woven throughout my story are a few underlying beliefs and theories on life that I'd like to share with you. The first of these is called the sine wave theory. Sometime in my late teens, I came up with this idea that I have often called upon in different stages of my life. It is such a part of me that it even found its way into my first marriage vows and into my mind as everything was falling apart around me. It is something that I regularly think about when things are going particularly well. *Life is like a sine wave—the amplitude is what you have the courage to risk.*

The amplitude varies from person to person. The majority hover around a comfortable, albeit boring, 5 out of 10. I believe that it takes courage to risk everything (including failure) to shoot for a 10 knowing that you may not make it and may swing all the way down to a 1. I believe that there is beauty in knowing that you have the strength to withstand and bounce back from a 1 and the courage to allow yourself to experience a 10. So I have chosen to live my life literally going for it! That said, I am not advocating being a loose cannon! As I write this, you find me currently bouncing out of a 0 or 1 on an upswing. The key is to never stay in the 0–1 range too long!

Another theory that I have found comforting is the seed planting theory. Having been an athlete pretty much my entire life, I am a big believer in goal-setting and adjustment. I think that it provides you with something to work toward and gauge your progress against. But even beyond that, I think that it's *critical* to allow yourself to dream.

> *Plant your seed.*
> *Water it.*
> *Take good care of it.*
> *Make sure it's in sun and has food.*
> *Dream Big! Dream Small! Dream the impossible! Just allow yourself to stretch and reach beyond what you thought you were capable of . . .*

I believe that thoughts and ideas are often like planting seeds. Your soft hopes and dreams are constantly guiding and directing you even subconsciously when you are not aware of it. I have had so many instances where even merely thinking that "something was cool" has helped to indirectly and subconsciously guide me toward it. Each day, we make thousands of choices—some of them big and some of them everyday mundane choices with seemingly no consequences. The point is that every single small choice adds up and amounts to something much greater than the sum of the parts.

Choose to plant a seed. It starts with a small thought and grows from there. Set a goal. Allow yourself to dream the big, scary, amazing dream. Honestly, there are times that you won't even realize that you are making choices that take you closer to that thought and your desired destination—your subconscious can gently guide you through the sum of all of those little choices. Of course, it also takes action, care, and being deliberate in order to make your dreams a reality.

Allow yourself to chart your own personal course to get there. Some people call this manifesting. I like to surround myself with people who have amazing green thumbs when it comes to their seeds.

Beyond the courage to achieve your dreams, there is also a courage in loving someone. My next theory I call the vase theory.

Everyone has their own precious, priceless vase—much like their own emotional fingerprint. I see a parallel between love and your own special vase.

Many people choose to keep their vases locked up tightly and safely. They rarely ever take their vase out and surely would never put it in the hands of a reckless toddler to watch it shatter into a thousand pieces. Part of maturing is being able to get the glue out in order to put your vase back together after a difficult breakup or challenging life event. I believe that those glue lines can make your vase even stronger than it was at first. Beauty lies in our cracks and scar tissue as they tell the story of when you lived, felt deeply, and had to survive.

To me, really loving someone is when you let them see and hold your fragile vase. The beauty in your apparent vulnerability at allowing someone to see, hold and touch such a big part of you.

In February 1994, I set out on a real mission to seek my own literal vase out. I went to an antique show in Northern Virginia with my sponsor mom, Nora, and found my vase at a small booth among hundreds of antique dealers. It was over one hundred years old and was perfect in every way for me—it was made of metal on the inside (emotionally strong like me) with an intricate, beautiful cloisonné design around its skin of a vibrant hummingbird, greenest of green reeds, and a scarab all surrounded by delicate white. This vase felt right in my hand as I gently spun it around. I made a good choice—especially with its strong metal interior and ability to withstand falls and harsh treatment.

The final theory I'd like to share is called the settling theory. You know when you've got a huge test and everyone's inclination is to cram and pull an all-nighter to make sure you're ready for it? At the Academy, *so many* of my classmates succumbed to this study model. I abhor this idea!

I believe that you should study until it no longer makes sense to you. If you keep catching the book about to fall on your head, notice that you've dozed off in the *Iliad* and thirty minutes have passed with the book soundly on your chest, or you can't see straight or make sense of what you're reading or doing—you need to stop!

You *need* to sleep. Everything will settle in its right place in your mind and be easily called upon when you need it.

Give your mind the gift of rest. It will in turn give you the gift of sifting through everything you've learned and putting it in the right place in your brain to be easily called upon during the exam. Your mind will sift and settle all of the information that may have become jumbled and allow you to succeed in the morning. I didn't always follow this, but more times than not, it worked well for me in an incredibly stressful, pressure-cooker environment.

US Naval Academy
or Bust

Two roads diverged in a wood, and I—I took the one less traveled by, And that has made all the difference.
—Robert Frost

Everyone seems to go to the Naval Academy for a different reason: some following in the footsteps of a father (or mother!); some out to prove what strong, noble warriors they are; some for a higher purpose—what they call their God; others for a free ride to college; and then there was me. Perhaps my reason was not to immediately be willing to die for my country . . . or the idiot standing next to me (as I had to repeatedly chant as a plebe), but rather the more selfish reason of wanting desperately to become the person that I was meant to become—even if that equated to painfully forcing myself to become her!

My journey to the Naval Academy began in my sophomore year of high school. I had a guidance counselor who felt that the Service Academies were one of the best-kept secrets in the country. Where else could you go to one of the most prestigious schools in the country, earn a fantastic education, get paid to go there, and have a meaningful, exciting job guaranteed after graduation? I was sold! The good news was that I had actually been recruited to swim by the Naval Academy, West Point, and the Air Force Academy. By the time I was a sophomore in high school, I had performed really well on the national scene in swimming and was noticed by many college coaches around the country and began receiving serious letters of interest. By my junior year, I had become an All-American, just missed the US Olympic Trials, and placed in the top three at the US Nationals while training with some of the best athletes in the world. Swimming had been a *huge* part of my life and something that I dedicated countless hours to, in and out of the pool.

My guidance counselor, Dr. Guerra, had been the counselor of a star student-athlete who got an appointment to the US Air Force Academy. Dr. Guerra was a huge advocate of all the Academies and helped to plant the proverbial seed for me. Although he was very helpful to me as I was making my decision (go to an Academy *or* one of the best swimming schools in the country?), the truth is that nobody can do all the work necessary to get into an Academy but you.

Many of the girls that I swam with laughed at the Academy letters of interest because they came from extremely liberal families that scoffed at a military education or career—parents who were hippies when they raised their children. My father had been a Marine and I was raised to be patriotic. But attending an Academy was not something that had crossed my mind or been a lifelong goal. I did not grow up memorizing *The Naval Institute's Guide to Ships & Aircraft of the US Fleet* or *Jane's* as some of my classmates had. In other words, I didn't grow up in a military family fantasizing about someday being in the captain's seat. I didn't get inspired by watching *The Right Stuff* or *Magnum, P.I.* or have some compelling family history of attending an Academy. I came from a very solid, upper middle-class family from a very middle-class Chicago suburb called Berwyn, and was an athlete.

My interest ebbed and flowed through my junior year. Although the athlete in me toyed with the idea of swimming for one of the best swimming schools in the country, I couldn't quell the small voice in my head that had been listening to Dr. Guerra. I decided to do the "Early Action Plan" and actually finished the *entire* package the summer *before* my senior year of high school. The entire package included lengthy essays, letters of recommendation, and taking medical tests and physical fitness tests, as well as interviews with my Congressman. This application is *not* for the lazy person. I honestly had no idea what the hell I was getting myself into, to be honest.

Dick Purdy was Navy's swim coach—and was he ever persistent! Ray Bosse was West Point's coach along with his wife, Cheri. I really liked her a lot—she was a Division I backstroker from Nebraska and we had really connected. I thought for certain that I was going to go to West Point and so did Ray and Cheri. They were so certain that they had me in the bag that they stopped calling me and assumed that I was a done deal. What they didn't know was that I was being heavily pursued by Navy.

Just before my birthday, I got a call from the Navy coach. Coach Purdy said, "Happy birthday, Joanna! How would you like this nice birthday present: You got into the academy!" Shortly after that, I received a similar call from Ray Bosse wishing me a "Merry Christmas and a Happy Birthday," but more importantly a "Congratulations for getting into West Point." Both appointments were delivered at my home with much fanfare. They were packaged in such a way that they looked like beautiful gold embossed diplomas (Navy's in a little blue case and West Point's in a little green case) and had the feel of something very significant.

It was such a great feeling to know that I had gotten into both schools and to not have to worry the whole second half of my senior year. On that particular birthday, I was easily at a high 9 on the life scale. I never expected to be faced with having to make such a huge life decision by getting accepted to two of the most prestigious schools in the country. I liked both coaches and didn't quite know what to do. In the end, Coach Purdy's persistence won me over, as I could easily talk myself into Annapolis and being near the ocean since I've always been a huge lover of the water. The real clincher for me was the fact that I believed the academics to be a little stronger at Navy *and* I thought that there were more options available to women. There was also this small, quiet voice that rather liked the option of going Marine Corps if I chose to. So with those things in mind, I accepted the appointment to the Naval Academy.

Berwyn

Dreaming, after all, is a form of planning.
—Gloria Steinem

I sure hit the jackpot when parents were divvied up! My mom's name was originally Julia Margie—though nobody ever called her that. She went by Margie and that nickname suited her just fine. She was a Southside-Chicago bred, tell-it-like-it-is "tough cookie." You always knew exactly where you stood with my mom— good or bad, she let you know. She had the courage to often say what most people would just think but be afraid to verbalize. Margie had to become a fighter at a very young age in order to survive. Margie was a first-generation American born to two immigrants from Slovakia: Anna, a housekeeper, and Joseph, a carpenter and handyman. During the Depression, my mom had to steal food in order to eat. When she was quite young, my mom found her father drunk and passed out on the lawn in front of her house. Little Margie was terrified that her daddy was dead and went into shock. She could not feel the entire right side of her body and became paralyzed with St. Vitus paralysis. Margie couldn't move the right side of her body for close to two years—we all know how mean kids can be when someone is "different."

When she finally overcame the paralysis, she ended up taking to folk dancing and became quite good, often performing around the Midwest and even in Europe. For her to eventually become the "Queen" of her nationality—of the Czechoslovakian people of the Chicagoland area—was a major accomplishment for a girl from the south side of Chicago with a drunk father and cleaning-lady mother who had once been paralyzed.

During the famous Houbi Day Celebration, my mother was asked to lead the parade through the streets of her town. Dressed in traditional costume with a flower wreath in her hair and two horses at her side, she led the parade. By all accounts, this should have been her special day—a day for her alone to shine. There was an excitement in the air as she stepped off. The soft pleats of her Slovak costume swayed and colorful ribbons flowed behind her as she waved at the cheering crowds and smiled warmly. Everything was perfect until she spotted her father sitting off to the side on the gutter of the street with his arm outstretched. Drunk. For a moment, she faltered and wasn't sure what to do.

With conviction and certainty, she stopped. The procession behind her came to halt and watched as she walked over to gently kiss her father on the forehead and help him up. She swallowed hard, picked her head up and turned back to the empty spot between the horses. Margie swiftly went back to her place and was able to gracefully continue leading the parade.

My mom ran a construction company in the '60s and early '70s until she had me. She wasn't afraid to get her hands dirty, be it labor or firing staff. The company she worked for, Ryerson Steel, put up the foundation for the Playboy Club in Wisconsin and the Sears Tower in Chicago. It was through this job that she developed "construction mouth" (she swore quite a bit) and a penchant for smoking in order to fit in and be one of the guys. By the time my mom had met my dad, she was thirty-eight years old while he was ten years younger. She knew that she wanted to have children badly and within two years, they had me very early on Christmas morning in 1972. My mom left her job to be home with me.

I grew up in a small middle-class town called Berwyn about twelve miles west of Chicago. In the '70s and '80s, my neighborhood was a very ethnic community with strong Czech, Slovak, and Polish roots until it began to turn more Hispanic. In fact, the Son of Svengoolie used to broadcast very hokey movies and reviews from Berwyn. Anyone who grew up in the Chicagoland area during the '80s would have remembered the long-haired, scary-looking guy with the annoying voice who opened every show from "Berrrrrwyyyyn." Berwyn was bordered by Cicero, Al Capone's stomping grounds, to the east, Oak Park to the north, Riverside to the west and Stickney to the south. As neighborhoods often do change and "roll" in a certain direction, things got better and better as you either went west or north. I am not at all doing the way in which Rich Koz would enunciate Berwyn justice—it made my city sound like some complete hick town and it became very easy for my peers to remind me where I'm from.

I started grade school at Komensky, a public school about two blocks from where we lived. I liked the school enough until third grade when I got Mrs. Ondrasek. She had just taken a special course on how to improve her teaching skills and decided to break the classroom up into three different groups in an effort to show what she had learned. I'm not sure exactly what the official labeling of each group was, but let's just call it what it really was: the smart kids and her favorites, the ones she didn't quite know what to do with in the middle, and those kids that were constantly disruptive and seemed to struggle with basic skills such as reading, writing, and math. Mrs. Ondrasek had decided to put me into the line-straddling "middle group," stuck between watching her favorites color great pictures and silently read happy books and the over-hyper, class-clown troublemakers work on icky math problems. I was green with envy! I terribly wanted to be in the group closest to the windows and longed to be with the "smart kids." So I began to pay attention to what they did that I wasn't doing. They were generally quiet, respectful, and non-fidgety. Mrs. Ondrasek had accused me of having ants in my pants in the bathroom line just days before, so surely that must have been it!

I began to put more effort into printing neater and re-checked my spelling over and over. I studied hard. *Really* hard. I was pretty darn competitive and didn't like being labeled a limbo kid. So I changed it! About two weeks before the school year was over, she called me and my parents in to talk to her about my progress. I had sweat my way into straight As and finally got moved into the smart group days before the end of the school year. By the time I finally had a window seat, it didn't matter to me anymore.

One could make the argument that her classroom strategy was brilliant, but my mom had had enough of the public school system for a while. In an effort to give me more opportunity, my parents decided to move me into a local private Catholic school. I was to begin fourth grade at St. Odilo's about a mile away.

I ended up attending St. Odilo's from fourth to eighth grade and, as an added bonus, got my first real taste of what cliques felt like. At Odilo's we looked like the unsexy '80s version of a Britney Spears video. We were only allowed to wear green tartan pleated skirts with white bobby socks pulled up to our knees (better not show any skin!) topped with short-sleeved, white cotton collared shirts and a forest-green polyester vest. I hated having to wear the same ugly thing every day. But the uniform was the least of my concerns.

There's always someone who just doesn't fit in and unfortunately, at Odilo's, that was me. At first the jokes centered around me being "Spurtle Gurdle" (a *funny* take on my last name that lacked vowels *and* my size)—I was on the chunkier side despite being a pretty competitive swimmer. It hurt a lot, but I tried to just let it roll off my back as best I could. At first, that seemed to work OK since it was just the dumb boys that were making the jokes and singing the made-up songs.

In the spring of fourth grade, my family took an amazing trip to Hawaii together. We visited both Maui and Oahu and had planned the trip for months—I even did my very first report on Hawaii so that I could learn all about it. My dad and I spent our days snorkeling, swimming, boogie-boarding, playing around on the massive slides, and visiting the early morning tide pools. As a family we explored the more cultural parts of the islands. I did all athletic pursuits with my dad enhanced by my mom's enthusiastic background support. This pretty much became a common theme in my life.

I think that oftentimes we don't see ourselves exactly as we are until something shocks us into reality. For me, that "shock" came in the form of a picture from Hawaii that I couldn't even talk myself into thinking was OK. I remember being very excited to get the pictures back from the big trip. There was one picture in particular that made me cringe when I saw it. My legs did not look at all how they did in my head—they looked massive to me as I peered down at the image. Adding to that was my distaste for shorts that rode up and the feeling of my inner thighs rubbing together in the heat as I wore a dress. I decided then and there to make a change.

How does a nine-year-old just decide to not be *the bigger girl* anymore? I already swam two hours a day on a very competitive team, had begun to see some success placing in the recent State Championships, and ate pretty healthy for the most part (my mom cooked all of our meals from scratch and I very rarely drank soda). Because it never occurred to me to ask anybody, I decided to just watch what my skinny friends did (this method seemed to serve me well in the past). The first thing that I noticed was that if we were eating something together, I had a tendency to be the first one done with what I was eating.

My first private goal became to be the last one finished when we had a snack. I was determined to master this simple task. I soon found out that it wasn't exactly easy or as simple as I thought! My neighbors, skinny gymnast sisters Sharon and Chris Deck, were in my mint green basement, a color I loathed, having a snack and I sat there talking and slowly chewing each and every bite while my stomach quietly rumbled inside of me. With each rumble, it reminded me of how much I wanted to take a bigger bite and stuff it into my mouth. But I didn't. I smiled and ignored the rumble and figured that it would go away eventually. It was a loud hungry rumble that didn't want to be ignored, but it was no match for me—Ms. Stubborn Determination. *Finishing last* was my first small victory. Really tasting my food, chewing it, and eating it slowly became a deliberate, conscious effort for me. I started to eat less and to get full faster as I listened to my body more.

The next thing that I began to notice was what I was putting into my mouth versus what they were putting into theirs. I had been eating a lot more—oftentimes not even because I was hungrier, but more because I had been eating so fast that I never stopped to taste my food . . . or *stopped* when I was full, as opposed to being a constant member of the "clean plate club" that my dad had touted for so many years. The slower I ate, the less I ended up eating and the better choices I made.

That summer, I became a master of controlling myself. I began the extended break at nine and a half years old and a rather high 104 pounds. Not only did I adjust my intake, selection of food, and speed with which I consumed it, but also summer swimming training ramped up considerably with double practices. After swim practice, I'd eat my breakfast and then go about my day. I vividly remember lying on the couch during a lazy, hot Chicago afternoon reading a book when that first annoying pang of hunger would surface. I tried a little experiment to see what would happen if I ignored that nagging hollow feeling. I noticed that if I waited long enough, it'd go away within five to ten minutes for what seemed like quite a while. But then, within an hour or two, *pang* would resurface, bearing its now-starving, angry head and would not leave as quickly as before, refusing to be ignored. So then I'd cave and grab a healthy snack and be on with it!

The combination of self-control, moderation (I still ate the things that I liked, just not as much), and swimming at a very competitive level had amazing results for me. I entered fifth grade weighing about seventy pounds and fitting into the coveted slim jeans. My swimming also benefited greatly as I became stronger, leaner, and faster in the water. My times dropped (along with my weight) significantly as I worked harder and harder each practice and became a force to be reckoned with in Illinois age-group swimming.

It was with this that I entered fifth grade hoping for the fat-joke songs to end. I longed to be one of the first girls picked for sports teams in class, not the last. Competitive team leaders pick their teams based upon athletic ability, while the more social kids pick the popular kids first. At first, my classmates didn't know what to make of my transformation. But mean kids still find a way to be mean. If the fat has gone away, something else becomes the focus. The next couple of years were a blur—I excelled academically and in the pool. But, socially, as I finished up seventh grade things began to change.

I didn't seem to fit into either group of girls that had begun to form—I wasn't silly and I wasn't a slut. I didn't want to fit into either of those groups as I couldn't bring myself to giggle at the letter E (in reference to Bruce Springsteen and the E Street Band) and had no idea what the hell a blow job was. I stood there in this little circle of girls as one girl discussed blow jobs and the other three laughed as if *they* knew exactly what she was talking about. I stood there just fidgeting with my hands and cracked a smile. I didn't want to be the only one not laughing at something that was obviously hilarious. The girls in this group had begun to not only experiment with boys—some of them with much older boys and even with sex—but also with alcohol and drugs. I knew that I had to get out of there as quickly as possible. I was literally saved by the bell.

After school, I went to swim practice as usual. When I finally got home after practice and ate my snack, I really wanted to get to the bottom of what all the fuss was about. I was in our dining room when my dad walked in. I really threw him a zinger when I said "Dad, what's a blow job?"

He looked at me, turned his head away for just a moment—likely trying to not panic or show any distress—spun back around and very quickly and abruptly blurted out, "It's when a woman sucks a man's dick." Just as quickly as he managed to get those words out, he disappeared.

I was completely shocked that these eighth-grade girls were discussing and laughing about blow jobs. I had barely even been kissed at all!

After this incident, I felt funny sitting with any of them at lunch. So I didn't. This choice, though sound, made lunch a particularly difficult time for me.

The room was set up with two very long large tables smack dab in the middle. You either sat at the girl table or at the boy table. No girls *ever* ventured over to the boy table—it was the *never-never land*. This left me in quite the predicament of exactly where to eat my lunch and how to keep myself busy to not feel . . . so alone.

Eighth grade couldn't come to a close fast enough for me. Even though it was hard for me, I learned many important lessons about myself and was ultimately able to do quite well and have fun in high school. The more difficult experiences made me appreciate high school and the good friends I made even more.

Swimming History

I began swimming competitively at the age of four and a half with a small AAU team run by the high school coach, Coach Ellinger. I loved swimming! My mom tried to put me into ballet like all of the other little princess girls, but I was much better suited for swimming and was quite a sight as I forcefully flopped my leg up on the barre in a little pink tutu (almost a precursor to the way in which Junie B. Jones would have done it years later).

I recall hearing Coach Ellinger tell the best swimmer on the men's high school team, Gary Simms, that he "was gonna get you a scholarship." I had no idea what a scholarship was, but I knew that I wanted one if Gary wanted one. Of course, I also had no idea that a coach has no part in getting a swimmer a scholarship except for helping him or her to train hard and achieve their goals. Gary had earned a sixth-place finish in the 50 free at that year's Men's Illinois High School State and got a full ride to a local Midwest college.

I was a pretty strong swimmer in the state of Illinois, often winning my major events at the State Championships and placing in the top three in zoned multi-state events by the age of twelve. I loved the sport to the point that every time I had to print the word "swim" or "swimming," I took care to make it the best looking word on the page. I religiously read every *Swimming World* issue that showed up at my door. I could tell you my times (even now!) from the best practices that I had ever swum. I rarely missed practice and was my own worst critic—I have always been extremely hard on myself.

My mom had to give me *permission* to miss a practice and if I ever did, it was not something that I took lightly.

By the time I was twelve years old, I had made my first Y National Cuts in the 100 fly and in the 100 back. At the time, my dad had just lost his job and money was quite tight. So tight that it became a personal mission of mine to help fund my trip. As a fundraiser, our team was selling candy bars to help raise money. We got to keep ten percent of our sales toward funding our personal trips. I ended up selling two thousand candy bars in order to pay for my plane ticket to Orlando—a hard-earned $200.

Sadly, I ended up getting a severe upper respiratory infection that seemed to stick around for several weeks too long—I couldn't stop coughing no matter what I did, and my mom even resorted to home remedies of me drinking onion and garlic potions. I wouldn't allow myself to miss practice in order to properly heal, so it became a vicious circle. Competing on the national level added a completely new dimension to the sport—suddenly, I was a part of the *big time* in swimming and this was truly my first big meet. I was terribly nervous as I swam my two little events on such a big stage. Being sick didn't help either. I did the best that I could given the circumstances, but ended up not even getting a best time at my first nationals. Although I didn't kill it in the pool, some very important seeds were planted for me! As we watched the finals each night from the bleachers, I decided that someday I wanted to earn a spot in the top eight *myself*. I wondered what the spotlight would feel like on me if I were to walk the length of the pool in my team parka and hear the announcer say *my name* in front of thousands. Every couple of minutes the "human wave" went around the large stadium that looped the pool area as swimmers and fans from all over the country enthusiastically stood up with their hands in the air and their lungs full of cheer. That year, our team had no swimmers qualify for the finals and we all sat there watching the best of the best fight it out for their final positions.

I continued to swim each day with my goals in mind of someday making finals at a big meet. I had been doing double practices and lifting since the age of twelve and had continued to gain strength and speed. I would often go to school with breakfast (a bagel with cream cheese, piece of fruit, and a juice box), lunch (a home-made sandwich, pretzels, fruit, juice box, and note), and a snack. Although I went to school pretty prepared fuel-wise to make it through the day, 10:00 a.m. was always a difficult hurdle to get past as I would physically feel as if I were hitting the wall.

I continued to improve and was a force to be reckoned with in the state of Illinois, but I longed to be on a bigger stage and to really compete. During the Senior Championships Meet in late March 1987, I struck up a conversation with a girl who was a year older than me. Her name was Julie Adams. She was kind of fast, but not the best on her team and not the best in the state. However, what she had told me changed the course of my summer and swimming career.

Julie had been very close friends and teammates with a prominent Illinois swimmer whose family had relocated to Florida and she had relocated teams to the Bolles School Sharks, one of the best athletic prep schools in the country in Jacksonville. At the time, Gregg Troy was the head coach of Bolles and had successfully coached several National Champions and Olympians—he is now one of, if not *the*, most decorated coach in US Olympic history. Julie shared with me her experiences training the summer at Bolles and mentioned that I would come back completely different. What she couldn't have possibly known is that she helped me plant a big seed in my life. The very next day, I had my mom call Coach Troy at Bolles and quickly decided that I wanted to see if I could hack it there.

> *March 23, 1987*
>
> *I'm in history class right now. Last weekend was the Illinois Senior Championships! I had fun and swam pretty well—managed a 2:14 in my 200 fly and a 103.1 in my 100 back. Not bad for being unshaved and un-tapered.*
>
> *Last night, I was evaluating my swimming and attitude and noticed that something's different. I'm no longer nervous swimming next to stiff competition and I'm also no longer scared of a tough practice like I used to be. Of course I'm a little nervous, but I feel as though I'm just as good as they are and have just as good a chance to win. I feel now, that I'm finally established*

as a swimmer. Sasha tried like hell to psyche me out before the 100 fly, but it didn't work out at all! I was really proud of myself. All of my hard work is paying off. Julie Adams and I are becoming pretty good friends. She was telling me about how she went to Florida to train last summer and went super fast. While we were talking, she told me all about her experiences that summer and gave me all the information—a phone number— and my mom is going to call today at 9:30 a.m. I can't wait!

I hope hope hope that I can go this year. It would be a dream come true to be able to rub shoulders with people that are THAT GOOD. I mean, I could really improve. When I'm with people like that—really good—it starts to rub off on me. I mean, I know that I'll work as hard as I possibly can to get myself up with them. Then, I'll be really fast too.

GUESS WHAT?!!! (written after I got home from school and practice) Mom called Coach Troy and they have room for me. YAY!!!!

Training in Florida was a major departure from the norm of club swimming in Illinois and most definitely on my team, the Oak Park Tops. I had essentially chosen to give up my summer to get my ass kicked in Florida. My main goals before heading south to Jacksonville were to make my first Junior National Cuts in the 100 fly and to possibly attend my first Junior National swim meet.

Right after that Senior Championship meet, we began our final countdown to the Y Nationals in Orlando, Florida. We had close to two weeks of hard training left and then would begin our two-week taper to the big meet. Taper for a swimmer is the best time of year— about two to three weeks before your target event, you dramatically cut your swimming yardage down to twenty-five to thirty percent of what you would normally be doing and all focus is on mental preparation, feeling rested, swimming fast, and getting a good feel for the water. For example, if you have the choice between sitting or standing, you sit; between running or walking, you walk. As the workload goes down, the intensity in these shortened practices dramatically increases. For me, taper was the best time of year.

Another benefit of tapering was that you got to shave down for the meet—shave off all hair that stuck out of the suit (not just legs, but arms and back too) in order to feel sleek in the water. I was particularly excited about shaving since I hadn't shaved my legs in months and looked like a hairy beast! We were scheduled to leave for Florida the week of April 18, 1987, and return after the conclusion of the meet on April 26. I had big goals for the meet and hoped that this would be *my year* to make the finals and "jump" into the big time. Unfortunately, I was also battling another upper respiratory infection (déjà vu from the previous year's Nationals) and missed about a week of our taper.

Although my relationship with some of the girls on the team was OK most of the time, it became strained and left me feeling alone and left out. They all went to the same high school and trained together year round, OPRF (Oak Park River Forest), while I went to neighboring Morton West. My parents couldn't afford to move into that school district as they had planned to and I went to a different high school—a much more middle-class high school. Although we had all virtually grown up together and shared many sleepovers and parties over the years, things changed as we aged and the stakes in the pool got higher. Many of the girls came from a lot of money and were a little stuck up. But, more than that, we were all incredibly competitive with each other in our events and in every single practice leading up to the grand finale of the season.

The best way to say it is that the team was like *Mean Girls* on steroids, where different people were left out at different times. The coach, Jim Kesslering, even resorted to a "bitch and roses" session before the start of every Monday afternoon practice where all the girls on the women's team could air out their issues with each other and we could enter the water with no internal issues. This seemed to work except in the nastiest of cases where the bitches and roses session lasted the entire two-hour practice.

I wanted badly to fit in with the girls on the team, but didn't truly know exactly what that entailed until we were in Florida for the National Championships. I was acutely aware of the sheer quantity of expensive makeup and jewelry that most of the girls on the team had—some had so much that I was shocked that their parents would knowingly pay for thirty of the expensive five-dollar lipsticks from the grocery store, let alone the same in all other makeup types. This doesn't even take into account the obscene amount of jewelry that they all had. What I didn't realize until I was finally allowed into their little clique was that they had taken the swim team aspect one step further to a shoplifting team.

The girls would enter a store and one would "case" it to see where the cameras and mirrors were while the others innocently browsed. Although not anywhere near a pool, the competitive spirit burned fiercely in this clique as it was a game to see who could come out with more loot from each store. It became evident that their parents didn't spend hundreds of dollars on all of their makeup and jewelry—they had stolen it. What began as a freshman prank to steal packs of gum during the swim team initiation became a full-blown addiction for many of them.

I'm embarrassed to say that during that trip, I wanted to fit in so badly that I too took a couple of things from the unassuming shops on the strip near our pool. I was horrified at myself for the adrenaline rush it produced inside me as my palms sweated and heart raced through the rush of the act. I hated myself for it and vowed to never ever do it again and didn't.

> *April 26, 1987*
>
> *I write to you on the plane headed back to Chicago. We took off only seconds ago. I'm a little sad as I write this because I really wanted to do better than I did. But, when I think about it, I did pretty good under the circumstances of missing the four most important days of our taper. I was in tears yesterday. I mean, I got all best times, but I know that I could have done much better. I ended up getting a 59.7 in the 100 fly, a 102.4 in the 100 back and a 2:11.21 in the 200 fly. I think that I could have been faster if I didn't miss that week. I haven't had a good taper in almost two years. I know that someday I'll be up there and look back on these rough times and remember.*
>
> *Things for me managed to get better toward the end of the week at Nationals with the girls. I mean, I was included more, but then as the week went on it didn't seem to matter to me as*

much anymore. I was doing things with all of my other friends from the other Illinois teams.

I never told you about how they all steal, ALL OF THEM, and I was so stupid that I followed right with them. Yes, I did the shameful thing of stealing things. I'll NEVER do it again in my whole life. I felt so bad. They all do it all the time. One of the girls, who I must admit seemed to have impressive style and taste, took almost the entire store! This was the first time that I ever did it in my life. I felt so bad and ashamed of myself.

As soon as I got home, my mom went through my bag and what I came back with and immediately knew that she didn't give me *that much* money to buy stuff. She questioned me and made me swear on my grandmother's sacred holy bible that I would never ever do such a thing again. I learned a very valuable lesson about not ever again compromising myself and my values in order to fit in.

Training at the Bolles School, Jacksonville, Florida

After much anticipation, my dad and I boarded the plane to Jacksonville, Florida—he flew with me to meet the coach and left the next day in order to make sure that I was properly situated. My original roommate was to be a girl about my age named Jean who was not swimming with the Senior Team, but still swimming with the age groupers. We all went out to dinner together that evening before I hit the water for the first time with the Bolles Senior Team.

Much to my surprise, pretty much everyone on the Senior Team was older than me—and not just by a little bit. There was one girl who was within six months of my birthday named Nicole Haislett who was a sprint freestyler (and eventual three-time Olympic Gold Medalist) and another girl about a year older than me who was also a butterflyer named Laura DeVore. Many of my teammates were returning college students and international students who boarded and went to school at Bolles. I had missed the first part of our ramp-up in yardage sarcastically dubbed "hell week." Coach Troy's plan was to ramp us up in yardage to a peak of over 22,000 meters for the sprint lane—for those of you that aren't swimmers, 22,000 is a lot of yardage (over ten miles)—and then slowly back off on yardage until our official taper would begin and count down to our biggest races.

The first day of practice, I walked down to the parking lot to meet my ride, Ginger Petersen (a junior in college who was a prominent backstroker and also living in the dorms), over to the pool at 0520 as practice was to begin at 0530. It was dark and a little muggy outside as we rode the five minutes to the outdoor long-course pool. I had little butterflies in my stomach as I wondered what I would be in for that day at practice. As I hit the water and felt its coolness around my body, I decided that I would do whatever it took to keep up with them all—even if it meant sprinting through warm-up. As the practice progressed with unbelievable intervals and distances, I continued to hold on and managed to survive through the end. That first practice, we swam close to 10,000 meters and were scheduled to swim another two hours in the afternoon, preceded by an hour-long land training session.

I was completely exhausted, but also didn't want anyone to know just how much my body was hurting, being the new person on the team. I was the last to arrive for summer training and most of the team had been in the water together for over a week and had adjusted to the conditions. I was fortunate to not miss hell week, but would have to muscle through it somehow without the base that they all had going in. After practice we poured into the cafeteria and emptied it of its contents. You don't want to mess with the hungry swim team with regards to not having enough food!

That afternoon, we assembled at the track just outside the adjacent short course meters outdoor pool on campus. I had never run as part of my swim training before and this was a new experience for me. The entire team began dry-land training with a four-mile Indian Run around the track. Each time you dropped to the back of the line, you had to sprint up to the front of the line and repeat the cycle again and again. I didn't mind this part so much, but going from running no miles to four miles was a little challenging for me—especially in the heat and humidity of Florida.

After the run, we had to do a series of exercises *perfectly* before we were released to the pool. Specifically, we had to do 100 military-style "hello dollies" and "flutter kicks." The only way to continue on to the next exercise was to have the entire Senior Team do all 100 without a heel hitting the deck. If one heel hit the deck, we had to start over. Inadvertently, by the time that it was all over with, we had done close to 500 of each exercise with the entire team screaming and sweating in pain by the end. We all hurt together, bled together, ate together, and celebrated together. After this grueling land work-out, we swam another 8,000-plus meters during the afternoon work-out. At any chance of rain, the team would collectively pray for thunder and lightning to somehow lighten our load.

I barely managed to make it through my first day and stumbled up the stairs to my room completely exhausted and wondering what in the world I had gotten myself into. The second day, we only had one morning practice followed directly by an hour and a half of heavy weight lifting with the afternoon off before we were to reach our peak yardage on Wednesday. When I got to the weight room, I was told to not only follow Laura Devore around the gym, but to lift exactly the amount that she lifted on each exercise. Laura was an extremely strong butterflyer and freestyle sprinter who had qualified for the Senior Nationals in the 100 fly the year before and was one of the premier butterflyers on the team—she was one of the fastest girls in the state and in the country. While I had been lifting since I was twelve, I had never lifted *quite* that heavy. The only way that I could make it through each set of fifteen reps was to imagine myself out of my body on the ceiling watching someone else go through the pain as my already fatigued muscles were screaming at me. It was quite existentialist and something that I called upon later many times.

Having to follow Laura in the gym was an interesting experience because it also seemed to put some pressure on her. I got the sense that she felt a little threatened by me and was worried that I might give her competition. The coach intentionally set up the dynamic and it worked in both of our favors and created a small, healthy rivalry. Eventually, I was able to complete the weight reps without existentialism—after a few weeks of gaining strength.

The rest of the day we pretty much had free, but all that I could manage was laying out for a little bit, reading, and eating. The next day, only my third at Bolles, was the hardest training day that I would *ever* experience in my life. We swam 22,000 meters that day—and

I was in the sprint lane! Somehow I managed to survive the day's worth of practices and was still breathing in and out by the time I fell into bed. The truth was that I had never been away from home in such a physically demanding environment before and was wrestling with the pain that I felt all over my body . . . and I missed my parents who had always been my behind-the-scenes support. My room was on the fourth floor and even making the steps required a concerted effort and focus—I often stopped in the middle for my legs to stop screaming at me. Our weekly training regimen looked like this:

- Mondays, Wednesdays, and Fridays:
    - Morning swim practice in long course meters: 5:30–7:30
    - Dry-land work: 3:00–4:00 p.m. (four-mile run; calisthenics and core exercises to perfection)
    - Afternoon swim practice in short course meters: 4:00–6:00 p.m.
- Tuesdays and Thursdays:
    - Morning swim practice long course meters: 6:00–8:15 a.m.
    - Weights: 9:00–10:00 a.m.

I found myself fantasizing about being back home and even wanted to cut my six weeks at Bolles short.

> *June 17, 1987*
> *I'm so confused! I want to go home, but if I do, I'd feel so stupid unless I was here at least three weeks. Coach Troy is an amazing coach, but I don't know. I'm SO DEAD and tired that it's almost amusing. I've never felt this way before!*
> *I never realized how hard it could be with practices and all. It wouldn't be so bad if I could see my parents at the end of each day. I miss them so much that I could almost cry. I never knew that I'd even DREAM about them. But, if I went home, what would people say? How would I feel about myself? I know that what other people think shouldn't matter to me, but the truth is that it does sometimes. I bet they'd all think that I was stupid and way too young and naïve. That I have to go home to mommy.*

The ironic thing is that I do. I don't know—this whole thing is TOUGH. I wonder what if I only stayed through Regions?

My body HURTS. Everyone here is so much older than me too. Sometimes, I just feel so alone here. I remember how I was so excited and bragging about how fast I'd get and everything. Now, I'm EATING it! I feel so bad.

Want to know what I don't understand? Julie Adams made it seem like she and Gretchen were such great friends, but when I told Gretchen about Julie, she acted sort of pissed off. Then, it seemed as though everyone was making fun of me just because I was asking if they knew her. I guess that I was just talking about her because it was an easy way to make conversation. I had hoped to use it as a bridge to make new friends, but that clearly wasn't the right bridge. I didn't know ANYBODY when I got there. Man, this is hard!

In spite of how bad I felt, I didn't know if I could forgive myself for leaving such an amazing opportunity willfully. So, I swallowed the pain deep down inside of me and continued to push forward. The first weekend, we had a swim meet in Gainesville, Florida, and I managed to do quite well in all of my events *and* got to know my teammates better. I made some new friends and began to feel like the training was somehow doable and that I was no longer suffering alone.

I was training with the following swimming legends: David Zubero (1980 Olympic Silver Medalist from Spain in the 100 back), Anthony Nesty of Suriname (who touched out Matt Biondi in the 100 fly during the 1988 Seoul Olympics by one one-hundredth of a second), Martin Zubero (1992 Olympic Gold Medalist in the 200 back for Spain), Nicole Haislett (three-time US 1992 Olympic Gold Medalist), Gregg Burgess (1992 US Olympic Silver Medalist in the 200 back) and several other world-ranked athletes. Obviously, Coach Troy's training methods worked well. During the stroke sets, I'd get to swim in Anthony's lane and battle the wave behind his fly kick— his kick was so strong that it left a massive wave behind him and was difficult to maintain a smooth stroke. Somehow I gutted it out.

I changed roommates—my new roommate became Ginger, the junior collegiate backstroker. She was uncomplicated and very easy to live with, plus she had a refrigerator! My life became much less filled with drama and I could focus on surviving the next two weeks of my taper which was no small feat. I loved to taper. Coach Troy commented on how fast I was looking in practice and I could feel a difference too.

> *July 9, 1987*
> *I feel really great in the water! SUPER GREAT! I can't wait until tomorrow when I get to swim my 100 fly. I haven't ever felt this smooth and strong. Can you believe that on Saturday I'll have been here a month?! Coach Troy said that there's no way that I'd miss my Junior Cuts. He even said that "I might make a Senior Cut!"*

That evening, I shaved down my body and was finally rid of the long "barbarous" hair that was all over my legs—not a very attractive summer look! The process of shaving down was sacred for most swimmers that grew up in the '80s and a *huge* event. I went to bed imagining the perfect race, from the whistle blowing to getting out of the pool with a Junior Cut (or senior) time. Somehow I managed to get some rest and when I woke the next day, everything came together perfectly for me. In the prelims, I felt incredibly strong, smooth, and powerful in the water. I took out my first 50 pretty strong, but not an all-out sprint so that I still had some energy left in my tank to bring the last 50 home. I remembered to shut my eyes on the turn and draft on the lane lines off the girl next to me. I blasted into wall at the finish and looked up at the clock with excitement and surprise. I had to do a complete double take of my time—I looked at the clock, looked back at my lane, and then back at the clock in disbelief—because I had dropped over two seconds and had not only made my Junior National Cuts, but was within a second of my Senior National Cuts in a very tough field and even earned a spot in the finals. I could barely eat anything between prelims and finals and was astounded that I was swimming *in the same water at the same time* as the Olympian Angel (Myers) Martino. I called my parents briefly to tell them the news and could hear their joy from thousands of miles away—I wished that they could have been there to see me swim that fast. I ended up getting another best time in finals by a couple hundredths and hit the wall eighth. I was exhausted, but thrilled with the results and watched in awe as Angel exited the pool to the waiting TV cameramen and interviewers.

During that meet's regular competition, I just missed cuts in the 100 back, 200 back, and 200 fly. I ended up time-trialing the 100 back and was able to make Junior Cuts in that event! I was very happy and planned to try the 200 fly again in a time trial since I was so close to the cut. I felt invincible in the water and for the first time, could see a clear path toward swimming greatness and finally felt that I was fast.

> *July 11, 1987*
> *I always wondered what it would feel like to have Junior Cuts and be close to Seniors. Now I finally know! I feel the same, but slightly more confident in myself. Now I know that I can be as good as I ever wanted to if I'm willing to do the work. I swam with some of the fastest women in the world and got 8th! I never thought I'd ever get to meet, let alone swim with, some of these people.*

Reaching My Swimming Goals

After that summer of training at Bolles, my body changed—a lot. I left Chicago a lean fourteen-year-old and returned an extremely strong athlete with new muscles and Junior Cuts to boot. I also came back much less naïve and was focused on my swimming goals. My perspective had dramatically changed training with Gregg Troy and the Bolles School Sharks. I became aware of all that was possible with the sport and also had hard-won knowledge about what it would take to accomplish those goals. I realized that none of the swimmers on my club team even had Senior National cuts on their radar screen, let alone the US Open or the Pan American Games. And . . . I also lacked the maturity to tactfully handle that knowledge without sounding stuck up or full of myself.

I continued to improve that year and went into the spring Y National Training in the best shape of my life. One day during our taper, the coach, Jim, called on me to do a "get out swim." In this particular challenge, if I could do a 2:12 in the 200 fly in practice, the entire team would "get out" of practice that day. I had about a minute to prepare as he sprang it upon me directly after warmup. I didn't have much time to get nervous, and instead just stepped on the blocks and waited for him to start me. I began the 200 feeling smooth and strong. I didn't take it out too fast and managed to hold on. I think that the coach was as surprised as the entire team was when I hit the wall at 2:12. Everyone was excited as they didn't have to swim practice that afternoon and I was stoked because I had matched my best time *in practice*. If I could match my best time in practice, what would I do at Nationals in less than two weeks when I was shaved and tapered?

I finally reached my goal of making the finals at the Spring Y Nationals—in almost all of my events! I was in the best shape of my life and my swimming showed it as we arrived in Florida for the tail end of our taper and the beginning of the meet. Although the relays were pretty much set, the fly and back positions could be changed based upon how we all did in our individual events. Relays are the only team event in swimming, where four women (or men) compete together with each person doing a different leg or part of the race. Going into the meet, I was not slated to be on a relay and had to earn my position. I knew that I wanted to be on that relay more than anything and hoped that my training would pay off and that I could earn a spot in either the backstroke leg or the fly leg.

Although we had all swum together for over five years, the team was very competitive and catty, especially the closer we got to the meet. The two girls on the team that I was competing against for a spot on the relay had very strong personalities and acted as the leaders of the "Mean Girls" clique—Sasha was a butterflyer and Cass was a backstroker. Both were set to be on the relay *unless* I beat them in their events and earned a position. While Rainne and I had had a tumultuous best friend/adversary relationship over the years, she had spent much of her time on the outside looking into their group—when it suited them they allowed her in, and when it didn't they would talk behind her back and make fun of her. Despite this, she still wanted badly to be a part of them since they were on the same high school record-setting state championship team and, well, the cool group *is* the cool group even if it requires doing some things you're not completely proud of at the end of the day.

> *April 16, 1988*
>
> *Well, I'm finally here—FLORIDA! My mom gave me three small violets when I left home for good luck. Sort of like what she did for me last summer when I left for Bolles. I kept them and now they smell really nice and make me feel not so far away from her.*
>
> *Swimming is going really well—today was our first day back in the water at the Justus Aquatic Center (God, I love this pool—IT'S SO FAST!). Today, I did a 13.5 for a 25 back and a 12.7 for a 25 fly, but it felt SO SMOOTH! I know what I have to and want to do to get where I want to get. I want so badly to look up at that clock and to be surprised and happy. Seniors would be awesome. My stroke's totally back. Now, it's up to me to be as good as I let myself be!*

My 25 times were very fast and enough to really get Sasha and Casss scratching their heads as they both knew that their relay spots were in jeopardy. My 25 back was just a tenth slower than Cass's and my 25 fly split was faster than Sasha's. My first events of the meet were on April 20—the 200 fly and the 100 back. I could barely contain myself and tried hard to get enough rest and do everything in my power to be ready. Apparently, those fast 25 times had really gotten to the girls because as I was falling asleep, they all barged into my room on the night of the 17th to have an "important conversation."

Rainne and I had talked during the first day of the meet about the relays and she told me how they were "pretty much set." She knew that I wanted desperately to earn a spot and she wanted desperately to earn a permanent spot in their Mean Girls Cool Group. So she told them every detail of what we had discussed. The Mean Girls were out for blood and wanted to make sure that I was completely aware of who was running the show. The fact that they were even discussing the relays and how "set" they were meant that they both were completely threatened by me. It took me a little bit of time to digest what ensued as all that I could feel in the beginning was completely alone and hurt, not to mention tired and groggy.

Cass began the conversation with, "I know that you said you hate things that are unfinished and I think there's something we all ought to talk about."

She then proceeded to tell me about how "a tenth is what makes the difference." In a final race, absolutely! A hundredth makes the difference. But in terms of measuring ability, we both could see the rather large elephant in the room—the open spot on the relay.

Then Sasha decided that it was her turn to step in and she said that "things with me weren't exactly peachy . . . as if you haven't noticed, we don't get along too well with you and obviously you don't get along too well with us. As if you haven't noticed, we've got exactly what we want—we've pretty much got all the friends that we want and you're not on our top list of priorities."

Although the personal attack hurt me quite a bit and made me really question if I wanted to continue swimming on that team in the future, it also fueled my competitive fire and made swimming even more important to me (as if that were possible!). I hung out with all of my friends on the other teams and poured everything into my races.

My first day of competition was on April 22, about mid-way through the meet, where I swam the 200 fly and the 100 back. The 200 fly was first and I was quite nervous—it was my toughest race to prepare for mentally and the most grueling physically. If not swum properly, the 200 can really kick your ass. About thirty minutes before my race, I met Jim at the designated rub-down area where all the coaches from teams around the country were getting their swimmers ready for their big events. I had my Walkman blasting New Order and was overcome by the smell of wintergreen as the butterflies began to build deep within my stomach. Jim said very little as he sprayed the wintergreen solution onto by back and rubbed it into my newly shaved skin. Less than ten minutes later and I was back in my team parka, headed to the blocks with cap on and goggles at the ready on my forehead.

That particular race ended up being my best 200 fly ever. Once the whistle blew and I stepped up on the blocks, I was filled with a little bit of everything: excitement, fear, focus—and it all converged at that very moment. There was complete silence as the starter announced, "This is heat eight of the women's 200 yard butterfly, that's eight lengths of the pool butterfly. Swimmers, take your marks."

I fluidly bent down and grabbed the blocks with my hands as my left foot shot back into the track start position waiting for the gun.

Bang!

Everything fell away from me as I hit the cool water and felt completely strong, fluid, and in control. I managed to contain my excitement and how great I felt and split the "perfect race" of:

- First 50: 30 seconds
- Second 50: 32 seconds
- Third 50: 32 seconds
- Fourth 50: 32 seconds

For a final time of 2:06.18 and a spot in the finals. When I surged into the wall and searched the clock for my lane, I had to do a double-take because the time was *amazing* for me and the feeling of *swimming out of my head* was well worth the wait. I almost couldn't believe what I had just done!

The 100 back was next on my agenda and I missed breaking a minute by less than one-tenth of a second. I had beaten Cass in the 100 back and thought that I had just eked into the consolation finals in sixteenth position. Regardless of what happened now with the 100 fly, I had just earned a spot on the relay! I was completely stoked. I spent the rest of the day trying to relax and not think too much—which proved to be quite a challenge. My parents were not there to keep me grounded and I missed them terribly, plus it would have been great to pick my dad's voice out of thousands during the race. I was the first swimmer from our team to make the finals in an individual event and I was finally getting to fulfill one of my secret goals from two years ago.

We arrived back to the pool at 4:45 p.m. for warm-ups and the meet was to begin at 6:00 p.m. I slipped into the water with opaque panty hose on under my suit to provide a little bit of drag and had re-shaved my body just to make sure that no hair had grown in the past day. I had never swum in such a venue—all lights were focused on the pool with the rest dark—it felt almost like a stage where all eyes were on us. I began to warm-up for both the 100 back and the 200 fly when Jim ran up and told me that I had been seventeenth by two-hundredths of a second in the 100 back and would only be swimming the 200 fly.

This was my second race in the big time after last summer's Tuscaloosa Regions final in the 100 fly when I was with Bolles. The feeling was one of the best ever as I walked along the side of the pool with the spotlight on me and waited for my name to be announced to the crowd as I shook out my arms and legs and waved. I put my goggles on, pushing the fear from my mind. This second race was about four-tenths of a second slower than my morning swim, but respectable in such a tough field with so much pressure *and* I still had my best event to come.

I swam my 100 fly on the last day of the meet along with the medley relay. In the 100 fly, I qualified for the finals in fourth position and just missed my Senior Nationals cuts by less than two-tenths of a second and ended up swimming the fly leg on the relay. I was thrilled to have earned a spot on the relay, but had secretly hoped for another chance to break a minute in the 100 back. In the finals, I got third place in my 100 fly and had the opportunity to shake future US Olympic Silver Medalist Janel Jorgensen's hand as we received our medals. I was very happy with the experience and looked forward to training for the summer and, hopefully, the US Olympic Trials for the upcoming 1988 Summer Olympics in Seoul, South Korea.

April 24, 1988
Well, it's all over, unfortunately. Actually, I really don't know exactly how I feel about it. I'm glad because of the pressure finally being released and I loved swimming—I would have given up a tan any day for that feeling. Personally, I think it's the best feeling in the world! I want to cry and be happy at the same time.

My 200 fly didn't go very well in the finals. I choked. I don't even know how to explain it. I was nervous, scared, happy and in awe at the same time. I'm so glad that I got to swim in the final heat. It made my 100 so much easier. I choked in the 200 because I couldn't believe that I was good enough to swim with them . . . next to the best. But in the finals I choked and went four-tenths slower and moved down four places. But it's a learning experience and I'd never trade it. Subconsciously, I knew in order to keep my place I'd have to go a 2:04. With another taper I should be able to make Seniors and that 2:04.

In my 100 fly, I got third and missed Seniors by eighteen-hundredths of a second. I know I could have done a 56—I did on the relay! In the waiting room, I was talking to Janel Jorgensen—she was very nice and seemed to be every bit a true champion. I hope that someday I can be just like her. Now, I've got my foot in the door and what I do with it is up to me. Also, during our awards ceremony, the top three in each event got a poster and a letter inviting us to the YMCA All Star Training Camp at the US Olympic Training Center in Colorado Springs June 15–26. If I'm accepted, I'll definitely go. I'm so excited to be included in such a thing! It'd be really tough training with doubles every day and many lactic acid tests.

Oh, our medley relay also got third place at Y Nationals and dropped two seconds between prelims and finals. I was so happy to be a part of it!

After two weeks off of swimming, I was ready to get back in the water and into shape for the summer season. I enjoyed the time off and was able to go out more with friends and explore more of a social life, but I yearned to be chlorinated (back in the water). I was able to pick up where I left off at Nationals and regained my strength quickly. That summer, my schedule was insane:

- Ride bike to morning swim practice 6:40 a.m.
- Morning swim practice 7:00–9:00 a.m.
- 8:45 a.m. ride bike to job of teaching swim lessons
- 9:00 a.m.–noon: teach swim lessons to little kids + privates

- Ride bike home and try to eat something
- Ride bike back for (Mon/Wed/Fri) weights and dry-land work 3:00–4:00 p.m.
- Afternoon long course swim practice 4:00–6:00 p.m.
- 6:15 p.m., Mom picks me up and puts bike in Subaru and drives me home. Eat. A lot.

Whew! I'm exhausted just reading the schedule above. Somehow, I managed to thrive in that environment and I was able to match my previous summer's best time in the 100m fly before my taper while wearing two suits. My focus and goal was to make the US Olympic Trials to be held in mid-August. Because my parents couldn't afford both trips to combined Junior/Senior nationals and the Olympic Trials, they opted to stay home for the Junior/Senior meet in hopes of all of us attending the Trials together a week later. If by some chance I didn't manage to make my cuts, we were headed on vacation together—win/win!

> *July 17, 1988*
> *Taper begins on Thursday!! TAPER is the MAGIC WORD because I ALWAYS go crazy on taper. I'm starting to feel my strokes again and feel very smooth and strong. If there's one event that I know that I can swim well in, it's the 100m fly! It's going to be so much fun—especially looking up at the clock. That's the best feeling! Being happy and surprised at the same time. The whole key is believing that you're good enough to be in the top eight. It's the passion in your eyes and the acceptance of the pain that surges you forward. Sometimes, I wonder what I'm doing here, but it all is answered in the end because when you get the feeling of satisfaction, it makes all the pain worth it ten-fold.*
> *God . . . I HOPE I make it. We leave for Orlando, Florida in eleven days for the combined US JR/SR Nationals.*

This meet was the last meet in the United States before the US Olympic Trials where the United States would pick the Olympic Team for the impending 1988 Seoul Olympics. Literally, this was the last stop. The meet was held at the Justus Aquatic Center again—a pool that I had a lot of big meet experience in. The field was incredibly competitive and I ran into all of my old Bolles School training friends and Coach Troy at the meet. It was fun to catch up with everyone, but there was little time as we were all incredibly focused on the task at hand—making trials.

My club coach, Jim, was the Mean Girls high school coach and was very close to all of the girls on the team. Not only had he coached them all since they were ten years old, but he had personally led them to the team's first Illinois High School State victory. I found myself feeling like an outsider looking into the inner circle, which is a difficult place to be with your coach. I never felt like I had his full support and always sensed that he wanted Sasha and Cass to do better. He encouraged them in ways that he didn't encourage me.

I swam my 200m fly and my 100m back at JR/SRs *adequately*, but didn't set the pool on fire with my performance. The 200 fly is a very difficult event that requires perfect execution of your plan in order to swim it well. In fact, I felt amazing the first 100 of my 200 fly, but did not swim a smart race. I took it out too fast and wasn't able to hold onto my stroke the last 75 meters and ended up dying. If I had swum the first 100 even a second slower, I would have been able to have enough gas left in my tank to finish strong.

There were two days between my 200 fly and my 100 fly. I wrestled with the desire to do the 200 again in a time-trial just to prove to myself that I could do better. I was scared and my coach didn't really help me deal with it as he had the other girls on our team. Cass had swum her 200m back similarly and our coach encouraged her to do it again smarter. She ended up time time-trialing it at least once and dropped over four seconds in her time. The 200 fly gnawed at me those two days as I watched everyone else swim their events—and so did the fact that my coach didn't care either way if I swam it again while I watched him work hard to convince Cass that it was worth it for her to try again. Increasingly throughout the meet, I questioned my longevity on that team.

The truth of the matter was that I didn't want to risk doing anything that would possibly hurt my chances in the 100m fly on the last day of the meet and I didn't have anyone in my corner to assure me that everything would be OK either way. My parents were

2,000 miles away and required lots of quarters to talk to them on a pay phone. August 4, 1988, felt like the culmination of everything that I'd been training for all these years—my own personal moment of truth. I woke up early and immediately felt the butterflies in my tummy. I could barely manage a half a piece of bread during that early morning breakfast and accidentally left my racing paper race suit in my room. I didn't realize the swimsuit mistake until after warm-ups when I went to go put it on for my race. Although several of the Mean Girls had their paper suits with them and were done swimming, no one offered to let me use theirs. In fact, they reasoned that they didn't want me to "stretch theirs out" even though I was smaller than most of them.

I was disappointed at the "no paper suit" since I wanted this race to be perfect. But even a paper suit couldn't stand in the way of me that day! The meet was winding down, but I was ready to go. Up until this point, no one on our team had made finals in an individual event or relay event. I was hungry, literally and figuratively . . . and ready to go for it. I met Jim in the rub-down area for my dose of his special wintergreen concoction and listened to him as he described the perfect race.

As I stood behind my lane watching the heats before me go, I did the swimmer shake and took off my parka, watching the heat before me enter the water. My skin was hot and tingly and my stomach was abuzz with butterflies as I watched the girls in front of me hit the wall and silently watched them exit the water. I had just enough time to glance at the clock (and their times) before I heard my whistle blow, the signal to step up on the block.

The moment before the announcer begins is such a pregnant pause where you almost feel stripped and vulnerable . . . waiting for the ritual of his words and the gun.

"This is the women's 100m butterfly. That's two lengths of the pool butterfly. Swimmers, take your marks."

Bang! went the gun.

I flew off the blocks with a fury and immediately did three powerful fly kicks to the surface. Suddenly, it was just me and the water I loved so much—and the beginning guitar riff of "Lola" cycling through my consciousness. I did three strokes until I took my first breath and settled into my stroke. I felt smooth and strong. Out of my peripheral vision, I could see the girls on either side of me and fought the urge to completely sprint the first 50. As I got closer to the wall, I could see my friends screaming for me at the end of my lane and felt my speed build into the wall. I shut my eyes on the turn as Coach Troy had taught me, and began to race home. I couldn't see the girls anymore and knew that all I had to do was put my head down and surge to the wall. The second my hands pounded into the wall, I spun around to match my lane to the large clock to see how I had done. I got a 1:04.29 and was within four-tenths of a second of the Olympic Trial cuts.

I had been watching all of the other heats and knew that nobody had made Olympic Trial cuts yet, but this was a very tough field. I ended up tying for seventh place in the prelims and earned a spot in one of the closest finals ever. There was only two-tenths of a second between first and seventh. That morning, I still had to swim the fly leg of the 400m medley relay—less than fifteen minutes after the 100m fly prelim race. I hopped into the diving well and warmed down for a few minutes and met my team for the relay. Because relays only swam once, we were not seeded high enough to swim in the finals.

Although we didn't all love each other, we worked well together and all got best times on the relay. I ended up splitting the fastest relay split of the fly leg of the meet (of all teams) with a 1:03.2 and was thrilled. I still had to somehow make it through the afternoon and prepare for my final race. It was very hard for me to eat anything (or keep it down) as I was terribly nervous. I missed the emotional support of my parents and wished that I were part of a more supportive team. I think the Mean Girls were angry that I had made finals and refused to talk to me, which left me alone with my thoughts most of the day—kind of a dangerous place to be.

It was finally time to head back to the Aquatic Center for warm-ups for my final race. While I was warming up, the team had all gone and gotten dinner—sadly, nobody really thought about getting anything for me. Warm-ups went by quickly and all I had to do was wait to be called to the ready room for my last shot at Trials. All of my protruding skin was freshly shaved and wintergreened up as I headed to the ready room—a very small room where all eight of us sat together. It was interesting for me to be there and observe everyone's unique reaction to stress as well as my own. My eyes briefly moved from girl to girl and wondered which one of us would win this tight race since only two-tenths of a second separated us all. Finally, an official opened the door and all the lights were turned out in the natatorium. The pool was lit up with spotlights on the side as we walked the entire length of the pool and prepared to hear our short bios and names announced in front of thousands.

I wore a funky bright blue and gold jumper as I nervously followed the line of women to our lanes. The consolation finalists had just finished and it was our turn to show our stuff. I was in Lane 1 since I had tied for seventh. I could hear the announcer's deep voice as he said, "In Lane 1, making her first appearance, is Joanna Sprtel of the Oak Park Tops." I waved, removed my bold outfit and took in a large hot breath of air as I methodically shook out my tingly arms and legs. I waited for the whistle and looked at the calm water right in front of me and knew that it all came down to this. On the side of the pool, I could see the coach of the Joliet Jets and he gave me the thumbs up.

I had nothing to lose and knew that I had to go out as fast as I dared and hoped that I could just make it home in one piece. After the announcer finished with all eight lanes, the whistle blew and the entire natatorium was filled with complete silence.

"This is the final heat of the women's 100 meter butterfly. That's two lengths of the pool butterfly. Swimmers, take your marks."

Bang! roared the gun as my reflexes threw me off the blocks with every ounce of strength that I had. I felt amazing and strong and didn't hold back this time. Instead, I fearlessly went for it and hit the wall first on the turn. I was able to continue building the next 50 until I hit an awful wall halfway back to the finish. My lungs seared with pain as I struggled to continue building speed to the flags and into the wall. I put my head down and hit the wall for the finish, but knew that they had overtaken me in the end. I managed to hold my seventh place, but fell short of my Olympic Trials cuts by a few tenths of a second. Sadly, nobody made it at that meet in the 100m fly and fewer than twenty-five women had qualified that year for the Olympic Trials.

I won't lie, I was disappointed, and I wanted a hug from someone who cared, but that wasn't on the menu for me that evening. Right after my 100m fly, the final heats of the women's relays all swam and we were pleasantly surprised to see that our time was good enough for second place at Nationals! We were thrilled—we were the only team on the awards stand in our dry clothes (that didn't swim in the evening).

By the time I had showered and put my clothes on, the team was ready to leave for the huge US Swimming party at Wet 'n Wild—US Swimming had rented out Wet 'n Wild water park for all swimmers and coaches directly following the meet. Everyone was very excited about the fun that lay ahead. When I finally stopped to breathe, an unimaginable hunger overcame me as I finally realized how famished I was. The rest of the team had already eaten and I was left to try and figure something out for myself or go hungry.

When we finally got to the Wet 'n Wild park, I was the last in line to get my ticket. Everyone on my team including my coach had gone through the gate as I was wearily searching for my ticket. As soon as I stepped through the gate and looked up to search for everyone, they had all vanished. It took me a moment to realize that on the most important evening of my life up to that point, I had been ditched by my team of Mean Girls at a large water park! My eyes began to sting as the reality set in. I scanned the park looking for any open food options and was disheartened to see that all concessions were closed at this late hour.

Just when I was about to begin feeling sorry for myself, I ran into one of my good friends from another Illinois team and we proceeded to have a great time on all the rides together. She was the life-preserver that I needed that evening to keep it all together and I will forever be grateful to her. We zipped down the slides and bumped into each other in the large wave pool, laughing all the while enjoying the moment of the culmination of so much hard work. Somehow I managed to meet up with my Mean Girl team to get a ride back to the hotel. At 11:00 p.m., I finally ordered a Domino's

Pizza that missed the thirty-minute deadline and arrived at 11:45. I ate my cold pizza out of the box alone and slipped into bed.

The next day, we left for home early in the morning. Although I was a little disappointed, I knew that I had given my race everything that I had and that I didn't have anything left over—that was really all that I could ask of myself.

> *August 4, 1988*
>
> *Well, I took my 100 fly out like never before . . . except the piano kind of fell on my back at around the 75. That makes me mad because I had a chance—I mean, I was in the race at that point, but I kind of died. I learned a lot on this trip from the Joliet Jets coach. I like him a lot and respect him. He helps me almost more than my own coach, Jim. I mean, Jim never really talks to me like he does to the other girls. That pisses me off just as the whole team does. I don't even know if I want to swim there anymore. I don't think that it's true that you have to hurt in order to swim fast. I didn't hurt (emotionally at least) in Florida with Bolles, but I sure have hurt repeatedly by the BITCH Mean Girls. I'll have to have a serious talk with my parents about what I'd like to do.*
>
> *My team made it seem like it was no big deal that I was swimming in the finals. But I knew that if it had been someone else in the finals, they all would have fawned all over her and been busy psyching the person up all day long. They didn't even talk to me the whole day! I don't know. I am just so confused because I hate feeling this way. I think I've finally had enough from them and am sick of it.*

And that was the last time that I swam with the Oak Park Tops and the last time I ever *had* to be with the Mean Girls. We landed safely at O'Hare and my parents greeted me with a bouquet of flowers and big hugs and kisses. My mom had tears streaming down her cheeks and my dad had the type of smile that filled the room. I felt like me again, safe and loved.

We left on our vacation less than a week after that trip and played a lot together. I could finally exhale and rest some and be a fifteen-year-old. We had a week-long summer vacation up at a Midwest lake similar to the famous *Dirty Dancing* scene.

I went on to become an All-American athlete and entertained many scholarship offers from swimming schools around the country. But by the time I was a senior, I wasn't sure that I wanted my college education to be contingent upon how fast I swam, and that's what it would have been had I accepted one of the other full-ride offers I had received. Navy ended up being the perfect option for me.

Plebe Year

Nothing is impossible, the word itself says, "I'm possible!"
–Audrey Hepburn

After graduating from high school, my family and I went to St. Thomas on vacation before I had to report in for my plebe summer on July 2, 1990. Induction day! Although I had been given a copy of *Reef Points* prior to getting to the Academy, I really didn't spend the time necessary to memorize it prior to going—I was far too busy tromping around Chicago and enjoying what was left of the summer with one of my best friends growing up, Rainne. Man, was I in for a rude awakening—I should have opened that small black book that would become my Plebe year bible.

All of the future midshipmen from the Midwest met at O'Hare International Airport. I had this one tiny, dark blue carry-on bag filled *only* with the things that they put on the list for us to bring— underwear, bras, some white T-shirts, and nothing else except for my swimsuit, cap, and goggles. I didn't even slip in my journal!

After we got off the plane and boarded a bus to Annapolis, we were left to a long line of people whose faces were much like my own: a mixture of fear, excitement and dread—all bound together by the realization that today was the last day of our *old life* and the first day of an entire new life. Everything smelled of starchy newness (kind of like us), and we didn't really know what to expect. Many girls that I had just met were in the bathroom discussing if they would be OK with the pregnancy test part of the urinalysis that we all had to do upon Induction Day—some were a little worried . . . Had they been found pregnant, they would have had to immediately forfeit their appointment and go in a different life direction.

As soon as the urinalysis was done, we were whisked off together in small groups of twelve by people with khaki uniforms on. They all examined us with their eyes full of questions, probing for answers—the human microscope at its best. We were all poked and prodded with needles. Just when we thought it was over, we realized it had only just begun. We were rushed here, there and everywhere. We picked up uniforms and got our first issue (of books, supplies, sundries, etc.) and all became part of our initial companies. I was to be a part of 29th Company which was in the eighth wing, on floor four (8-4). We chopped (ran) up the stairs and squared every corner with huge bags in tow filled to the brim with new clothes, books, and shoes. As a plebe, you were required to chop everywhere unless it was after-hours after 2000 (8:00 p.m.), and under no circumstances were you allowed to directly walk to where you were going. Plebes were required to square every corner at a perfect ninety-degree angle and exuberantly yell either "Go Navy, Sir" or "Beat Army, Sir" with each turn. It was regular to be dripping in sweat by the time you reached the fourth floor. This was my first experience with chopping up to 8-4 and it was tough!

Within a matter of minutes, we were transformed into different people. Although many sleeves were drooping and trousers were dragging on the floor (those of us that didn't properly duct-tape them up), we managed to form up for our very first formation. Being only five feet four and a half inches tall, my issued white works were way too long. I was lucky because a prior enlisted guy in my company, Brett "Nelson," helped me to duct-tape the hem on my pants so that I could quickly make it to formation without tripping all over myself or getting yelled at for looking sloppy and unkempt. I chopped down the stairs as best I could following the person in front of me—since I really had no idea where I was going. Luckily, I picked someone in my squad to follow and made it to formation the first time.

After 29th Company chopped down the four flights of steps, we formed up outside of Mother B (our affectionate term for Bancroft Hall, which was to be our home for the next four years) and marched toward Tecumseh Court for our induction ceremony. Tecumseh Court is a majestic courtyard right in front of the grand entrance to Bancroft Hall. This was the very beginning of a long journey. As one class, we raised our right palms and confidently repeated the oath of office. It had been a very long day and many people hugged their parents one last time (mine weren't there) before that first step toward their new home and away from their old life.

I remember being scared and acutely aware that I was in *way* over my head as we marched back to our company area. In a wild change of events, everything was turned upside down and inside out as a guy with brown hair and a tan uniform was standing directly in front of me yelling at the top of his lungs. Because I had to maintain a brace, all that I could see of him was his red neck bulging as he belted out the orders. When he ordered me to look at him, I noticed that his eyes bugged out as his face turned a tomato red and he yelled, "This isn't camp Tecumseh, you are no longer a civilian!"

His words hit me like a brick flying through a glass window. The shattered pieces of that window stuck with me for many days afterward, as that single day had an effect on every day that followed it. Everything was a blur and my stomach a knot as I struggled to memorize as quickly as possible everyone's name in my squad. We were expected to know everyone's name and where they were from by the end of the day. This may seem simple enough, but during the day, everyone in our class got their hair cut. All the men's hair was completely shaved while all women's hair was cut to, at the very least, a bob. Everyone looked so similar without distinguishing features such as hair or personal style—and we weren't allowed to talk socially much . . . yet.

The uniform for plebe summer consisted of standard issue Physical Training (PT) gear (blue rim Naval Academy crest shirt neatly tucked into blue and gold Navy polyester shorts, old-school tube socks pulled as high up as possible (just below the knees) with a blue and gold stripe at the top, gym shoes and the blue rim Dixie cup worn beneath a loose fitting two-piece jumper uniform) referred to as white works. Even the most attractive members of my class looked like complete dweebs in this getup, especially when sporting the all-important brace, which required pulling your chin back into your neck to create as much of a double (or triple) chin as possible. As the summer went on, those white works became looser and looser for most of my class, as we all shrunk quite a bit from the stress of each day, Coach Lenz's workouts, virtual workouts all day long, and little time to eat—with no time to eat in a relaxed setting whatsoever.

My platoon commander was Midshipman 2/c Doyle, a USNA hockey player, and my company CDR was Midn 1/c McNeally. Our company was originally assigned four women: me, Mikki, Amelia Gargoyle, and Katie. Katie and Mikki were roommates during plebe summer and I was stuck with Gargoyle from Maine.

Before going into college, everyone has a vision of what their first college roommate will be—cute, smart, fun, and of course your best friend. The kind of girl who could be a sister and who you could trade fun boy stories and share clothes with if you were ever allowed out of your uniform. When I met Gargoyle, she was none of those things. She was rather tall, completely un-athletic, with stringy, greasy hair, and pale blue bug eyes hidden behind big brown birth control glasses that slid down her greasy nose. She had one of those receding chin lines, with a large mole and one long hair sticking out of it. All of these things do not make the person, just help to package her up. Unfortunately, her personality matched her appearance. She was *mean* and we never meshed or worked well together. I felt alone in my room and in my new space, which made plebe summer that much more challenging.

Every morning—except for Sunday—we were expected to be up and "all turned out" (beds stripped and standing in our PT gear) by 0520, ready to head to morning physical training (PT) with the legendary Heinz Lenz. Coach Lenz was born in Berlin in 1925 and immigrated to the United States at the age of fifteen. He served in the US Navy and became a part of the Naval Academy's staff and began leading PEP, the physical education program for all incoming plebes, in 1968. My class managed to catch him at the very twilight of his career, as he retired in 1992.

By 0530, our entire class was on the athletic field waiting to hear Coach Lenz's stiff German accent as he urged us to "stretch to the Severn 94" and to run "five laps at 94-second pace." He was very mindful to have us all begin our exercises with stretching together—1200 midshipmen all united by being the class of 1994— and exercises resembling a duck walk to prevent shin splints, since we were running virtually everywhere throughout the day. We were all pushed to our personal limits and rewarded for a moment by the beautiful mid-Atlantic sunrise (for those who dared to steal a glimpse out of the corner of their eye) at the end of our sweat-drenched workout.

The heat and humidity of Annapolis were enough to do any-one in, even a girl used to Chicago's summers. I remember chop-ping back up to my room dripping in sweat after a hour-long Coach Lenz session filled with sprints, push-ups, sit-ups, burpies, and many other military exercises. Every moment of our day was strategically planned out with all fat completely trimmed out of the day. Free time was a commodity, and the only true day where we had any time to sleep or breathe was Sunday morning, which most of us spent either sleeping, going to church, or standing in line for the row of old wooden phone booths for a chance to talk to our loved ones back at home. Who am I kidding? We all wanted our mommies— even for a moment—to try and make some of this dreadful summer better. The booths themselves were incredibly uncomfortable and took the heat and humidity of an Annapolis summer to another level.

As each week went by, we grew as a class and began to develop our base of professional knowledge and our individual and collective strengths. We were taught the importance always being on time—the hard way. The very moment that a mem-ber of our platoon was late, the entire platoon dropped to the plank push-up position and began doing push-ups until the last person arrived. Sometimes, instead of push-ups, we "watched TV" (a modified plank position where your weight is on your elbows and your chin rests in your hands) or merely stayed in plank with little pools of water collecting beneath us and hands ablaze from the hot asphalt. Before every formation, we were all required to do chow calls in order to announce the formation to all upper class in the hall. There was a seven-minute chow and a five-minute chow call recited as loudly and confidently as possible—all while having an upper class stare you down, practically daring you to mess it up. A good chow call is loud, clear, and fast, not lasting more than thirty seconds. A seven-minute chow call looks like this:

> *"Sir, you now have XXX minutes until morning/noon/evening meal-formation. Formation goes (inside/outside at Tecumseh court). The uniform for (morning/noon/evening) meal is XXX. The officers of the watch are: the Officer of the Watch is XXX, the Midshipman Officer of the Watch is XXX. The professional topic of the day is XXX, major events on the yard are XXX. You now have XXX minutes, Sir."*

A five-minute chow call is exactly the same, except slightly abbreviated. Instead of saying the professional topic part, a plebe belts out:

> *"All hands are reminded to shut off all lights, running water, electrical appliances, lock all confidential lockers, and open all doors. Time, tide, and formation wait for no one. I am now shoving off, you now have XXX minutes, Sir."*

The intrinsic idea behind plebe summer is that the Academy will very quickly break you down and then build you up to be a stronger version of yourself—able to quickly filter a plethora of information and perform in a very high-stress environment. The Academy builds leaders—some of our country's best military and business leaders. This lesson or knowledge is hard-won in that an entire year is dedicated to putting as much stress as possible on a young adult and teaching them how to either sink or swim. Everything is taken away from you when you enter and then slowly doled back out to you in small portions as a privilege. The whole purpose of plebe year is to teach you that you can thrive in a high-pressure environment because someday you may be called upon make life-or-death decisions and need to very quickly filter all information available and *act.* The best explanation that I have found is from a US Military Academy (West Point) '83 grad:

> *It was during this little slice of heaven [while in battle in the first Gulf War on a particularly "challenging" evening when his entire platoon was put in jeopardy] that the Fourth Class System was illuminated to me in all its glory. Its goal was not harassment, ridicule, or punishment. Its goal was to train the neural network to deal with an overwhelming amount of disjointed information, quickly process that information, categorize it, and make rapid, sound decisions. At that moment, I would have gladly given a month's pay to the genius who devised the Fourth Class System. It provided me with a priceless gift to sort the significant from the insignificant and do my job in a much better fashion. From my perspective, that is the rationale behind the system. It trains your brain in a non-lethal environment to sort through the mess, bring some order to it, and continue functioning.[1]*

Plebe year helps to unify your class and build up class spirit, and also gives you this amazing common denominator with all Academy Grads that have ever gone before you, including many historical and inspirational figures in our country's history.

Where else in the world (except of course for West Point, the Air Force Academy, the Coast Guard Academy, or the Merchant Marine Academy) would you have to get your ass handed to you for two months before you *even start* your freshman year? As a USNA plebe, you must: square every single corner in a perfect ninety-degree angle with a loud and exuberant "GO NAVY, SIR!," or "BEAT ARMY, SIR," eat meals in squares while maintaining a brace . . . on the last three inches of your seat sitting straight up as if there were an imaginary pole along your spine, run to the bathroom with the same squared corners (regardless of how badly you have to go), have a very full and challenging academic load of fifteen hours on the very

---

[1] Bo Friesen, 1983 USMA Graduate. http://www.usna-parents.org/resources/plebeyear.html

light side and twenty-one hours on the heavier side, be responsible for all of your professional knowledge at any given moment, and wear a uniform every day (which doesn't even touch on the fact that your room must be kept inspection ready at all times). It is most definitely not the typical college experience, at all.

Plebe summer came to an end with a visit from my parents during Parent's Weekend and my first real boyfriend, Adam, in late August. He had been an amazing boyfriend during that summer and wrote me *every single day* that we were apart—I must have received over forty letters where he filled page after page with his elegant handwriting and heartfelt words of the kind of life he'd like to build with me. His letters helped to get me through that difficult summer and gave me something to look forward to and work toward. I didn't even notice any of the men that surrounded me, because he had been in my heart.

The other event that traditionally signals the end of plebe summer is the famous dance dubbed the "Pig Push" by the very mature men of my school. The Pig Push was a dance where women were bused in from schools around the surrounding area—Baltimore, Philadelphia, etc., to dance with and entertain the new midshipmen. The midshipman who danced with the biggest girl would win the "Pig Push" pool of money at the end of the dance, amounting to over a thousand dollars. The tradition of the dance was sexist and I felt bad for the girl who had danced with my winning classmate. This was the beginning to a long road of my fellow female classmates' and my just "sucking it up" and "taking it" for fear of appearing weak or overly feminine among our male classmates.

Finally, the Beginning of AC (Academic) Year

Plebe summer is officially over when the brigade returns and the new class is "introduced" to all the upper class in their company and in the brigade. This happens just before the start of Academic Year. "Meeting" my company's upper class was a daunting task for me because during plebe summer, we only had four upper classmen for every thirty-four plebes and we all had gotten used to their leadership styles and expectations. But, once the brigade returned, we were completely out of our comfort zone again as there would be three upper class to each one of us. To put it mildly, the return of the brigade scared the shit out of me!

Leading up to "Hell Night," we received special "invitations" from our upper class. The care the class of 1992 in 29th Company took in order to instill the fear of God in us was quite impressive. The edges of my "invitation" were burned in an ominous manner. Per the note, we were required to bring a canteen and needed to be ready for virtually anything—except a fun time. I hoped that I had studied enough for this first meeting and had no idea which 2/c would be in my squad or what they would be like. I only hoped that they didn't flame too hard and that no matter what, they wouldn't see me cry.

As soon as the evening formation was over, the lights went out in our hallway and the 2/c began kicking doors open and screaming. We knew that that was our formal call to the passageway. They were like a pack of hungry wolves ready to devour us, and I was scared. I didn't shake, but I just couldn't wait for that night to be over with.

The entire class of '92 filed out in a scary pack like bloodthirsty wolves and began firing questions at us and rates at us.

"Sprtel, name all of the carriers in the Navy."

"Sprtel, how the hell do you pronounce that?"

"Sprtel, Chain of Command top to bottom, go."

"Sprtel, how many days until my Ring Dance?"

"Sprtel . . ."

And the questions went on and on—I was responsible for an impressive array of professional and practical knowledge that any one of them could have asked. I could hear all of my beloved classmates barking out their answers as loudly and confidently as they possibly could. We all began to smell and sweat was dripping down our bodies as the night continued for what felt like hours while '92 *flamed* on. The word *flamed* was specifically used because someone who screamed a lot as an upper class was referred to as a "flamer." Some of our 2/c got right into our faces—only inches away from our noses and sternly asked rates while others screamed down upon us trying to make us crack, testing our military bearing. Smiles were not allowed and laughing would have been grounds for many push-ups, not to mention being surrounded by more than one 2/c who could inflict any form of punishment and humiliation upon you.

The class of '92 was very fired up, as this was their first tangible leadership experience—we were *theirs* this year, and a complete reflection of their leadership ability. At the Academy, a special relationship forms between all of the even years and the odd years. 1992 trained '94, and we trained '96. So, in a way, we're all "related." 1992 seemed ready and able to take their responsibility to a new level. The year that we went through plebe summer, none of our plebe summer squad leaders were in our company, so all of the faces on that evening were new.

The 2/c midshipmen in my squad were Mr. Lancer and Mr. Hampden. They were roommates and seemed to be decent guys except when they were around us. Mr. Lancer quickly became my nemesis. I think that he smelled blood when he looked at me and decided that I would be his special "project." I began to fear meals with my squad and wondered what he would ask me that day and hoped that I'd get it right. Many times, I left the table feeling flustered and disappointed in myself for forgetting some obscure piece of data that I remembered learning but couldn't quite spit out as fast or confidently as possible. On the rare occasion that I got his unrelenting questions right, I privately rejoiced and let loose in my room as it was a small victory during a time when there were very few for me.

As soon as my classes began, I was drinking from a proverbial fire-hose trying to juggle twenty credit hours, every possible piece of professional knowledge that Mr. Lancer could ask me, and a Division I sport that I loved. I took classes in English, history, calculus, naval leadership, chemistry, and computer science. That didn't leave me much time to breathe at all. Although I had always been a good student and earned very good grades, I struggled in the beginning of my plebe year and my performance was mediocre at best.

The first part of plebe year was a big blur of squared corners, chopping, getting shit on by Mr. Lancer who would flame up one side and down the other, and getting my ass kicked academically (it was very sobering for me)—my only respite being my time in the pool with the swim team and the weekly care packages from my mom. My mom was such a gem! She sent me care package *every single week* that I was at the Academy and I lived out of them. I ate all of my dinners out of them so that I wouldn't have to brave King Hall (where 4,400 midshipmen all ate at the same time) and being shit on by some random upper class—or put my uniform on. It was already a long enough day with twenty credit hours' worth of classes, double swim practices on an NCAA Division I team, and professional knowledge/rates that needed to be memorized daily so that they were available and at the ready should any upper class question you. I spent many of my days just trying to be breathing in and out to sing "Navy Blue and Gold" at 10:00 p.m. in our blue robes and corduroy slippers. Not many college freshmen are expected to be in bed at 10:00 p.m. and can actually get twenty credit hours worth of homework done in that time period!

On one particular day in September, in order to compound my stress and angst, I accidentally left my locker unlocked. Much to my chagrin, Mr. Lancer managed to find my locker and decided to teach me a major lesson. He made me sign a locker log every single time that I opened or closed my locker for a week straight. The worst part of the punishment was that I had to chop over to his room to sign his log before and after getting into my locker, which exponentially increased the possibility that I could run into him—I was already trying to avoid seeing him at all costs (even not going to the bathroom until the last possible moment) and then was forced to see him even more. He could hear me coming around the corner as I yelled "GO NAVY, SIR" and again "BEAT ARMY, SIR" as I squared the corner to get to his door to sign the log. In the beginning he would be standing there with his hands on his hips and his critical eye taking in every detail of the state of my uniform and my hair. His piercing gaze terrified me, but I kept with it. When he had time, he would ask me some obscure question that I was expected to know. Somewhere in the middle of that week, I began to answer all of his questions correctly and he began to look at me differently. The best feeling was when I overheard him tell one of his classmates that "that Sprtel is pretty squared away—she's *my plebe!*"

Hearing Mr. Lancer speak of me in such a positive manner was the one catalyst I needed to change my plebe year. I began to have more confidence in myself and stopped questioning why I was there and if I could not only survive, but someday thrive there. I had to dig out of the academic hole that I had managed to get myself into with all of my stressing, but somehow I did!

Just before October of plebe year, my mom sent me a clipping of "Who's Who" from the *Chicago Sun Times*. She clipped this article about then-Captain Anthony Wilson, a Chicagoan who had come from Cabrini Green to graduate from the US Naval Academy, command nuclear submarines, and eventually become the Deputy Commandant of Midshipmen. As soon as I got through the care package, I placed the article into my Navy-issue book bag to read when I had a lull in my schedule. With the clipping in my heavy bag, I headed off to my afternoon classes via Red Beach—a red tiled area outside of sixth wing.

Just as I opened the big glass doors and relaxed from chopping down three flights of stairs, I noticed a group of very high-ranking naval officers and a very big, very senior naval officer with four big stripes—a Captain (O6) in the Navy. I was a little nervous about making sure that I saluted them all properly and contemplated if I should group-salute them all by confidently saying "Good Afternoon, Gentlemen" or if I should salute each one individually. I was very nervous about the impending saluting situation.

I decided on an upbeat "Good Afternoon, Gentlemen" and tried too quickly and swiftly get it over with. Looking up at the Captain, I tried to display my best salute possible. The other officers returned my salute and kept moving toward where they were going, but the Captain stopped to actually talk to me.

He was a rather tall, dark man with warm eyes and a big white smile—Captain Wilson, the Deputy Commandant of Midshipmen from Chicago! The irony was that I actually had the clipping in my bag *about* him! He looked down at me and said "Midshipman 4/c Sssss—how do I pronounce that?"

"It's Sprtel, sir!" I said with much exuberance.

"Where are you from, Midshipman 4/c Sprtel?" Captain Wilson asked.

"I'm from Chicago, sir!" I managed to reply.

Captain Wilson then explained that we were both from Chicago and that he would like to have me come and visit him and his wife on Captain's Row (where all of the O6s and above lived at the Academy). This chance meeting began a very healthy mentorship and friendship that I would call upon many times over the course of my life. Very few people actually follow up on the true connections that they have made—I have always valued these connections and many have developed into lifelong friendships and relationships.

Swimming was a safe haven for me during plebe year and remained a very important part of my life. The biggest meet of the season for us—aside from NCAAs (the National Championships)—was the Army-Navy meet held during Army-Navy week in November. I was slated to swim the 100 fly and the 100 back as well as the medley relay. I had earned a spot on the top relay and was completely pumped to beat Army! I was nervous as we began our taper, but felt strong and very smooth in the water. Because the meet was held the week after the Thanksgiving holiday, we weren't allowed to go home for the break and all found places to stay over the holiday.

I was invited to stay at the sponsor's home of one of the 2/c (second class/Junior) girls on the team during that Thanksgiving taper training week. Although it was nice to be able to exhale some away from school and my uniform, I still had the nervous butterflies of preparing for my first collegiate taper and longed to feel my stroke in the water. Toward the middle of that week, I began to feel better in my taper—my fly began to pop and my 25 splits really came down. I was a little nervous and excited to swim my events at my first Army/Navy swim meet. To me, representing Navy during this big event made all of those corners that I squared mean something because I was finally going to see if I could beat Army in the pool.

The Monday after Thanksgiving, the brigade returned from the holiday and the energy and enthusiasm level around the yard was higher than I'd ever seen it. All the mids were excited as many performed "spirit missions," and each fall Navy sport prepared to face off against Army. Each year, we'd switch off which home-pool the meet would be swum at, and this particular year, we were scheduled to swim at West Point in their pool.

The morning our Navy Blue and Gold bus departed for West Point, we ate with the Superintendent (Sup) and Commandant of Midshipmen. I got to sit next to the Sup, Admiral Hill, and served him his food—it felt like such a privilege to be able to sit next to and talk to him. They were all so supportive of our team and wished us well and of course, that we Beat Army! The Brigade of Midshipmen formed up to send us off and the Navy band was playing "Anchors Aweigh" as we boarded the large blue and gold bus in our Service Dress Blues and drove north toward West Point and what we'd been training so hard for. I imagine that's how professional athletes feel when they are heading to the Super Bowl!

The night that we arrived, we all shaved down together and got to bed early in order to be as prepared as possible. Although I was used to performing under the pressure of a big meet situation, I had never cared for a *team* as much as I did for Navy. I was very proud to be a part of Navy's team and wanted more than anything to do my part. I felt strong and smooth in the water and was able to win all of my events and we were able to win the meet claiming a star for our lettermen's sweater for beating Army! Tears shamelessly rolled down our cheeks as we sang "Navy Blue and Gold" and respectfully stood at attention while the West Point girls sang their song. We were also all granted a free weekend to celebrate our victory. This was big deal as weekends were unheard of as a plebe.

The last part of the week culminated with the legendary Army-Navy football game to be held in Philadelphia. All of a sudden, all of those corners I squared seemed to mean something to me personally and I began to completely own being there and decided that I wanted to be there.

The entire Army week, plebes risked "recon" missions to exhibit their Navy Blue and Gold spirit—conducting a late-night mission was a rite of passage and expected to show not only your class spirit, but also your company spirit. My company was no exception and we met around 2:00 a.m. in the dark, quiet hallway of our company area to hang our sheet poster somewhere in the yard (the large Naval Academy campus) where all of our upper class would be proud to see it. Part of the excitement was in not getting caught by the "jimmy-leggers"—Annapolis police department. We had a very small run-in with the jimmy-leggers (we saw the car rounding a corner and dodged into the cover of a nearby tree), but managed to lose them quickly and display our hard-earned work. The best form of appreciation for us was overhearing our upper class brag to their friends and classmates about how "shit hot" their plebes were.

The entire yard was abuzz with excitement as everything culminated in the big Army-Navy game to be held at Veterans Stadium in Philadelphia. All midshipmen were bused up to Philadelphia, where we were to march on as one impressive brigade of 4,400 in our black and gold winter O-Coats hiding the many layers beneath our Service Dress Blues. March-on is an impressive sight as everyone moves in quiet, steadfast unison. After the presentation of colors and the national anthem, the coin was tossed and our team got down to business!

As plebes, you are expected to run down to the field and pump out push-ups for every single touchdown or score—fortunately (or unfortunately!), that year we only had to do twenty push-ups. During the halftime ceremony, all plebes from both Army and Navy carried the largest American flag that I had ever seen—it literally filled the entire field as Lee Greenwood belted out his famous song, "Proud to Be an American," for all to hear. I will never forget the crisp air billowing through our beautiful flag as I held my small, foot-long piece of the material tightly next to Mikki for those five minutes. The flag and the song that day represented everything that we were working toward and made all of those squared corners mean something to me and to us. Navy ended up losing the game that year and we were all slightly dejected as we headed back to A-town to finish out the semester.

Sadly, Adam and I weren't destined to be part of the two-percent club. Somewhere in the middle of that first semester, he "kissed" a girl at a frat party and felt so bad about it, he told me. Although the kiss (or whatever it really was) likely didn't matter at all, I began to question our relationship—a lot. All of a sudden, I started to notice all of the attractive, smart and athletic men *literally surrounding* me. I ended up breaking Adam's heart when I returned home for Christmas break that year and could no longer feel for him what I had before. For me, the magic was gone and I was looking to my own "what next." I learned a valuable lesson from that experience— sometimes you burden someone with the truth in order to selfishly make yourself feel better about what you did. Not all truths need to be shared. It was a tough lesson to learn and one that I've thought of often since as I've struggled to release myself of the burden of it. Sometimes, the harder thing is to hold onto the truth you created as was the case for Adam and me.

Although very challenging, I somehow managed to get through my first set of finals at the Academy (limping by with barely over a 2.5 GPA) and, eventually, my plebe year. I continued to pick up my grades through the second semester.

Perhaps one of the most important relationships that I developed was with one of my classmates named Elise. Elise had dishwater blonde hair, big blue eyes, and was a midwesterner like me—except she was from Ohio. We shared calculus and chemistry classes together as well as one of our PE classes, where we both had fun learning personal defense. Elise and I were different enough to complement each other and similar enough to get each other on the level that matters most—in the heart. I no longer felt alone at USNA and had someone to become my partner in crime, confidant, and study buddy all built into one person. If there were a test that had to be taken to save our country's future or assets, I would send Elise in to represent the United States. She was simply brilliant when it came to test taking and I happened to be one of the only people who helped to break her out of her shell and tapped into the outgoing side that she didn't know she was capable of.

Elise and I quickly became friends through our three shared classes and both dreamed of someday being like our chemistry professor, Anne B. Frost. Dr. Frost was a beautiful middle-aged woman with short frosty white hair, colorful glasses, an amazingly sharp intellect, and who was completely charming with her southern accent. She would sweep into the room like a cool breeze on a hot day and tell us of her adventures with her husband as they would often fly abroad to Paris for the weekend if they fancied it. She was classy, elegant, and very successful, and seemed to us to be the epitome of what we both someday hoped to become. Elise and I became lab partners and completed all of our experiments together. Despite knowing the honor code by heart, we were naively under the impression that since we were partners, we could divide and conquer the experimental follow-up problems whereby I would do half and she would do the other half. We should have known that this solution was too easy and too good to be true. Unfortunately, it put us into the precariously gray area of the honor code.

This is not how it works in a school with a strictly enforceable honor code. At the Academy, "midshipmen do not lie, cheat, or steal nor tolerate those who do." Was sharing experimental data with your lab partner and team member a gray area? Perhaps. Was testing the limits on this something we wished to tackle as plebes? No! When Dr. Frost called us into her office after class one afternoon, my palms began to sweat as we sat in the two chairs facing her. When she pushed two papers with red ink at us across the table, a sick feeling came over me. We both fought off tears when she told us that she would not turn us into the Academy authorities, but that we would both receive an incomplete grade on that particular lab. As we sat in her office together, not only was I embarrassed at what we had done, but also worried that I had changed Dr. Frost's opinion of us, which was a tough pill to swallow since we both emulated her so much. In retrospect, it was likely because she genuinely liked us that she chose to not press charges and turn us in on honor code offenses. At its most serious, midshipmen are kicked out for honor offenses. Both Elise and I felt like we had dodged a major bullet that day, and we had.

This was an incredibly stressful time in my life as I was juggling a Division I sport, twenty-plus credit hours, and a wealth of professional knowledge that had finally just begun to really click for me. I wasn't prepared to deal with what happened next when a very close friend of mine became pregnant by one of our classmates. The only option in this situation was to either leave (by being kicked out) or get an abortion. Leaving wasn't an option for my friend, as she desperately wanted to live out her dream of graduating and someday becoming an officer.

Abortions were very difficult to obtain from inside the walls of the Naval Academy—especially as a plebe. The only place that she was able to find ended up being a chop shop of sorts and required a major operation to get her there unnoticed and with the cash necessary to get it done. When she finally got there, she had to endure an abortion *without anesthesia* and return to the brigade the same day—and suffer in silence. Luckily, she was able to be SIQ (Sick in Quarters) for at least a few days to recover internally without having too much exposure to our upper class. This does not even begin to address what she went through emotionally, as she was the type of woman who loved children and dreamed of someday having her own. My friend had to endure this entire ordeal by herself, as our male classmate quietly walked away from the "issue." She was so brave in the face of such a difficult decision. I admired her for her courage and strength during such a rough time and tried to be there for her as best I could.

That year, Elise and I planted the seeds to grow the healthiest friendship of my life and I still consider her to be a part of the family that I choose. I swam in the NCAAs in the early springtime at the Walter Schroeder complex in Brown Deer, Wisconsin (where Mary T. Meagher had set her long-standing 200m fly world record) and many of my family members came to cheer us on. My swimming was just OK at NCAAs, as other things seemed to take priority—improving my grades, surviving plebe year, and having some semblance of a social life. Elise and I began to chart our respective courses together and helped each other through many challenges as well as small victories, but the best thing that she and I could do together was dream big dreams . . . and actually see them come to fruition.

We actively counted down the days to Herndon and the end of our plebe year. The day before Herndon, I was swimming in Le-Jeune Hall to do some training when I noticed the guy in the lane next to me wearing Swedish goggles (only *real* swimmers wore those!). He swam pretty fast, seemed pretty cute, and we began talking. His name was Cody and he was a class of '93 water polo player from Long Beach, California. At first, we did some sets together, but quickly decided to actually play in the pool—something neither one of us had done in a very long time. It was nice to have fun in the pool again and to enjoy time with someone so easily in our element. Cody was about five-foot-nine with happy eyes and curly brown hair. He seemed a little playful and silly to me—we enjoyed our time and played until we both had pruned fingers (which is no small feat for two chlorinated athletes). We quickly made plans to meet up before we each left on our respective cruises.

We ended up meeting for a clandestine "inner" run (a three-mile run around the inside perimeter of the yard) out to the cemetery that evening. We got to the cemetery and ducked into the trees where we were hidden by the shadows of the creepy tombstones. Cody pointed up to the full moon in the sky through the trees and brushed his cheek against mine en route to our very first kiss. He made my stomach dance in circles with that kiss and I quickly became smitten. Although we only had a short time in the cemetery as we had to run back to our respective company areas for taps (our curfew was at midnight and we all had to muster and be accounted for physically), our time was special and stayed with me.

Plebe year ended with the class of '94 climbing Herndon, the final rite of passage before no longer being a plebe. Herndon is a twenty-one-foot tall granite obelisk statue that had taunted us since Induction Day. The upper class midshipmen coat Herndon with hundreds of pounds of lard and place the plebe blue rim Dixie cup squarely on top of the statue—our last plebe task was to replace that Dixie cup with a Midshipman cover. Once the cannon blew, we stormed the statue. Our strategy was to try and remove as much lard as possible early on. That lard had to go somewhere and it ended up all over our bodies, melting into our hair and down our hot skin. We were pushed together like sardines and tried to build a human pyramid to climb the statue, but each time we got close someone slipped down into the hot mess. At first glance, the task appears to be not so difficult, but the truth of the matter was that it was pretty damn awful! We (women) all wore swimsuits beneath our PT gear in order to remain "decent." It was very difficult to leave a shirt on with the mid-Atlantic late May heat and humidity when we were all smashed together so closely. As one class, we climbed the statue with only the brute force of our bodies and eventually made it to the top in one hour and forty-four minutes, but our classmate forgot to pull off the Dixie cup! He just hurled the midshipman cover on top of it and thought we were done. The class of '92 wasn't pleased, so we had to make another attempt to the top to remove the Dixie cup beneath the midshipman cover. It took us another excruciating hour, but '94 persevered together! We were proud to have finally earned the right to be "youngsters" (the term used to describe a Naval Academy Sophomore, or 3/c midshipman) and no longer plebes.

I was giddy with excitement (a definite 10 on my sine wave) and left the next day for my Youngster YP cruise filled with anticipation for the adventure ahead and some fleeting thoughts of my cemetery kiss.

Youngster Year

*The only person you are destined to become is the person
you decide to be.*

—*Ralph Waldo Emerson*

For me, youngster year kicked off with my YP Cruise with
the Naval Academy's small fleet of Yard Patrol training
ships. These YPs were quite petite at 102 feet long and could
reach a maximum speed of close to thirteen knots (thirteen miles
per hour, less than half the speed of most naval vessels). Each of
the six ships in our little pretend Battle Group had a crew of one
officer, four firsties (senior, 1/c midshipmen), four youngsters, and
a small handful of enlisted support personnel. Although not as *sexy*
as doing a *real Navy* cruise (most midshipmen typically spend eight
weeks during the summer on two separate ships somewhere in the
world), the YP cruise was considered to be a good deal because you
ended up with an extra two weeks of summer vacation.

The YP Cruise of the summer of 1991 went to such ports as
Key West, Florida; Nassau, Bahamas; Cozumel, Mexico; and New
Orleans, Louisiana. The seas were rough much of the time and I
found myself filling many bags (puking) while on watch. Some of
my classmates had such a bad go of it that they managed to puke
up parts of their stomach lining. Forty-five-degree rolls are never
fun for anyone—especially those of us with weaker stomachs. The
first time that we pulled into port, I stood in formation and felt my
body involuntarily swaying as if I were still onboard taking rolls. It
took me a while to get my equilibrium back and I prayed that my
fate would not be out at sea—because I wasn't sure that I could
handle it.

The watches were fun and the destination ports were a blast as we were allowed to explore and wear civilian clothes—a privilege that had been taken away for an entire year. I started to feel like a real person again and became excited about what the future held. I bonded with my fellow classmates and enjoyed the small taste of freedom that the youngster cruise allowed. Elise got to do a Mediterranean cruise followed up by a sailing cruise to Bermuda, which she had been completely stoked about. I was a little jealous of the places she got to experience, but was happy for her and excited to see her again.

Even though plebe year was a complete struggle (which I survived), I never realized how much Bancroft Hall had become "Mother B" to me and my new home. I couldn't wait to see Mikki and all of my company mates and to swap juicy summer cruise stories. I plotted and planned just how long I would wait to go and *happen* to bump into Cody. I was looking forward to living with Mikki this next year alone and hoped that that would be the case. As soon as I walked onto our deck (company area), Gargoyle grabbed me and told me that Mikki didn't want to live with me anymore and that I was supposed to live with Dolly Devereaux (the Utz Princess) from a neighboring company. I was terribly hurt by what Gargoyle said as I had always felt very close to Mikki.

But, in typical Joanna fashion, I just sucked it up, put my head down, and silently tried to not let my weak hurt show. I moved into the room with Utz and tried to put it behind me. I was pleasantly surprised when I did finally see Mikki and we were able to talk and she explained that Gargoyle had told her the same story—that I didn't want to live with her at all anymore. We were relieved to at least know the truth and looked forward to the next semester when we could try and find a way to live together.

I decided to wait three days before hunting down Cody's company area and looked in vain for the door bearing his nameplate. I was shocked when I couldn't find it and was reduced to asking one of his classmates where he had gone. I was even more shocked when they told me that he had decided to leave that very morning on the eve of his "Two for Seven Night" where he was to commit the next seven years of his life to the Navy in exchange for the two that he had already served. Two for Seven Night is a huge rite of passage for midshipmen. If they decide to leave the Academy (or Navy) after that point, they would owe the government money for the education they'd received.

While he struggled academically, I believed wholeheartedly that Cody would be an excellent officer. What I didn't know was just how big the shoes were that he was trying to fill—his great-grand-father and great-great-grandfather had both been Admirals, with an entire class of Cruisers named after his family. It hurt his pride to struggle so much academically in a place where he was expected to set the world on fire and do his family name proud. The same girl who told me that he had left scribbled down his mother's phone number for me on a scrap of paper. That single slip of paper began a phone relationship accented by handfuls of visits on stolen time through the years.

It was with Utz Princess as my roommate, and with a Cody-less Academy, that I began my youngster year. Utz was a slightly overweight red-headed woman who was a third-generation Naval Academy Mid expected to inherit millions of dollars if she managed to graduate. The Academy was an often unforgiving environment for young college women—being only ten percent of the population, most male midshipmen were very quick to notice even a three-pound weight gain in our uniforms. When I was there, women were sarcastically referred to as WUBAs. Professionally, WUBA referred to the common uniform that all midshipmen wore throughout the school year, Winter Working Blue Uniform Alfa. However, when used in reference to a female midshipman, it meant either "Woman Used By All" or "Women with Unusually Big Asses." The term became an offensive, ironic badge of honor among female grads that still rustles strong emotion among many of us.

Being slightly overweight made Utz an even bigger target than she already was as a WUBA. Utz struggled academically as well as with passing the semi-annual physical fitness test, but she wanted to graduate more than anything. I sensed that the money was only a very small part her resolve to graduate no matter what—the real reason in her heart was to make her late father proud. I liked her well enough, but we were very different and she always seemed to be trying to get into my personal business. Even more than that, she could never manage to keep her side of the room clean, which put our room on a perennial watch (it was inspected much more than normal by our seniors) despite the fact that my side was squared away (neat and well kept). She seemed to be sick quite often and had some pretty serious female issues going on that threatened her future there.

I came back from youngster cruise completely out of swim shape and had to fight to get my stroke back in time for the Army-Navy meet. This was the first time that I had ever been away from the pool longer than a month! It was a big uphill battle for me—the first time that getting into shape took more than a month of hard work. The stressful professional and academic environment didn't lend itself to the optimal conditions that many Division I athletes enjoy. In 1991, we hosted Army in our own pool and my company came out in full force to cheer me on. I managed to win my 100 fly, but not the 100 back as we had a new plebe who was a super strong backstroker. We won the meet and I was thrilled with that, even if my times weren't Personal Records (PRs).

Cody and I began a long-distance phone relationship and decided to meet up right before my Christmas training in Coronado. I must have imagined the moment hundreds of times and hoped that he'd live up to the word-pictures that I had eagerly created with my imagination. I didn't have time for a real local boyfriend, so the emotional support that he offered via long-distance seemed to work for me. He was adjusting to becoming a civilian again and worked hard to bring up his grades in order to pursue becoming a veterinarian while I was trying to improve my GPA and somehow survive the Academy.

I tried hard to make the best of the roommate situation and did so until things spiraled out of control in my room. On an early December Monday morning, I was headed to my room after finishing my third-period class when I was stopped by our Battalion Officer, CDR Adams. I very rarely had contact with CDR Adams, so having him deliberately stop *me* was cause for concern.

He quickly put his arm in front of me as I started to reach for my door and said, "Midn 3/c Sprtel, your door is locked."

Alarm swept through my body as I quickly went through the events of the morning in my head—wondering if our room was somehow that UNSAT that it would be locked and grounds for inspection by the Battalion Officer? I was worried as nothing like this had ever happened before.

When he opened up the door, I had no idea how to respond. Our entire room was in shambles. Someone had broken Utz's printer, dropped her radio, and taken out the contents of her purse. They found her makeup and wrote "FAT BITCH LEAVE" on the mirror and on the desk. They poured her base all over her dad's picture and wrote some more nasty stuff on her rack.

I was completely speechless. God, it was so degrading. I can only imagine how horrible she must have felt about it.

Another interesting point—none of my things were touched at all. For about a week after the incident, I had to navigate yellow police tape around my door and answer countless questions as they ruled me out of the suspect list in the formal *investigation*.

> *Dec. 14, 1991*
> *Last Monday, our room was "vandalized." No matter how much I dislike her and don't trust her, NO ONE DESERVES THAT. It was just horrible. I feel so bad for her—to have to go through something so blatantly hurtful and personally vindictive is just awful. This has been such a stressful time for Utz . . . and for me. I never thought that I'd have to navigate yellow police tape just to get into my own room!*

The level of degradation that Utz had to silently swallow was almost insurmountable. The Academy is hard enough without the feeling of being placed under a microscope and deemed unwanted by your company-mates. My heart went out to her and her unique situation. And yet, I still had to figure out how survive there *myself* somehow.

Shortly after that incident, I was able to complete my first semester and to still be breathing in and out after the final exams. Elise came home with me for almost a week of the first part of Christmas break and we had a blast—enjoying Chicago's Greek Town and Satorini's for saganaki; dancing to the wee hours of the morning at Mother's and then skiing the weekend at Lake Geneva. She fit in perfectly with my family and chased my dad and me down the slopes as we zipped in and out of the trees and down the midwestern black diamond runs. Elise left in time to be back in Ohio with her family for Christmas and I celebrated my nineteenth birthday with one foot in Chicago and the other in Long Beach to visit Cody for a couple of days before meeting the swim team for Christmas training in Coronado.

Once I got back to the yard, Mikki had figured out a way to permanently become my roommate and we were able to move in immediately. We were thrilled to finally have the chance to live together—and both appreciated how lucky we were to have each other in such a tough place. Going through a year of not-so-nice roommates ensured that neither one of us would ever take the other for granted again.

Whenever someone would ask me "how the roommate situation" was going for me (since the last semester had been so hellish), I would beam from ear to ear and say that "I had the *best* roommate ever. Period." I meant every single word for the rest of my time at Mother B with Mikki.

The rest of youngster year continued on an upslope for me as my grades climbed toward a 3.0, my social life improved dramatically, and I was finally settling into Academy life. I began to love and even defend my school. I was very proud to be selected to be a part of the plebe detail for training the incoming class of 1996. As a detail member, I was slated to be a part of the first set of the summer detail indoctrinating the new class of plebes just as they came into the Academy. Detail was not considered to be an easy summer "cruise" option as it was often incredibly demanding—I would soon also find out just how rewarding it also could be.

2/c Year

Challenges are what make life interesting and overcoming them is what makes life meaningful.

—Joshua J. Marine

2/c year technically begins when the outgoing class graduates and the plebes climb Herndon. At that moment, tentative youngsters become important 2/c midshipmen with the responsibility of training the incoming class. Every plebe fantasizes about what it will be like to someday become an upper class (2/c—Junior) midshipman! Not just for the payback opportunity, but more for the overall chance to hone your leadership skills and actually start putting to use all that training—and I was no different. An elite group of midshipmen get selected to do plebe detail to train the incoming plebe class—I was personally a part of training the class of 1996 by doing the first set of summer plebe detail. In order to do plebe detail, you had to give up four weeks of precious summer vacation. But, to me, it was completely worth it. Every even class at the Academy has a special bond with the other "evens" and every odd class has a special bond with the "odds." It's an intangible bond between the even and odd classes—like a familial blood line of sorts.

I worked hard to remember all of the things that I wanted to emulate from my experiences as a plebe as we got ready for the arrival of the class of 1996 on July 2, 1992.

July 1, 1992
   Induction Day is tomorrow. I can hardly believe that it's here and I hope that I do as good of a job with the plebes as Rich

Doyle did with us. As I sit and watch the rain fall outside, I
thought of something inspirational that I believe:
    PEOPLE LIVE UP TO EXPECTATIONS! There's
so much to do and to teach them. It's such a big responsibility! I
guess this is how new parents must feel.

On July 2, the incoming class of 1996 arrived. Plebe summer
was a completely different experience for me from the 2/c side.
I wanted to earn their respect and teach them all of the valuable
skills that I had learned, while still remaining true to myself and my
values. The class of '96 was *ours* and we very much wanted to make
our mark. In my particular company, we had several recruited varsity
athletes and I tried to take them under my wing as best I could.

It always amazed me to see large recruited athletes fear my
presence—*me*, five-foot-four-and-a-half-inch me. I was the first
person that they saw that very beginning of their plebe summer as
they gathered up their sea bags filled with hundreds of miscella-
neous items and rushed to their next station. I learned the importance of being confident, loud, and very direct with my orders.
Whenever we dropped for push-ups, I led by example and did
every single one alongside them and with them. It became my
cornerstone to never ask them to do something that I myself was
not willing to do alongside them. I think that it helped me to earn
their respect.

There were also many comical moments. Although I know it's
difficult to quickly change an automatic response from "Aye aye, sir"
to "Aye aye, ma'am" when under complete stress trying to perfectly
remember thousands of small details while maintaining a locked-on
military bearing, I still had to teach them not to call me sir. I would
intensely look up at my plebes and demand that they look at me and
forcefully ask, "Do I look like a man to you?" They would begin
shaking and quiver back, "Ma'am, no ma'am."

On one particular occasion, we were conducting their first formal room inspections. By this point, my plebes knew to take me seriously—very seriously. My other classmate, Harry, and I went from
room to room inspecting our plebes' work. As soon as I entered the
room of my Greek God-like recruited volleyball player from Cali-

fornia and his future Marine roommate, I had to immediately exit lest they see me openly laughing at the sight I beheld.

Greek God and Marine both stood at attention with their large paws outstretched, awaiting my inspection. This all sounds perfectly normal except when you looked closer, they were both beginning to stoop over as sweat rolled down their faces and snot hung from their noses. Not just a little snot. A very long stream of snot swung as Greek God and Marine breathed in and out waiting for my re-arrival. They tried not to break their military bearing as I stood beneath them. I strained not to laugh at the sight of them and to maintain my military composure.

I quickly ordered them to "clean themselves."

Greek God and Marine shouted in unison, "Aye aye, ma'am!" and proceeded to wipe the mucus, sweat, and spit from their faces. They somehow made it through their first room inspection and eventually through the rest of the summer. I felt like I was part mom, part 2/c mentor to these new midshipmen. It was a very empowering position to be in after having gone through so much myself.

The feeling of pride in my plebes ebbed and flowed as did their performance. Sometimes they really struggled to perform under the pressure as I showed them just how far they needed to come by beating them in their own chow calls and also by knowing their rates (the basic knowledge that all plebes are expected to know) better than they did (which is to be expected considering that I'd been there eating, sleeping, and drinking the material for over two years!). This subpar performance was not the norm, and, all in all, I was proud of our new plebes and protective of them like a parent would be.

July 14, 1992

You know, I do love it here. Although it takes me a while to realize it sometimes, I do love it. I can't imagine going to school anywhere else.

I find myself in a time warp—we're at the shooting range with the plebes. The only difference is that I'm the one in the khakis. God, this is so weird—being on the other side of the table. I never thought that I would get to be here. Honestly, I get to go home for a small break in seven days. I'm really excited to see my parents, but then I also am sort of sad too. Sometimes I feel like their (my plebes') mother and as if only I can reprimand them. Really, what it is is that I feel like I should protect them somehow. This is such an interesting experience for me.

Everything that we learned in Naval Leadership class is now practical—leadership and how best to deal with people. I enjoy this! It's very difficult, perhaps one of the most difficult things that I've ever done because of the immense responsibility. But, at the same time, it's very rewarding too. I'm in the middle of doing their counseling sessions right now and I've had them each bring with them a list of what they perceive their strengths and weaknesses to be as well as mine. It's proven to be a good training tool for them and for me too. I just hope that I'm doing a good job!

I was able to finish up my portion of Plebe Detail and then headed home for a few weeks of leave where I could reconnect with friends and family. My favorite part of those breaks was the time I spent with my favorite Auntie and Uncle, Auntie Alice and Uncle Fred. It was with them on Lake Nagawicka, Wisconsin, that I was able to get back into the real me by writing more, *breathing,* and even swimming for fun. Uncle Fred would often get in his boat while I swam the two-mile lake. He would keep a vigilant watch on me to make sure that no boaters ran over me while I was training. For me the setting was idyllic and a time that I'll never forget, even though it was fleeting.

I returned to the brigade re-energized and ready to do well in my 2/c year. Although 2/c year at USNA is one of the best years ever for a midshipman, with the $12,000 interest-free loan and ring dance on the horizon, the academic load is quite strenuous to say the least. Every academic year is challenging, but the year that most non-engineers dread is 2/c year because of the required heavy technical class-load which includes Electrical Engineering, Thermo Dynamics, and a tougher Weapons class. Electrical Engineering was widely considered to be one of the hardest classes at the Academy.

I fumbled through the first semester of EE with a solid B leading into the final exam—*even* after caving in to Elise's desire to go to the Renaissance Festival the day before the EE six-week exam. Elise is perhaps the best test-taker that I have *ever* met. If the future of our country depended on someone's ability to perform on an exam, then Elise would be my very first choice. I had had several technical studying experiences with Elise where we had both studied the exact same material and seemed to know it the same way, only to have her break the entire class's curve while I was just scraping by. The Renaissance Festival was fun and worth the stress that it added to my life that evening, but I was a bit on edge watching her walk around so lightheartedly in full-on period costume while I felt incredibly guilty for not studying and that I should be eating, sleeping, and drinking EE in order to keep my B and be OK in the class. I envied Elise that day as she thoroughly enjoyed the day and what it had to offer while I was worried sick about the exam. I studied until my eyes could no longer remain open—practicing my settling technique in hopes that all the information would come to me at just the right moment during the exam.

My parents came out to share Thanksgiving with me, because the Army-Navy swim meet was the following week and we were in the middle of our taper. I tried to convince myself that I could still swim well, even though I hadn't swum particularly well leading up to the event.

Despite my growing questions in the pool, my parents really threw me a curve ball. On Thanksgiving Day, I had the surprise of my life. It felt like something that you read about in a book or see on TV that normally just doesn't happen in real life.

On Thanksgiving morning, my dad said, "Jo, I need you to get something out of the car for me."

He started walking out in front of me and I said, "Dad, I'll get it for you!"

I was so focused that I walked right past the surprise sign and the bows on the car, went to the trunk, opened it up, and held up the bag for my dad. I was wondering why he was snapping pictures of me.

My mom walked out to the trunk with tears in her eyes and said, "Honey, no! THIS is for you . . ."

My initial response was "NO! This is Dad's car. Dad loves this car. What's he going to drive? You can't possibly be sure about this!"

My mom then said, "Yes, honey. We're flying home and you are taking us to the airport."

I was in complete shock and disbelief. I was speechless. It was the best surprise of my life so far. It was very ironic because the first thing that I said when I saw the car upon their arrival was "Gosh, I love this car." It's kind of funny because I honestly do love the car. It's exactly what I wanted! Having a car as a second class midshipman gave me a lot of new freedom and helped me to feel more independent.

December 3, 1992

A week ago today, I was with my parents and having such a great time! Today was quite a sobering day for me—I write to you from the Navy Blue and Gold bus heading back from the Army-Navy swim meet at West Point.

I am not all that happy right now. In fact, I could very easily cry if the lights were out and I could do it quietly without anyone knowing, or if I were alone instead of on a bus . . . My head hurts like hell AND I have an EE exam tomorrow that I am not prepared for at all.

Today we swam Army at their pool. It was quite sobering for me, because this time I didn't taper well and I didn't swim so hot either. I suppose it's my own fault and maybe I didn't even give myself a chance. It still hurt after winning my events two years in a row. Maybe I'm just feeling sorry for myself? Part of me would love to be able to come back the last part of the season and kill it while the other isn't so sure I want to continue swimming. I am frustrated and embarrassed with my performance. It's just hard for me to swallow.

Cody confuses the shit out of me—he's so hot and cold. My love life sucks, or rather completely feels nonexistent.

Right after returning from the Army-Navy meet and then the subsequent game, the brigade buckled down for final exams and then the coveted Christmas break. Being an English major, I had to really work my tail off to muster up some type of grade that I could live with in all of my technical classes (namely, EE and Weapons)— for me, that was a C.

EE Scandal

By the time X-week rolled around in December of 1992, many of the 2/c non-engineers were seriously concerned about the EE final exam. Mids were allowed to put formulas onto one index card to use through the exam, *but of course not the actual solutions to the exam.* One of my more industrious football player classmates managed to acquire some extremely good "gouge" (the "really reallys" of what you need to know—in this case it was the *actual questions* to the test, beta). He managed to get a copy of the actual exam from the printers that we were about to be given the evening before. The EE exam is no joking matter—and as evidenced by the six- and twelve-week midterm exams, nothing to be taken lightly. In an extremely competitive environment such as the Naval Academy, every little bit helps to boost your class ranking, which will dictate what you get to do in the fleet.

Once this classmate of mine acquired the exam, he quickly realized that he needed the help of some of our smartest EE minds in order to come up with the solutions. He couldn't solve the problems on his own without help. He set about finding the smartest/coolest members of our class, who wouldn't mind bending the rules some by providing the solutions. Once the problems were solved, the gouge spread like wildfire and touched every company in the brigade of midshipmen in the class of '94. Doors were knocked all through the night as classmates shared the gouge from friend to friend, classmate to classmate. The exam reached every part of our class, from the dirt-bag geniuses to the Division I athletes and all the in-betweens. I am lucky that the knock never came to my door, because I likely would have accepted any gouge that could have helped me on that exam.

I ended up sitting that exam with my fuzzy neon yellow "good luck" bug placed directly in front of me. My mom sent the cute little non-military thing in a care package to cheer me up before my huge exams. I was quite a WUBA sight in my winter working blues, surrounded by fifty male classmates, with a bright, happy, fuzzy little bug in front of me. The good news is that, after much stress and little sleep, the power of the bug worked and I earned my solid C fair and square.

Just as strong as the honor code was within the Academy, there was this very strong sense of class and not "bilging your class-mate" because it was thought that you live or die with your team. In nautical terms, the bilge is in the bowels of a ship where dirty water, oil, and rust collect. "Bilging" a classmate is the equivalent to "throwing someone under the bus" and would often breed half-truths in an effort to protect oneself and one's classmate. Nobody wanted to be seen as a bilge that screwed everyone else over. These two opposing forces—honor and loyalty—directly converged at this crucial tipping point of the EE exam. My classmates were faced with the tough decision of either "coming clean" and possibly bilg-ing another classmate or covering up the truth and breaching the honor code. In many cases, there was no right answer and no possi-ble way out of the mess ahead.

All in all, this was touted as "the worst cheating scandal in the history of the United States Naval Academy," per the *New York Times*. The Navy investigation found that nearly seven percent of the class of 1994, including the class president, had advance knowledge of the Electrical Engineering final exam given in December 1992. The worst offenders sold classmates copies of the test for as much as $50 apiece, while other midshipmen cheated with information from the copies and then lied to investigators, Navy officials said.[2]

"After 16 months of investigations, the final tally in April 1994 implicated 134 members of the Class of 1994, including 88 mid-shipmen found guilty of cheating or lying to investigators. Of those 134, 24 were expelled, 64 received lesser punishments and 38 were cleared; eight left the academy for reasons unrelated to the incident."[3] In the end, the Navy's Inspector General found that

---

[2] Eric Schmidt, "Expulsions Urged in Navy Cheating Case," *New York Times*, April 1, 1994

[3] Fern Shen, "Expelled for Cheating on Exam, Ex-Midshipmen Blame System," *The Washington Post*, June 4, 1994

midshipmen not only cheated, but lied to protect themselves and each other.

Normally a two-star Admiral's position, the Pentagon recommended that a four-star admiral, Charles R. Larson, be installed as the Academy's next Superintendent in an effort to get USNA back onto the right course with regards to honor.

In my opinion, perhaps one of the worst parts of the Cheating Scandal was that there were many classmates that were strung along all the way to the end of their 1/c year fighting to retain a commission, only to have it slip away days before graduation. Yes, they had made a big mistake, but wanted more than anything to become the officers that they had trained and worked so hard to become. It was hard to watch them walk around in limbo for over a year and half only to have the rug pulled out from under them at the very last possible moment.

Jay

Although I went into Christmas training trying to motivate myself into swimming redemption, the truth was that the sport that had been such a part of me had suddenly become a chore. I stopped liking it. My tipping point came a little over a week after we returned from Christmas Training in Coronado. I was in the middle of a very difficult fly set: 10 x 200 fly on the 3:00 (the pool was a short course meter pool). A girl on our team had injured herself and was studying on the pool deck—I think that she had broken her arm. After number six, and feeling like complete hell, I caught myself thinking, "I wish I could hurt myself so that I didn't have to do this anymore."

I decided directly after that practice to hang up my suits, as I realized that what I had loved most had become something that I now despised—for me to even consider getting hurt to be a better alternative spoke volumes to me. It was a very difficult decision for me, as swimming had been the one lifeline for me at the Academy and was a big part of my own self-identity. I also knew that hurting myself was not an option and realized how ridiculous my thought had been.

I had a hard time adjusting to all the free time, altering my own self-worth equation and my relationship with exercise. At first, I worked out several hours a day because that was what I was accustomed to for the last twelve years! I would run for over an hour at less than an eight-minute pace, lift for an hour, and even still play around in the pool for "fun." I took a water polo course taught by the men's Division I water polo coach (Navy loosely began a women's club team that I played on that spring).

I enjoyed the class immensely, as it allowed me to have fun in the pool again—something that I dearly missed. Most of the people in the class were not swimmers and didn't know much about water polo except for one of my classmates, Jay. Jay and I quickly became friends and even started swimming together two or three times per week on our off periods to stay in shape. We had what I can only describe as "good clean fun"—we thoroughly enjoyed each other's company and respected each other immensely. It didn't hurt that I also found him to be incredibly attractive, but I tried hard not to notice the spark that was forming because he had a serious girlfriend at the time who happened to be on Navy's track team. I always secretly wondered "what if" and wondered what it would be like to date him. Jay was just one of those guys who seemed to excel at whatever he put his mind to—he was currently wrapping his mind around the possibility of becoming a Navy SEAL.

Jay and I spent most of the spring swimming a few times a week together, goofing off in the pool, until one evening when he came to my room after hours to tell me that he probably wouldn't be able to swim in the morning—he was scheduled to be on watch until 3:00 a.m. and thought he'd be too tired. What happened next completely blew me away!

Jay sat beside me as I lay in my rack and familiarly put his hand on my hip bone as if he'd done it hundreds of times. This was the first time that he had ever deliberately touched me. Although I tried not to act differently, I completely noticed his touch—all of my senses were on end. We just kept easily talking right through it all. We both seemed to be hyper-aware of the other's small movements.

Jay's hand lingered along the side of my body for a few seconds too long as I pushed the sleep out of my eyes and tried to make out what he was saying. Our conversation started out innocent enough, but ended up being so incredibly intimate. There was *much more* going on than the words that passed between us. His fingertips barely touched my skin, yet it made me tingle with every trace. I could feel the heat coming off of his body and feel his heart beating rapidly beneath his chest. We both trembled at each other's touch. Perhaps part of why it was so intense was because I had stubbornly denied that "it" was there between us because I was trying to be respectful of his relationship.

But, *damn,* was "it" ever there in the room with us. My body responded in ways that I never knew were possible. The way he traced my skin was incredibly sensual on a level that I was not used to moving in.

And yet, Jay did not kiss my lips with his. It was as if he were channeling *Pretty Woman* and that that act alone would make what was between us real.

Jay had to abruptly leave to check back in for watch. He told me to fall back asleep and that he'd come back as soon as he could.

I fell asleep again until he slipped back into my room. I felt like I was lodged somewhere between an amazing dream and reality which allowed me more brazenness than normal. When Jay came back, he wasn't tentative at all, but rather held me for real this time.

I softly said, "Have you ever wondered about things with me?"

I was very surprised when Jay quickly replied, "Are you kidding me? I used to secretly watch your legs while we were swimming and sometimes even have a hard time standing next to you in the pool because I'm so attracted to you.

"Not sure if you're aware of this, Jo, but she is even jealous of our friendship," whispered Jay. I think that Jay's girlfriend could feel the connection that we had, even if we hadn't yet fully acknowledged it.

He then put my hand on his heart. I could feel it rapidly beating beneath the thin material of his shirt. I felt so intimate with him, feeling him next to me. It was like we were both shaking because we felt the same and we couldn't believe that it was happening after thinking about it for so long.

He opened his mouth to say something important and I could feel him struggle to get the words out. He slowly and thoughtfully said, "Do you think that we could be 'friends of potential?' My heart is divided and split—I care for both of you very much and am not sure how to handle *this*."

I was silent at first, taking his words in and thinking about how it made me feel and how I wanted to handle it. I had never really been "the other woman" and didn't like the connotations—and had never felt so strongly before either.

Finally I said, "This isn't going to go away, you know. If it's really there, then it's going to happen. Please promise me that you won't regret what's happened between us—and the closeness that we've shared."

His arms circled around me tighter and he brushed his nose against my face and said, "Of course not, Jo. Honestly, I would love to someday make love to you—only if you'd want to."

He completely took my breath away with his words and little flowers began blooming in my stomach. I think I reacted that way because I could feel that he really meant it in all senses of the word—not the kooky, gushy way that people make fun of.

All I could muster in response was "maybe someday." Thinking about it didn't scare me or make me feel cheap, because I genuinely trusted and respected him. We slipped in and out of consciousness together that evening until he absolutely had to go . . . and I had to wake up from my dream.

We reluctantly became friends of potential.

May 3, 1993

O dear book of mine. Calamity Jane am I! Distraught . . . Confused . . . Happy . . . Overwhelmed . . . This whole thing has made me catch my breath—last night, this morning. I feel so much.

I've secretly had a little crush on Jay all this time and wondered what it would be like if we were ever to cross the friend line. Wondered how SHE felt to have him look at her with his heart in his eyes. That was the problem, the reason that we never connected before on a physical level . . . not that I haven't wanted to.

I don't feel bad about anything at all! In fact, it felt amazing to be next to him, touching him . . . feeling his heart beat. It was

*very comfortable and intense at the same time. I don't know how
else to explain it.*

*It was just SO SPECIAL between the two of us regardless
of what happens in the future. I feel so much better at least now
that it's out in the open instead of lingering like undercurrents
which are always there but not visible to all. Things got . . . interesting and through it all, I felt natural and comfortable, not bad.*

Jay wasn't ready for me and for what "it" was—we both knew
inherently what was in the room with us that night/morning. We
fumbled around each other the last remaining weeks of 2/c year
and even spent some special moments together, but nothing on
the same plane as that evening (we'd have to wait years for that).
He went through the motions of his relationship for a few months
more and I pretended to be OK.

For me, Ring Dance ended up becoming a non-event. Cody
wouldn't allow himself to go with me because he thought it would
hurt him too much to come back to the Academy when he never
attended his own class of '93 Ring Dance. And while Jay already
had a date all locked up, I was stuck fumbling around for a date at
the last minute. There was one class of '93 hot SEAL guy that had
been flirting with me as I helped him improve his skills in the water.
1993 SEAL guy was like an Italian-stallion Guido who was clearly
into impressing the ladies—he even managed to get away with slick-
ing his hair back while in uniform. He was not my first choice as a
date and I honestly felt nothing for him. His graduation was about
four days after my Ring Dance and he had friends and family coming into town and explained that there was going to be one girl "visiting" that was just a good friend of his. He told me that she really
wasn't a big deal and asked if I was cool with it.

The day before the dance, as I sat in King Hall eating lunch, one
of my classmates sat next to me. Glen was a very ethnic-looking
individual who was a little bit different. He was nice and kind, but
not at all someone that I could ever connect with on any level other
than distant, platonic friendship. He was not my type of guy at all!
There we sat together, eating our lunch.

More out of being conversational than anything else, I asked, "What are your big Ring Dance plans?"

We had all looked forward to the Ring Dance for over two years and it was one of the biggest events of the Academy experience. It was natural to talk about the details with it being so close.

Glen just looked down at his food and quietly said, "I'm not really planning on going—I don't have a date."

The thought of one of my classmates missing one of the biggest dances of his life seemed wrong to me and I almost felt obligated to make sure that he attended. I decided in that split second that I would go with him to the dance and very quickly changed my plans with Guido.

"That's not true, Glen! You can't miss this dance! In fact, I won't let you miss this dance. I'm not going with anyone special, so will you go with me?"

"Really? I'd love to go," beamed Glen, and we were off and running to the dance.

Good thing I nixed the Guido idea, because as Elise and I tromped around the DC dance scene that evening, I walked past this strong, slick-looking guy pinned against a wall groping on a girl. The kind of groping that made you wonder what their sex would be like later—his mouth was devouring her and his hands were all over her ass. He opened his eyes while his mouth was on hers and looked up at me. To my surprise, it was Guido sucking down every drop of his "friend." I laughed heartily inside and was happy with my decision.

The dance was bittersweet for me. I got to dip my ring into the water of the seven seas but was only allowed to put on my beautiful gown for about thirty minutes during pictures. Otherwise, all female midshipmen were required to wear dinner dress blues the entire time. I found it difficult to feel beautiful and sexy with my hair tied tightly in a bun in our most formal uniform. Men look dapper and hunky in their uniforms, but we women do not. Most of us WUBAs wanted to leave as quickly as possible and barely danced at all since we would have had to do so in the confines of uniform. I caught a glimpse of Jay with his girlfriend as they happily smiled into the cameras. I felt wistful, but also was ultimately happy with my decision to save Ring Dance for Glen.

It was a delicate balance for me to be kind to Glen and keep his advances at bay. He had the hope that we could really be dates to the dance and I . . . well, could not go there with him. We had a nice time and enjoyed the anticipated moment as friends, much to his chagrin.

Leatherneck

My dad was a Marine—it's more proper to say that he is a Marine, because as the saying goes, "once a Marine, always a Marine." Although he only served for a handful of years in his very early 20s, he always looked fondly upon that time and felt that it helped to shape him into the man he became. Since you can select Marine Corps out of the Academy, I always kept it in my mind as a real possibility. As a way to keep the option available to me, I elected to do Leatherneck during the first half of my first class summer and won a scholarship with the Cox Fund to study in Guadalajara, Mexico for the last half. This decision left me only two weekends free that summer, but the opportunity seemed to be well worth the vacation time to me.

Leatherneck was a short, condensed version of TBS (The Basic School), designed to give midshipmen a taste of what they could anticipate experiencing in Quantico and out in the fleet if they chose to become Marines. The Basic School (TBS) is a six-month school in Quantico, Virginia, considered to be a rite of passage for *all* future Marine Corps officers, regardless of their commissioning source. TBS is where all basic Marine Corps Officer training occurs. A Military Occupational Specialty, MOS, is selected during TBS and dictates your career in the Marine Corps.

Leatherneck was challenging on many levels for me. Although I excelled athletically and had a very strong athletic background, I certainly hadn't spent my formative years playing GI Joe or fantasizing about becoming one with my rifle.

June 1, 1993

Hello from Quantico! Right now, we're about a week into training and I have about nine minutes to write to you before we have to form up to run the E-Course, Obstacle Course, Echo Trail and Stamina Course all wrapped up into one nice hellish run. I feel like it's the morning before my 100 fly at nationals *or something—or even worse yet, like it's the 200 fly. I know that once I get started, it'll be OK, it's just this horrible waiting. I honestly can't wait until it's <u>OVER</u>. This definitely is a challenge for me (this whole Marine Corps thing).*

I feel like I've grown up a lot. It's funny because sometimes I honestly feel like that and then all of a sudden, in the midst of all of my supposed maturity, I go ahead and do something really stupid like leave the water on all night at Joanne's house (she was one of my sponsor moms).

The hellish run ended up going OK, but was completely physically and mentally taxing as we had to run the course in our small squads of four and all finish together and figure out how to go beyond what we thought we were capable of. One of my squad mates decided that he had shin splints and couldn't run at all which made it easier for me. It was a little frustrating, but we all stuck together and made it to the final push past the "yellow brick road" to the finish line. The last five yards of the course is actually painted yellow, bringing you back to when you were a kid watching *The Wizard of Oz*—except never in so much sweat, pain, or dirt. Much of that summer's training focused on stretching beyond your preconceived limits.

For example, I found myself in quite a pickle on two separate occasions of Leatherneck training. My first real brush with fear came on the Confidence Course and the "Stairway to Heaven" challenge. On this particular obstacle, you had to climb to the top *and over* the final rung of a massive two-and-a-half story *ladder* made of telephone pole wood *without any form of protection* (i.e., no harness, no rope, no nothing to stop you from falling). The "Stairway to Heaven" seemed to inch its way up toward the blue sky as I watched classmate after classmate make their way up, over, and down it.

As a five-foot four-and-a-half-inch girl with shorter legs, I was in trouble on the top rung, which seemed to be just a tad further than the other rungs. In fact, when I got to the top rung and managed to get my waist up to it in an attempt to get my body over and around it, I got stuck. In order for me to get over it, I had to completely release my feet from the rung below. I froze and became very scared. I knew that if I slipped and fell, I would severely injure myself—possibly fatally. My legs dangled from the top rung and could not reach the one directly below.

One of my classmates, James Petit, saw me stuck up there and quickly climbed to the top like a monkey. He nonchalantly got to the top and got in the exact same position that I was in. James looked over at me and smiled and said "Hey Joanna, how's it going?"

I said, "OK, James . . ." with fear in my voice and written all over my face. "Can you just stay here and talk me through this?"

"Of course," James said. "Just listen to my voice and slowly inch your body down to the next rung. We've got this!"

"OK, James. I believe you," I said, more trying to convince myself. I slowly inched my body down for my feet to make contact with the next rung. James never left my side as I made my way down to safety. That top first rung was the scariest and once I was off of that one, I sailed down the rest. I never forgot James's selflessness as he helped me in my time of serious need.

My next amusing experience occurred when we were doing something called MOUT (Military Operations on Urban Terrain) training: practicing how to attack in an urban/city environment with many close buildings. MOUT is considered to be a very difficult warfare environment because there are so many places to hide. In this particular exercise, we were supposed to scale the side of the building and hang like a spider, holding on with one arm and one leg off the roof of the building. In a very stealthy manner, we were to have one leg down the side of the building and the other free arm was supposed to hold the rifle in the prone position ready to strike at the window when the marine would effortlessly land on both feet and be ready to strike or pounce like a cat. I watched anxiously as my LT showed us the technique that he expected us to master—I wasn't convinced at all that I could complete this task and was hoping that I would get the opportunity to watch how some of my classmates handled it before I even thought about doing it myself.

But that was not in the cards for me! My LT yelled, "*Sprtel*, You are up first. Show everyone the technique."

With as much excitement as I could muster, I yelled, "Yes, Sir!"

I got to the roof of the building and peered down. I had on my steel-toed boots, a Kevlar jacket, and a steel helmet that just didn't fit properly on my head. To be perfectly honest, I was quite scared. But I didn't have a choice; everyone was watching me. I slowly got into position and held on to the roof with one hand and one foot and tried to slowly slide the right half of my body down the building with rifle up near the window as he had. What happened next is . . . quite embarrassing.

I slipped off the roof, landed flat on my buns, broke my rifle, and watched my helmet roll around on the ground next to me. Not only was I shaken up, but was also quite humiliated. My entire platoon was doing everything that they could to not completely bust out laughing at my gross lack of military decorum and professionalism. I would definitely need Extra Instruction (EI) to ever master MOUT training.

After four weeks in Quantico, we got to move onto the Marine Corps Fleet for another two weeks and experience what real-life Marines do. I went to Camp Lejeune in North Carolina and really hit the jackpot with the Marine that I was hooked up with. Her name was Crystal Pelletier and she was incredibly inspirational. Crystal was a prior enlisted Marine, but was completely squared away in every sense. She was a ripped athlete, very neat and detailed in her job, and seemed to be a force to be reckoned with. Her integrity was incredibly high and I felt that I was in the presence of excellence—she made me feel like more being around her as well. For the week that I spent shadowing her, I learned how to press my uniform better than the Laundromat! On one particular occasion, I had just pressed my uniform and felt particularly sharp as I was next heading to meet up with many of my classmates to watch a helicopter operation where they were moving large objects (twenty-plus-foot bells) from one location to another. I drove my Acura Legend as far up the sandy road as I thought I could go and then was forced to decide which landing zone (LZ) everyone was at.

I watched as the helicopter hovered to pick up a large load and then rise up and make the mile trek over to the other LZ. The helo kept going back and forth between the two points. I made the choice to head to the right position and began to make my way there by foot since I was certain that my car wouldn't make it through the soft sandy road. About a quarter-mile into my trek, I noticed a large marsh that I needed to cross in order to reach the LZ. As I passed the halfway mark and was about thirty or forty feet from the end of the marsh, I began to sink quickly into the mud. Before I could react, I was up to my crotch in mud and began to panic. I was ALONE in a marsh and sinking quickly (not to mention my frustration with the state of my uniform). I made a command decision to try and get myself horizontal to stop sinking any further—this seemed to be the only option available to me to stop sinking. I grasped at some branches around me and "swam" my way out, only to realize that I was in the wrong LZ. I was at the LZ where they were picking up the large items to move, but nobody was there.

In order to reach my classmates, I had to cross a small waterway and decided that that would be my only opportunity to attempt to clean myself up. I was completely covered in wet mud from my waist down. I sat down in the shallow water and tried to clean my now trashed uniform as best as I could. When I made my way up the bank and my classmates spotted me, they had fun teasing me and wondered what happened. I was embarrassed, but more than that, I was happy to have made it out of the marsh unscathed, and, I learned a big lesson about how unpredictable marshes can be!

Crystal and I worked out together in the gym, ran during lunch, and even managed to slip some girl talk in there too, as she fondly told me about her husband and how they had met. She was a fantastic example of how you could be a fiercely strong warrior and still be a beautiful, feminine woman. I knew that I wanted to be like her someday.

The Cox Fund Scholarship

July 18, 1993

Right now, I'm on Mexicana Flight 815 to Guadalajara, Mexico. This is so exciting for me and a bit scary too. I hope that I don't make too many mistakes. But I suppose that this whole thing is a huge learning experience for me. You know, this was one of my goals when I first got into the Academy. The idea started from a very quick conversation with a swimmer who was a year ahead of me—she was doing the program and raved about it. Now here I am, three years later, on my way to Guadalajara for one of the best opportunities of my life.

When I step out of myself for an instant, I really do live an exciting life—flying home for a long weekend or off to a new country! I never thought I'd be doing that. I remember as a kid being kind of scared of the thought of flying all alone and here I am doing it all the time! You know, I never could have pictured my life would be like this five years ago.

When I flew out to Mexico, I flew out of Chicago to Guadalajara. I had no idea what to expect of the family that I would be living with. All I knew was that they had paired me with two other male midshipmen for this four-week adventure—Evan and Peyton. These two guys were in the same company and had both just completed Leatherneck as I had a week before. Evan was slated to become his Company Commander and was cute, athletic, smart, and blonde. Most of the girls liked him because of his easy personality and flirtatiousness. Peyton was a tough nut to crack—he also intended to become a Marine, but was colder and not very interested in becoming friends.

Little did I know that the family was only expecting three boys (especially considering that part of their ulterior motive for hosting the Academy Midshipmen was bi-fold: (1) for the large sum of money involved; (2) also for the slight possibility that one of these athletic, successful young future officers would fall for their daughter). Needless to say, we were all quite surprised to know the intended sleeping arrangements.

They walked us down the tiled hallway to a small room with three twin beds in it and a small bathroom. They expected all three of us to sleep in that tiny room together. I barely knew the other two guys that I would be living in the same room with! Here are just a few small things I considered regarding this situation:

- What happens if someone has to pass gas in the middle of the night? (there's nowhere to go)
- What about taking care of all of your bathroom business?

- How do we get dressed in the morning quickly—this is where being a swimmer comes in handy and having grown up in my swimsuit.
- What if you don't really get along with them and you have to spend all of your down time in the same small, confined space with them?

I was afraid to make waves in the household when they asked me if I was OK with this situation. I wasn't happy about it, but figured that I could suck it up for the summer if it would make things easier for the family. I could tell that they really didn't want to move me out of that room and that they also didn't really have anywhere else to put me. I decided to just suck it up and make do. (In retrospect, I should have spoken up for myself and not been so overly concerned about if it would hurt their feelings—especially considering how much money I was paying them to be there.)

The arrangement started out as well as possible, considering the circumstances and the fact that the three of us didn't have a prior relationship going into the summer. Evan and Peyton had been buddies the last three years, so for them it was a perfect scenario, but for the three of us together—not so much.

Our first evening there, their daughter Ani took us out to Tequilas (the place to see and be seen) for a quick bite with her girlfriend to get to know us better, tentatively flirt on the dance floor with the boys, and to have some good clean fun.

They (Ani and her friend Lis) both had some serious decisions to make regarding which guy each one wanted. I could see the wheels turning even on that first evening as they shyly flirted and worked on their English while we all worked on our Spanish. This was my first foray into authentic queso fundido and home-made tortillas . . . and of course, the true Mexican culture. We stayed until the wee hours of the morning and danced until our feet could no longer take another step.

July 21, 1993
I found a swim team to practice with! In order to get there, I have to take two buses (about a thirty- or forty-minute trip each

way), but it's a good workout for me. The team runs for an hour before practice and then swims for about two hours. It's a different experience for me—practicing in a different language is a challenge. I've just learned how to say all of the strokes, but I've got a long way to go with my language and with my swimming. Maybe instead of taking the bus, I'll run there . . . But I don't like the idea of dodging traffic so much.

As I came across this passage, I forgot the minor detail that I had only waited three days to find a team to swim with upon arrival. While everyone in the house took a siesta, I hopped my buses and went to practice. Swimming was something that was in my veins! It was such a part of me—even though I had made the hard decision to stop swimming with the USNA team at the end of 2/c year. It still was a big part of my personal identity and helped me to get in touch with *me* when everything around me was so foreign.

The mother of the house didn't know what to make of me—it wasn't typical in their family to have someone so dedicated to their sport to forgo siesta for such a major workout. Also, it's not like the place was so easy to get to either. I think that she actually quietly admired my boldness to get on two buses and go swim with a team in a foreign country. (I was kinda proud of myself too.)

One afternoon when I came back home from practice, the host mother sat down and had a very heartfelt conversation with me. She assured me that she didn't mind holding some food back for me and told me that she knew that I would someday do something big and make something of myself.

That experience turned out to be one of my most memorable. I got a chance to see how their elite team trained and to get in there and kick it with them! It was also validating from the standpoint that I was able to not only keep up, but lead the lane. It made me realize what an amazing athletic background I had and the exposure to some of the world's best coaches. At the end of the swim team, the Mexican men's water polo team would get in and begin practicing. Sometimes, they would let me do drills with them which I enjoyed immensely. The velocity with which they threw the ball was astounding—way harder than the girls threw! I was happy to just be allowed in for a few moments. On my way back home, between the two bus rides, I would stop at a little street vendor to buy a treat—Peñafiel (like a sparkling cider). I really looked forward to that treat during my practices! The host mom would leave some food out for me to eat when I got back and I was *so* grateful to her for that.

> *23 Julio 1993*
> *This whole living situation is extremely weird for me. I mean, living in the same room for a month with two other guys . . . I think that the worst part for me is the whole "pairs" thing.*
> *I talked to my other half last night—whoever he is or wherever he is right now.*

I remember that evening so vividly—the white wash of the stucco against the twilight blue sky with the local church in the distance. I sat on the rooftop of the family home alone with my thoughts. Willing them (my thoughts) up to the "someone" I hoped to meet someday. The moon was so bright in the sky and, somehow, I felt like maybe he was out there thinking of me too. I wanted "him" to know that I would work hard for us and do the very best that I could.

The *pairs thing* refers to the two budding romances in my room/ house between Ani and Evan and Lis and Peyton. It wasn't even three's a crowd—try five! It made for a particularly awkward time for me as I struggled with interpreting if they really wanted me along when they'd invite me on outings.

> *26 Julio 1993*
> *The past weekend was very nice (at most times, that is). On Saturday, we went to the Quincañera of the niece of our family. At first, we went to the church—all of the women had their hair done for the event. I, personally, didn't have mine done, but that's OK. The church part was very different. The niece knelt at the altar the whole time as if she were getting married without a groom. She had an escort also (I'm not sure if he was her boyfriend or not). After church, we went to the reception/fiesta.*

It was held in an extremely beautiful area, in the middle of a canyon. The view was breathtaking with mountains in the background as well. I wish that I had brought you with me because the view was quite inspirational.

Before the dancing began, there was a ceremony where first, the parents brought out a pair of high-heeled shoes to replace the doll and flats that she was wearing. It was said that this was "the first day of the rest of her life" where the shoes of her childhood were replaced by women's shoes. They, she and her escort, danced an old, traditional dance very similar to our ball. After that, all of the men of the family cut in until everyone got a short dance with her. After that, the dancing began for everyone.

Talk about dancing! I danced for virtually six hours straight. By the end, my feet hurt <u>so much</u>. But I learned a lot about Mexican dancing. I learned that I need to learn how to let a guy lead me. It's just that I'm so used to dancing with guys that don't how to lead that when I get one that knows how to, I have to adjust!

Also, I was witness to one of the biggest SCOOPS of all time. Ani, the daughter of the family, has got it bad for Evan. It's quite comical to watch, to be honest, and a little awkward to observe. Anyway, we were sitting in church and she came in late because she was still getting ready. And when we saw her, she was wearing this incredibly tight, orange linen dress with a HUGE slit up the side. I must admit, she looked fantastic. But, it was kind of funny because she never let Evan out of her sight—God forbid he dance with anyone else (even the guest of honor!). It was fun to watch things unfold.

After the party, everyone came back to our house and sang songs and listened to Chabo and Oscar play the guitar until the early morning hours.

There were so many parts of the trip that were *amazing*. I loved drinking in the culture and appreciating its pure joy and expression. So much more fiery than ours here in the States. And committed to their families.

I'd like to think that Evan, Peyton, and I became great friends through sharing this space with each other. But the truth is that we really didn't stay in each other's lives at all past that month in Mexico. I had always liked Evan as a person—he seemed genuine and had depth. When we were hanging out in that little room and he was desperately trying to learn how to play the guitar, we shared quite a bit about what we were both looking for. He had become rather fond of this girl named Julie and thought that she was the coolest, most perfect girl—even though they had not even become more than friends yet. She had a voice like an angel, a terribly sweet personality, and was pretty athletic too. I remember hoping they would end up together because he thought so highly of her and respected her so much for who she was—it seemed so healthy. Of course, he probably didn't even realize that he was planting his own seeds that summer as he contemplated her while enjoying Mexico with Ani, the daughter of our host family. Years later, my heart went out to him as he had lost his beloved Julie to a car accident—they had married, started a family and were very happy together.

July 31, 1993

I'm on a bus headed to Los Altos. There's a big cultural fiesta there all weekend. I'm looking forward to it. It's very pretty here—every direction I look, there are faint outlines of mountains. I wish I could paint or take vivid pictures. I would be able to capture this view forever. I still can, but it's not tangible.

Everything is so green, SO ALIVE. Lost in a time warp where office buildings and sidewalks don't exist—just the rugged land moving, changing, adapting with time and surviving somehow with the handicap of technology.

August 1, 1993

A day later. A different city. Right now, I'm sitting in the lobby of a four-star hotel in Guadalajara. (I walked here and just decided that I liked the atmosphere.) I find it peaceful and inspirational at the same time.

I met someone last night. He was so much fun! Good looking, water polo player, studying to become an architect, a great dancer. I don't know—whenever I think about the fun we had together, I get this silly smile on my face.

We never did meet up again, deciding ultimately that the distance wasn't worth the effort. Martin became the source of a nice, sweet memory filled with warmth and genuine fun (it didn't hurt that he was a very good kisser). Part of why I had been drawn to him was because he reminded me of one of my big loves in life, Cody. His facial structure was very similar and he was a collegiate water polo player—definitely my type O guy.

All in all, my Cox Fund summer in Mexico was a most memorable experience—and one that I didn't have much time to reflect on. I immediately left Mexico, spent a weekend at home in Chicago, and flew back to A-Town to start my senior year.

First Class Year

The question isn't who is going to let me; it's who is going to stop me.

—Ayn Rand

After I got back from Mexico and rejoined the brigade, two things happened—(1) my face broke out in a manner that was worse than *ever* before, and (2) I needed to figure out how to differentiate myself from my peers who were going Marine Corps if I had any chance at getting Public Affairs. I was concerned about both equally even though one was very superficial and the other was career/life course kinda stuff.

What girl at the age of twenty doesn't care about her face? I always felt as though I were reasonably attractive (like in the above-average range when I tried), but the sudden breakout made me feel ugly. I didn't even want to take the senior picture with my company and secretly hoped that people (guys) could look past the zits that popped up on my face. I ended up seeing this completely inspirational dermatologist at the Bethesda Naval Hospital, Dr. Kallgren. She was beautiful, smart, compassionate, and athletic, not to mention the fact that she completely helped me. She made me think about becoming a dermatologist someday—if only I had enjoyed chemistry more, I might have seriously considered it.

She eventually put me on Accutane for a full course of treatment. I was on it for about six months. This drug is no joke—legally, you need to be on birth control in order to be on it because if you were to become pregnant, the baby would come out deformed! Accutane completely dries your body from the inside out. My biggest side effect was with regard to my workouts—I could no longer train at an extreme level. Prior to beginning Accutane, I was training for the Marine Corps Marathon. My body would physically hurt during any strenuous workout. For example, I had always represented my company in the annual Iron Mid competition of the brigade—a competition where each company would send their best athletes to compete in various challenges such as how many push-ups, sit-ups, and "Hello Dollies" you could complete in two minutes, pull-ups, a 5k run and even a swim. In the past, I used to pump out over 100 push-ups and over 130 sit-ups, but while on Accutane, I could barely complete seventy-five or eighty of each exercise. It was a tough pill to swallow being such a competitor, but one that I welcomed if it meant that my face would finally become pimple-free.

You can always tell when someone is on Accutane because they need to have lip balm with them at all times—otherwise, their lips start to literally peel off within an hour of no lubricant. All of the side effects aside, it completely works and has kept my face pimple-free since that time. I'm a believer. Finally, having clear skin gave me much more confidence in myself not only as a woman, but also as a leader. Accutane did more than just clear up my skin, it helped me to regain an essential part—my self-confidence

Finding My Second Family

Parent's Weekend occurs before homecoming of 1/c year—it's when all of the firsties (seniors) get to show their parents around *their* yard during the beginning of senior year. There are special dances and events all weekend long. But one of the biggest things that most firsties do while their parents are in A-town is look for a home to rent for the upcoming June Week's festivities.

We were no exception. I had done all the legwork prior to my parents' arrival and we were supposed to view five different homes in and around the Annapolis area. The home that stuck out the most was on Dividing Road and sat proudly on the Magothy River. It was the second home that we had seen and, conversely, the last home! Although the house was spectacular and filled with artistic charm, what resonated with me was the wonderful people who lived in it. It was on that day that I met Nora, Clay, and Ben Williams. Unbeknownst to me, I had met part of the family that I choose.

When we first walked into the house, their seven-year-old son, Ben was watching a kid's Saturday morning science show in his soccer uniform while Nora was showing us around. I was drawn to him from the beginning and found him to be a smart, witty, and sensitive boy who seemed to get the best of both of his parents. Nora and I immediately clicked as I found her to be a fun, creative, and inspirational mom. All told, our initial visit probably lasted thirty to forty-five minutes. We decided to rent their home for June Week. As we were leaving, Nora extended an invitation for me to come to dinner sometime with her family and we exchanged information.

Oftentimes, soft invitations end up going unrealized as many people do not follow up. But I believe that when you feel a connection, you need to follow up on it because those relationships could end up becoming something important in your life as was the case with the Williamses.

I ended up going over to the Williamses' house the following week for dinner and immediately became smitten with Ben. He and I began writing small notes to each other on a chalkboard that they kept by the front door—I would write him a note as I was leaving and he would read it and write me a new note to view upon my next arrival. Because my schedule had a lot more flexibility during my first class year, and I finally had a handle on my academics, I began spending a lot of time with the Williamses. They were a soft place for me to land during my senior year at the Academy. Nora became a true confidant and almost like a second mother to me, while Ben was the little brother that I never had. I fell in love with them all that year and enjoyed watching him grow and learn.

Ben brought me into his first grade class that fall when he was allowed to "bring a friend to school." I wore my uniform and he proudly showed me off to all of his little friends. He enjoyed trying on my Academy ring and would ask to put it on his little ring finger and dream big dreams. We had a very special friendship and I feel blessed to have been a part of his formative years.

Dion Debacle

A couple of months into firstie year, I had an interesting situation arise with one of my company mates. He was a large, very muscular guy who had been a part of my company the entire time that I had been at the Academy—so, in many ways, we grew up together. Dion was also from Chicago and had a very big personality: he wore flamboyant gold glasses with his uniform, played 150s football in his earlier years at the Academy, and was kind of an outspoken guy. Throughout the time that I knew him, he tried to "test the waters" with me on several different occasions, making comments that were just on the edge of appropriate. I always tried to brush off his comments as meaningless and went about my day as normal. I thought of all the guys in my company as brothers and wished him no ill-will.

One evening, while I was at the Mate's Desk waiting to use the company phone, he came up from behind me, wrapped his arms around me and proceeded to rub his penis up against my back. Dion was not a small guy. He was built like a very solid house and having his physical mass so close to me was startling. I was very surprised that he would do such a thing! When he finally released me, I looked at his shorts and could see the entire outline of his penis and it appeared as though he wasn't wearing any underwear.

I walked back to my room knowing that it just didn't sit well with me that he thought it was OK to rub up against me like that. Although it bothered me, I had no intention of filing an official complaint against him. I went in to talk to our Company Commander, Lief, later that evening to tell him about what had happened. While Lief was a good friend of Dion's, he and I were also friends. We were the type of friends who grow up together and know way too much about each other without being best friends. I honestly just hoped that Lief would take Dion aside and ask him what the hell he was thinking and tell him that it wasn't OK. Instead, Lief decided that the most appropriate thing to do was file an official complaint and launch an investigation regarding the incident.

By 6:30 the next morning, the case had already been forwarded to the Commandant of Midshipmen. My head was reeling and I was shocked that this thing had escalated so far so fast. This was a very difficult position for me to be in as it seemed to polarize my company and two sides formed. My friends versus Dion's friends—his story versus mine, as the onus fell upon me to prove that I was not a slut who deserved it. During that time period in the Navy, if a woman brought forward charges against someone for inappropriate behavior, she ultimately became the person defending her honor as her entire sexual history gets opened up to be examined.

The incident was very stressful for me and took a significant amount out of me emotionally. I was doing well academically and seemingly happy in other aspects of my life, but I worried about how things would end up with Dion. He had to hire an attorney to defend himself and to fight to stay at the Academy. This wasn't his first problem with conduct or with his grades—Dion was treading on thin ice and the incident with me just almost pushed him over the edge. Ultimately, I was saddened that it had been forced to go to such an extreme and supremely stressed about the process. It was not what either one of us wished for the first semester of our first class year.

Dion was eventually found guilty of this offense and spent a lot of time on restriction. His future was still in limbo due to the full picture of his Academy career. I had been very worried about what people would think of me for bilging my classmate, but in the end, I think they actually respected me for not allowing his behavior to go unnoticed.

Service Selection Brain Damage

As Service Selection loomed, I knew that I needed to make some very big life decisions in less than four months. After spending my summer doing Marine Corps training, I was seriously considering that option versus staying in the Navy. I knew that if I went Corps, the Military Occupational Specialty (MOS) or job that most interested me was Public Affairs, which would enable me to use my English degree and work with the media. Public Affairs is a fairly competitive MOS to get in the Marine Corps and I knew that I needed to differentiate myself somehow.

As soon as I got back from my summer of craziness, I set to the task of differentiating myself. Much to my chagrin, one of my other female classmates, Maddie, who also completed Leatherneck with me, decided to create the Naval Academy Public Affairs team immediately upon the return of the Brigade. She was getting some good press for her initiative and I was *green* with envy! As I thought about how I would feel working for her, I didn't like that idea so much—OK, not at all! At first I was mad at myself for not moving quicker to jump on that opportunity before she did.

But then I decided that there was more than one way to skin the same cat. I began to think about how close we were to Washington, DC, and the Pentagon, and decided to create my own opportunity where none had existed before.

I decided that since I was so close to the Pentagon and our country's capital, I should create an internship for myself at Head Quarters Marine Corps (HQMC) Public Affairs. Instead of first going through the proper channels at the Academy, my idea was to reach out to HQMC at the Pentagon and then figure out all of the logistical details (like the Academy's approval) afterwards. I somehow managed to find the right contact at HQMC and, with a flutter in my stomach, picked up the phone and confidently asked for what it was that I desired. It's a simple thing, yet very few people ever ask for what they *really* want.

I was giddy when I got off the phone because they loved the idea! Nobody had ever thought to create an internship at the Pentagon from the Academy before. It made sense—we were so close to Washington. Of course, getting HQMC's approval was only half the battle. I immediately sprang into action and contacted my Company Officer and our Battalion Officer and quickly got it approved through the Chain of Command (everyone at the Academy that I reported in to).

I was set to work at the Pentagon one day per week doing whatever the HQMC Public Affairs Office (PAO) requested of me. The first day that I drove into the Pentagon, I was quite nervous and didn't know what to expect. But I was also incredibly grateful for the opportunity and was in awe as I navigated DC beltway traffic with the bright orange sun coming up over our country's capital and all of the majestic monuments. I peered out the window of my Acura Legend and had to nearly pinch myself for my good fortune. I couldn't believe that I had created such an amazing opportunity. I was a little nervous, but that quickly subsided when I met the people that I was to be working with. They were all so warm and welcoming!

I was able to complete several unique assignments—especially for a very young 1/c midshipman from the Academy (not yet 21)! On one assignment, I met with another PAO down at The Basic School and got to dress as a civilian reporter. I met Captain X at

0730, when we were to meet with several young Marine Officers in the middle of their warfare training in Quantico. Their faces carried a mud-streaked film of war paint fresh with perspiration, as it was evident that they had been in the field for a couple of days and were completely exhausted. My mission was to help train them on how to deal with the press in their face—at the most inopportune moment.

I was tasked with shoving a microphone into their face and asking them all sorts of obtrusive questions to see just how they would react.

Although I thoroughly enjoyed my weekly assignments with HQMC, the honest truth of the matter was that I still was not completely convinced that I was going to select Marine Corps. There were a couple things that had happened during Leatherneck that I just couldn't shake and left me wondering if I would ultimately be happy as a Marine. I couldn't get the image of the young drill sergeant out of my head. He was running a PT session with Marines getting ready for Force Recon School (the Marine's Special Forces) and putting them through their paces: flutter kicks, hello dollies, etc. The marines were sweating and groaning and gutting it out, merely trying to survive this training session. A couple of my male classmates and I stopped to observe the training when the drill sergeant immediately stopped his session, looked squarely at me and yelled "WHAT'YA LOOKIN AT THERE, FEMALE?! WHY DON'T YOU JUST KEEP ON WALKIN', FEMALE?!" My face grew hot with embarrassment as I wasn't quite sure how to react to this abrasive call-out. I wished that I had had a brilliant comeback at the ready to really put him in his place, but instead, I just walked away.

As the semester was winding down and everyone was preparing for the upcoming holidays, I happened to run into (now) Admiral Wilson in the basement of the Pentagon in mid-November. I had just locked my car and was quickly walking through the dark parking garage when I looked up and noticed a familiar face—one that I had not seen in over a year and he had since made O-7, Admiral. The last time I saw Admiral Wilson, he was leaving the Naval Academy after doing the Electric Slide with all 4,400 midshipmen during our lunch in King Hall. He had reminded us all to not take things so seriously *and* that the Navy could be fun. It was a very big deal for me to be seeing and talking to an Admiral and very impressive to me that he remembered me!

Admiral Wilson smiled warmly and said, "Midn 1/c Sprtel, Joanna, is that you? What are you doing here?"

"It's so great to see you, Admiral Wilson! Congratulations on your big promotion. I am so happy for you! I'm at the Pentagon one day a week doing an internship with Head Quarters Marine Corps Public Affairs—my schedule has worked out that I can come every Tuesday. What is your new position here, sir?" I asked, smiling broadly.

"Right now, I'm working at the National Military Command Center," said Admiral Wilson.

Thinking quickly and feeling a little gutsy, I tentatively asked, "Do you think that one day while I'm here, I could come and visit you?"

I was a little blown away when he didn't hesitate at all and quickly responded with, "Sure, that's a great idea! Let me give you my card and let's set up a tour one afternoon." As quickly as we had reconnected, we parted ways again and both headed to our separate places within the massive Pentagon. Except this time, I had his new card burning a hole in my pocket.

I waited a couple of days before calling him to schedule my tour of the NMCC. I was excited to have the chance to see such an important part of our country's national defense, and from such an intimate view. Although I was supposed to be there at 1400 (2:00 p.m.), I got there a little early to make sure that nobody was waiting on me. At exactly 1400, I called Admiral Wilson at the official entryway point—a large glass door guarded by two shiny men. No one is allowed past that point without an official escort and cursory check where they double check your identity, eye you up, and finally give you a badge. The NMCC is a part of the Joint Chiefs of Staff office and is very official.

As I waited for my escort, the old familiar butterflies started building in my stomach. After about five or ten minutes, Admiral Wilson sent a LCDR (Lieutenant Commander) down to get me. I quickly rubbed my palms on my Service Dress Blue uniform skirt to make sure that they were not clammy to the touch as I confidently shook the nice LCDR's hand. He took me up and into the major watch station of the Joint Staff where I met Admiral Wilson. His office was in a room with a big wooden table and computer monitors and TV screens showing maps around the world of all our holdings and all of the "hot spots" in the world. All the screens went blank as soon as I entered the room. I got the feeling that I was seeing something that ninety-nine percent of our country never had the opportunity to witness and I felt very privileged.

Admiral Wilson was about to hold his daily staff meeting and I was told by the LCDR to quietly wait with him in his office while the meeting was going on. In fact, I overheard the LCDR telling one of his colleagues that he didn't have to attend that day's meeting because of me. He was very shocked when Admiral Wilson called me in to observe. The LCDR quickly told me that I should quietly observe near the window plants and not say anything.

Admiral Wilson had something completely different in mind! "Joanna, please come and sit next to me," he said, and asked the LCDR to bring me a chair next to the Admiral and his large desk. Shocked, the LCDR quickly did as he was told and brought the chair over for me. I think he was completely surprised at the chain of events.

I was in complete awe and became very mindful of every single detail, wanting to make sure that I put my best foot forward. Admiral Wilson then told all of the people at the tables—captains, colonels, majors, etc., to introduce themselves to me and to tell me briefly what they did there before giving him their reports.

As each one reported in and gave me their quick bio, I maintained laser focus and tried to hang on every single word. Honestly, I didn't know how to react to these people so senior to me telling me all about themselves. It was a very unique feeling, to be treated so specially when I was just a lowly midshipman. After their bios, they went around gave Admiral Wilson short news blurbs in their respective specialties. Because this was the top joint command office, all of the services work together at the top.

On the wall of Admiral Wilson's office was a small red phone on which, at the single push of a button, he could get in touch with the President, Secretary of Defense, Chairman of the Joint

Chiefs of Staff, and some other very important people. The Admiral was the one that would brief the President in the event of a crisis situation.

While I was in there for the brief, they had to escort me out when they discussed sensitive, classified information. And by "out," I mean *all the way* out to the big glass doors with the guards where I had originally began my afternoon.

When I was allowed back in, I got a tour of virtually everything. There was a room that they had a linkup directly to Russia. It hit satellites in the Caribbean and then went to Helsinki, Leningrad, and two other places. The US's Russian analyst was a major in the Army. He graduated from West Point and coincidentally one of his Russian teachers at West Point remembered him and "picked his name out of the hat" for the job. His professor was the man who had had the job before he did! Really shows how important and influential having the right contacts can be.

It was all just so exciting! The reason they have this linkup is to prevent another Cuban Missile Crisis so that we can communicate quickly in the event of an emergency. The messages that we send go out in English and somewhere along the way get translated to Russian and vice versa.

Another room of interest that I saw was the Crisis Room. Hanging from the ceiling were several placards of hot spots around the world: Bosnia, Nigeria, Haiti, etc. Underneath these placards were a bunch of desks with our country's specialists from all different services and even civilians too. These people are called in when needed and may stay anywhere from a day to nine months or more—as long as our country needs them.

After my tour, Admiral Wilson brought me into a large important-looking conference room and we chatted. This was the room where Desert Storm was fought by the President and Joint Chiefs of Staff—I felt almost eerily reverent in that room of such great historical significance. Our conversation stretched through many different topics as we talked about everything from my impending Service Selection to my own personal goals and dreams to guys and my love life—we must have talked for over two hours. And I wasn't the only one doing the talking! He shared many of his important life experiences with me and was very open, honest, and caring. Admiral Wilson made me feel better about myself than I had in a very long time, if ever.

We talked about my internal struggle with regards to service selection: the Marine Corps versus Navy. I shared my doubts about going Marine Corps and he mentioned some unique options in the Navy and even helped me to get excited about becoming a Surface Warfare Officer or SWO. According to him, "You could go SWO, do something to bring yourself a little bit ahead of everyone. Try to lateral transfer into Intelligence and on to Monterey Language School and then if you were to get all my boxes checked, possibly foreign service such as a military attaché." It was impossible not to be excited about the prospect listening to him *there*.

After we had exhausted all of the professional topics, Admiral Wilson opened up to me about some of his own personal experiences.

Coming from a fatherly place, he asked me if I had a boyfriend.

I very quickly said "No!" which was the truth at the moment. Cody and I were all over the place and, well, nothing else clicked.

"You know, Joanna, I made one of the biggest mistakes ever by getting married right after graduation. I just wasn't ready for that step yet and wish I had waited. I love my children from that marriage immensely, but on a more personal level wished that I had waited until I knew myself better," said Admiral Wilson.

I didn't know what to say to that and just listened as he shared more of his life story. I did share my very personal fear that guys were afraid of me sometimes.

When Admiral Wilson heard that, he said, "You have everything going for you, Joanna! You look great in uniform, you're very intelligent, athletic etc . . . and if a guy is going to be scared of you, then he's definitely not the one for you."

He said with a chuckle, "Wow, if I were only twenty years younger." And then he said that that was one of the things he loved most about his wife, Shari—that she's aggressive, beautiful, and smart.

Admiral Wilson then said, "You just wait! There are going to be so many guys after you. You just better be choosy."

Before wrapping up, he asked me, "In forty or fifty years, what would you like to be known most for? What would be the ultimate accomplishment for you that would make you most proud?"

I was a little thrown off-guard by such a big question posed by an Admiral. Even though we had a warm, familiar conversation, I was still acutely aware of the fact that he was an Admiral with one very large gold stripe, while I was just a young first class midshipman with the skinniest of skinny gold stripes on my uniform!

As if reading my thoughts, he looked at me and said, "You know, Joanna, I can remember the first time I ever met you. You were so scared and unconfident and timid. Now look at you! You are totally comfortable and at ease talking to an Admiral. You have grown into a woman. It makes me feel good to know that the Academy is doing its job."

He then looked at his watch and realized that if he didn't leave very soon, he'd be late for dinner with Shari—and I would be late in getting back to the Academy. That one afternoon turned out to be pivotal for me as I tried to come to my service selection decision—and built me up at a time when things were challenging for me. What started out as an hour or so tour lasted from 1400-1835 or so—and, it probably could have gone on longer if we both didn't really have to go.

I wrote him a thank-you card and crossed my fingers that we'd keep in touch. I hoped to keep in touch with him forever.

Nov. 24, 1993

I write this to you from a plane—this time headed back from my Thanksgiving visit in Chicago. One of the biggest things that I've learned this year is that if you want something, you have to ask for it. You have to make that scary move to actively try to get it. I'm so happy that I did that with Admiral Wilson! AND followed up!

I think that we're about to land. I can't see anything out the window. There's a lot of fog and I think rain outside. . . . The Dion thing is OVER. FINALLY! He was found guilty . . . I don't have much else to write about that now—I pretty much just feel empty about it inside.

Dion was ultimately found guilty of the "crime" and was kept in limbo for months as he fought to earn his commission and to graduate from the Academy. Sadly, the Navy left him treading water until deciding to separate him just before graduation. He was bitter and angry with me and blamed me for the Academy's ultimate decision. What he will never know is how conflicted I had been too—and what an awful ordeal it was for me.

Going into the Christmas holiday, I still had no idea which direction I was going to go with regards to my impending service selection. Combat Exclusion was lifted in November of 1993, dramatically changing our service selection—meaning that if a female was physically qualified, she had to select a warfare specialty. This had not been the case for every Academy graduate that had ever come before. Many women had planned on doing General Unrestricted Line or some other type of support role in the Navy. This was a groundbreaking time for women in the service and was a precursor to the 2013 legislation which opened up virtually all combat areas for women.

Laws prohibiting women from serving in combat units were repealed in the early 1990s. However, since then, it has been US military policy to restrict women from certain units and military occupations, especially ground combat units. In recent years, efforts have been underway to remove these restrictions.[4]

> *December 25, 1993 (my 21st birthday)*
> *When I was younger and couldn't sleep due to the stress of double practices, tough academics, and not fitting in with some of the mean girls at school, my dad would rub my head. Especially when my head hurt late at night, the only thing that would help is if he would sit next to my bed and rub my head. It seemed as though with each strand of hair that he released, a small bit of the tension disintegrated. And finally I could relax and get the rest my body and mind craved.*
>
> *Just a separate thought. Something I remember from years ago that I never appreciated until I actually pictured my mom threading the needle and spending hours to get her sweet message*

---

[4] http://www.fas.org/sgp/crs/natsec/R42075.pdf

across to me. She wove her heart into the thread that colored the picture. Sometimes I am critical of her, but it's not meant to be vicious or mean. I love her and consider her to be my true best friend—such a selfless true love that knows no bounds.

Over ten years have passed and I think that the impatient little girl inside (the now) woman in me needs to understand that God still isn't finished with her yet. She needs to let go of the pain strand by strand and live. Her parents are still filled with unconditional love . . . trying to make her happy somehow. Why can't she just realize that their selfless effort only helps to show what is already there?

This image doesn't make sense unless you realize just how hard needlepoint was for my mother. My mom was a nail-biter her entire life and she had no nails whatsoever, which made even threading the needle terribly difficult for her, let alone attempting to embroider a girl who looked like me. As an awkward nine-year-old, I didn't appreciate the gift—I wanted something flashy and more "commercial." Years later, I realize just how special her message was and how much more meaningful it was coming from her when it was such a difficult thing for her to do.

January 14, 1994

Service selection is coming up soon. I'm feeling better and better about my decision! I'm actually starting to get motivated about it. I need to work my ass off though because we will be the first women on combatants. We can either make it easier for future women or even harder. We are going to break new ground for women and I need to prepare myself for that all-encompassing challenge. Overwhelming. Exciting. Everything all balled up into one.

Part of this whole service selection process for me felt connected to my relationship with Cody. I considered him to be "Big Love #2" in my life. We had left so many things in limbo and I thought we had such great potential that I needed to *know* before I consciously chose a direction even further away from him.

In perhaps one of my most ballsy moments ever, I completely threw all caution to the wind and went for a "10." The Thursday before the Martin Luther King three-day weekend in January of 1994, I had no big plans for the holiday weekend and decided to step out on the proverbial ledge. At about 11:00 p.m. on Thursday evening, I called Cody with adrenaline coursing through my veins. I was direct and to the point in my desire to be spontaneous and to fly out to see him for the weekend. I didn't care that the ticket would cost me $600 (as a 1/c midshipman, I think we made something like $500/month)—all I needed to know was if he would be there and be available to see me.

He was thrilled by the idea of being in the same city together *tomorrow* and we just went with it. I purchased my ticket just before midnight and flew out less than twelve hours later. As my luck would have it, my flight ended up getting diverted to Portland and never made it into Spokane that evening. It was a complete mess in Portland as hundreds of stranded travelers waited to get their lodging for the evening in an airport ill-equipped for such massive delays. My USNA training kicked in as I took command of a group of ten stranded travelers. We managed to get our lodging and food vouchers before almost anyone. Instead of ten people standing in a line all doing the same things, I had taken responsibility for our group and we all quickly managed to get our logistics together. Perhaps one of the best compliments I received during that event was when one of the gentleman, a doctor, told me "how happy he was with our tax dollars and the training that I received." It made me feel like a million bucks.

I didn't make it into Spokane until the following morning, but Cody and I made the best of our fleeting time together. We had always worked well physically and this trip was no exception. We were older and more mature and more willing to see where we could take this thing. Cody's mom kept calling him and he wasn't answering his phone because we were busy sucking every drop out of every moment that we had together. We never turned the TV on or listened to the radio and clung to each other with such a visceral need. Finally, on Sunday afternoon, he relented and picked up the phone to call his mom back. There had been a massive earthquake in the Long Beach area where his mom lived (the Northridge earthquake was a 6.7 on the Richter scale) and she wanted to check in with her son to let him know that his family was OK. We felt a little guilty about being so self-indulgent during such a large natural disaster so close to his family.

Nobody can ever accuse me of not going after what I want. That's exactly what I did with my Cody weekend.

> *January 19, 1994*
> *Ten days til Service Selection. I need to become one with Ships & Air Craft. I don't think that I'll be able to get a Combatant. I hope so, but don't know. I need to do some research. Soon! Like tonight! Seattle is a lot closer to Cody, but he doesn't want me to wrap my career around his. I am so confused!*

I didn't want to be *that girl*—the girl who picks a ship or a job or moves cross-country because of some off-chance possibility that things will work out with a guy. I didn't want to just wrap my whole career and future around a relationship that had been on and off for the past three-plus years. I was worried about the pressure that it would put on the relationship, and yet, I also knew that if I didn't give us a chance, I would always be scratching my head wondering if I should have given us the best shot possible. So, as much as I hated to admit it, I was *that girl*.

> *Jan. 28, 1994*
> *One day until Service Selection. What a monumental day in my life. This week had been like a roller coaster for me emotionally. A few days ago, I was scared, confused . . . wondering if I was making the right decision. I talked to Cody about my worries and about what was bothering me. I'm glad that I did.*
> *I had remembered something that Cody had said ages ago. In one of our better conversations—before now, he said "that I didn't want to be married to the Navy. I left the Navy!" That phrase scared me, made me wonder if this whole thing was worth it because it's not going to be what you would call incredibly easy for us to get through. I felt as though I needed to know if he would support me if I decided to stay in—if I could handle him*

being a vet and living on a ranch and if he could handle me being an officer. What if I <u>liked it</u> (the Navy)? I needed to know if he was completely against it, because if he was, then that would mean that we could never have a healthy relationship because he wouldn't be able to let me grow in unison with him.

I felt as though I was jumping the gun. I don't know where I'm going to be in five years and neither does he. But I felt as though I really needed to know how he felt about this.

If I can't talk to him about things that bother me or eat away at me in our relationship, then we really don't have much of anything. And as it turns out, HE KNOWS I'm going to be a Naval Officer! (NO SHIT!) But he's not completely averse to it. I mean, if things were good between us, he would maybe even consider doing some international stuff. That sounds very exciting to me. Part of me wonders if we'll be enough for each other. . . . I guess I just got spooked.

I can't get over the fact that tomorrow is Service Selection. All of a sudden, everything is coming to a head. My life is actually going to start soon. I have so many questions. What am I going to do?? What type of graduate school am I going to go to? What sport am I going to pick up next? What ship will I get? Will I be Joanna Lynn Sprtel Howard someday? Interesting. What if it is him someday? Way in the future . . .

Hmmm. Tomorrow we'll know a little bit more of what my future holds.

The much-anticipated day came and went just as any other— except that I knew at least one concrete part of my future plans. I was able to service select the USS *Paul F. Foster* (DD-964) and was very excited to get my first choice! The ship was currently in Long Beach, California, and would be changing home ports to Everett, Washington, as soon as they successfully got through the shipyards. It was the best possible outcome to really give Cody and me a shot at something real and I was thrilled.

Jay ended up getting his first choice of SEALs. I celebrated with all of my classmates and cheered on my Marine friends as they all shaved their heads that evening to display their enthusiasm at officially making the choice to become a Marine. Although I was happy with my choice, there was a part of me that felt sad that I didn't fully use the opportunity that I had at HQMC—there was a soft voice in my head that felt as though I had betrayed the opportunity. But, in the end, I was true to myself and am still very grateful for the experience. It was a once-in-a-lifetime chance.

Meeting with a Pig

Rounding out the end of my first class year at the Academy, Cody and I again cooled off significantly as more time built up between our last weekend together. I could feel him pull away and had decided to stop trying so hard for it. Instead, I chose to enjoy my last few months at Mother B and play it out.

In the middle of March 1994, Rainne came to visit me for a long weekend. She and I had kept in very close contact over the years and now she was a six-foot-two sprinter (swimming) for Illinois State. I set out on the mission of finding a tall guy to her liking so that we could all go out dancing in DC. I walked up to the men's water polo team table during lunch one afternoon and picked a cute, tall guy (six-foot-five) with blonde curly hair and bright blue eyes. I boldly and confidently walked toward him, craned my neck to look up at him and boldly said, "Do you have a girlfriend?"

He flatly replied, "No!"

I quickly and animatedly said "One of my best friends is coming into town and she needs a suitable date to join us when we go out. She's a rather tall sprinter from U of I. Are you busy?"

He was completely thrown off-guard by my chutzpah and very quietly replied, "Uh, I'm busy."

I immediately spun on my heel and said, half under my breath, "It's your loss," as I walked out of King Hall and made my way to my afternoon classes.

Less than four hours later, I was summoned to the Mate's Desk when Will called. He shyly said, "Hey, it's Will, the tall water polo guy you talked to this afternoon at lunch. Does your friend still need that escort this weekend?"

I was very shocked to hear from him again as it really looked like he was taken aback by the suggestion and not interested at all.

I immediately said with a smile in my voice, "Sure! That would be great. How about I call you when she gets in and we'll make plans for the weekend."

I came to realize later that his reaction was one of shyness versus indifference. I had forgotten that she really only liked brunette boys and that this one just wouldn't do. While he didn't work for her, he sure worked for me! Will became my date for the weekend and we very quickly became a couple. I ended up asking one of my tall company-mates to be her date and so it was.

Some people are "growers" when it comes to love (someone needs to grow on them over time) while others are able to recognize it immediately when it's in the room and openly embrace it. I'm much more of an embracer kinda gal and can fall hard and fast when and if I do. Conversely, convincing myself does not work for me at all.

That Saturday night, Will went with Rainne, Bran, and me into DC where we went dancing at a New Orleans bar called Lulu's. We danced into the night and flirted our asses off until we were a hot mess of bodies touching and stolen kisses. All four of us ended up at my sponsor family's home that evening—picture three *very tall* people all above six-two, and me, the lone short girl, stuffed into a tiny room. Will and I crashed on the bed while Rainne and Bran managed to make the floor next to the bed work out just fine. The rest of that weekend was a blur for me as everything began to move fast toward graduation.

Will and I began making plans together—real life plans—and enjoying whatever small freedom we both found. I brought him home to Chicago, where I was able to share all of my favorite places with him and my favorite people—my parents over Easter weekend. We often ended up at the Williamses' house after classes and practice. We would try our hand at cooking meals together and often hung out with Ben. On one particular afternoon, Ben was working on how sound waves traveled through water. As a way to help demonstrate this, both boys—one very tall and one very, very short proceeded to fill the bath tub and stick their heads underwater to have a conversation. I walked in to see two butts in the air—a small one with brown shorts and a much bigger one with very long legs attached to it and blue shorts. As they both came up for air, an inexplicable smile and laugh exuded from both "boys" as a new camaraderie had begun. The sight warmed my heart.

Will and I had settled into the routine of being a happy couple in love as we headed into May. May was such a big month at the Academy—for me, it was the culmination of my entire Academy career as every firstie had been counting down the days to graduation and June Week for ages. For the 2/c midshipmen, it was the time in which they would finally get their 2/c rings and attend the elusive Ring Dance. Since Will was a year behind me, I got to attend his Ring Dance and he got to attend all of my graduation week festivities. About the only academic thing hanging over my head had been finishing up my final English project, a short story about a boy who went out crabbing with his Papa in the Chesapeake. As I was writing the book, I envisioned Ben as the main character. As with most writing and me, the words spilled out of me when they chose to. For this particular project, I had managed to get about seventy percent of the way done until I reached a point where the words just stopped. It wasn't until 2:00 the morning before it was due that I had the rest of the story nailed and the words finally poured out of me again. The story is one that I still hope to publish.

That story was the last thing that I needed to complete in order to graduate and I was completely relieved to be done (and happy with the results as I had earned the best grades of my Academy career that semester). I could finally exhale and was only mildly annoyed that I had duty that Thursday evening as Battalion Officer of the Watch (BOOW)—the senior person in my company and Battalion remaining. It was a pretty easy day to have duty, since the brigade had disbanded and only a skeleton crew of midshipmen remained on the yard—only those people with later finals. The yard was eerily quiet and I was so close to graduation that I almost felt invincible. I was graduating in twelve days and my parents and family were all scheduled to arrive in Annapolis in less than a week.

My large cruise box sat directly outside the door to my room and was a very real reminder that I was about to leave Mother B *and* graduate! The boxes were to be picked up very early the following Monday morning and I still had a lot to pack. The Navy ships one large cruise box per midshipman to their first duty station—inside it you place all of the things that you've accumulated the last four years—your life shoved into a box!

Will had been very sweet that evening and brought me some dinner to eat since I wasn't allowed to leave. We ate and talked and . . . lost track of time . . . consciously, almost on purpose. We ended up peacefully (and stupidly) falling asleep for far too long—with all of our clothes on—until I heard the sound of my door lightly rumble against my trash can very early in the morning. It must have been around 0400 in the morning on Friday, May 13, 1994—everything was quiet and dark in the hallway *except* for the bright light coming in from the hallway obstructed only by the figure of a tall, thin man.

I immediately sprang out of bed alarmed, as adrenaline coursed through my veins, and quickly headed toward the man standing in my doorway. Will just laid there still and not moving, appearing to be asleep. I was terrified of what might happen as I knew that I had allowed myself to be put in a very compromising position in the eyes of the Academy—even with all of my clothes on!

The guy standing in my doorway was a 2/c midshipman in my company and a part of my watch team. He was unassumingly dropping off the duty keys to my room before reveille, until he realized the position of power that he had gratuitously found himself in.

I stood at my doorway in bare feet, blue rim tee shirt and blue and gold shorts and looked up at him with just a little too much fear in my voice and said, "Please, please, *please* don't turn us in."

I was acutely aware of the big box next to him in the hallway and my future hanging in the balance.

He just stood there for a moment considering his options until he said, "OK. I won't turn you in if you have sex with me right now. Don't worry about your boyfriend, he's asleep. All you have to do is just lie there or suck it."

I was completely stunned and had never felt so degraded in my life. At first, I thought that for sure he was kidding.

But then, this sick pig continued to say, "I don't need money. I have $9,000 in the bank from my new 2/c loan. I need *this*. Now. I can get it on the weekend from anyone, but not *now*."

I had never looked into the eyes of a criminal before this time. This guy was a criminal disguised in the clothes of a future Naval

Officer at one of the best schools in the country. He was even junior to me! I couldn't believe what I was hearing come out of his mouth.

Being in bed with a member of the opposite sex would have been *no big deal* and even a rite of passage at any other school, but at the Naval Academy, it was cause for very serious disciplinary action that could result in a 6000 Series offense and even expulsion. For me, my graduation could have been taken away. Around that same time, there was also a very strong push toward limiting personal contact (fist fights) among all mids with an article called I-90, whereas someone could incur a very serious 5-6000 Series fry if they were ever found guilty of aggressive physical action toward someone else.

Through it all, Will just laid there pretending to be asleep. He was a ripped six-foot-five Division I collegiate athlete! He could have easily beat the shit out of Pig, but he was frozen and couldn't move.

After Pig gave me his ultimatum, I stood there considering my options in disbelief—just feet away from my cruise box. Everything that I had worked for sat hanging in the balance of the next ten minutes and which decision I would make. I think that only about thirty seconds passed by, but it felt like an eternity as I weighed both sides of the equation presented to me.

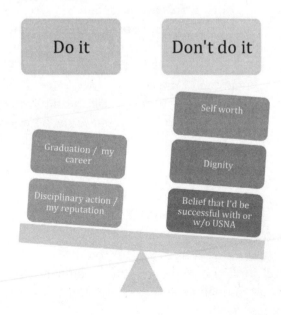

I quickly came to the conclusion that no matter what, I could not and would not touch him willfully. I knew then and there that if it meant I had to forgo my graduation even with my parents and family arriving in less than a week, I would do whatever it took to make him not touch me.

I decided that nothing was worth who I am and what I believe in . . . and that I'd be successful with or without a degree from the Naval Academy. And that if I had to take my lumps and be on restriction and not walk my graduation ceremony with all of my family there to share the experience, then so be it. I was strong enough to handle that too.

So . . . I looked up at him and nodded.

Pig said, "Meet me in *this* room in ten minutes."

The second that Pig left my room, Will shot out of the bed and grabbed my shoulders. He began shaking me and said, "Do whatever you have to do to make him not touch you."

He sent me into that room knowing that things could go badly for me. I was in shock that I was about to walk into such a buzz-saw of a situation. I was almost numb.

After ten minutes, I walked into the room and Pig sat on top of a desk that was in the center of the room with his pants off. He was very hard.

His dick seemed to take up the whole room.

Pig looked at me and very calmly said, "Think about it, ten minutes! You can just lie there or suck it. Everything you've worked for . . . or this."

This was the first time that I learned what my physiological response to major stress was. I got extremely parched—so parched that I could barely talk because my mouth felt like it was lined with cotton. The only plan that I had was to begin talking—rather hard to do when you are so parched—about anything that could possibly resonate with him!

Since I knew that he had gone to prep school prior to USNA and was quite religious, I began talking. Talking about minorities and how important a graduation from the Naval Academy was . . . I spoke about God and religion and anything that I could think of to get him to simply put his damn pants back on. Along with my mouth being completely parched, I began to shake inside as he was holding my entire future and career over my head in exchange for "ten minutes."

"What's it gonna be, your career or this?" sneered Pig, believing that he had me in a no-win situation.

"I love my boyfriend. I *cannot* do this and *will not* do this," I finally said. Surely that had to count for something? Yet still he didn't put his pants back on and persisted in trying to have his way.

I just sat there mentally scrambling for anything that I could say to get him to put his pants back on. I think that I might have been in the room with him for about half an hour, but time stands still in high stress moments such as this—it could have been only about ten or fifteen minutes.

Finally, Pig realized that the only way that he'd get *it* from me would be to rape me. Slowly, he pulled his summer khakis up, turned on his heel and looked at me and said, "I'll think about what I want from you this weekend. I'll call you or let you know at the end of the weekend."

As soon as I left the room, I knew that I needed to talk to my parents immediately—find out how they would handle this. They were one hour behind us on the east coast and it was a little after 4:00 a.m. for them. But I knew that I could call them at any hour—especially when in a situation like this. My dad was a former Marine! When I told my parents what had happened, my mom had to physically stop him from getting on a plane and: (1) going directly to the Commandant of Midshipmen and (2) personally wringing Pig's neck. We opted instead to sit back and see how things played out.

As soon as I was granted liberty, I headed over to the Williamses' house and told Nora everything that had happened. Nora encouraged me to call the civilian police to at least get some questions answered. I didn't even know what the legal term was for what Pig had done to me. I ended up anonymously calling the police station to find out what you would call such a thing—extortion! I knew as I was going through it that what I had done might have been bad in the eyes of the Academy, but what he had done was *completely illegal* and would have been due course for him to not only get kicked out of the Academy, but also be up to his eyeballs in severe legal action and possibly in jail.

I spent that entire weekend jumping every time the phone rang, worried that Pig was going to call me and tell me what he wanted in exchange for his silence. I fantasized about recording the call which never came . . . about how I could hurt him as he had hurt me. In the end, he never did call me. I returned to the brigade that Sunday early evening emotionally spent and on the cusp of one of the most exciting weeks of my life thus far.

When I got back, I pulled my roommate Mikki aside and told her what had happened. I asked her if she would mind not leaving me alone much that evening as I was worried about what would happen if I came face to face with Pig. I also had the deadline of taping up my cruise box looming. As the rest of our company rested, I sat outside in the dark hallway putting the last items of my life into the box.

At about 12:30 a.m., Pig walked down the empty, dark hallway toward me in a very cool fashion. Mikki was watching a movie with her best friend (and now husband), Bran, in the wardroom.

He stopped just in front of me with his hands in his pockets and said, "I've talked it over with my girlfriend and have decided not to do anything."

I was completely silent—stone cold silent—and looked at him with the hardest gaze that I could produce.

The kind of look that said, "If I could run your balls through a garlic press, I would."

Like hell he talked to his girlfriend about what he had tried to do to me!

I never spoke to him again or saw him again after that incident. I often wonder what would happen if our paths were to ever cross—and if I were the first of many he tried to do that to.

June Week

"You're off to Great Places! Today is your day! Your mountain is waiting, So . . . get on your way!"
—*Dr. Seuss,* Oh, The Places You'll Go

June Week began immediately after the Pig incident. My parents were due to arrive in Annapolis in mere days with many members of my family descending upon the city to help celebrate this major milestone. I was swept away by the force of the June Week wave which was the culmination of everything that I had endured at the Academy. It was filled with Ring Dance, several formal balls, the final parade and jumping off the 10m platform in our parade dress uniforms, countless parties, concerts, and of course our graduation ceremony which would be highlighted by President Bill Clinton.

The only way that I could cope with the enormity of what happened was to stuff it deep inside. I just charged ahead with my happy face on trying to embrace everything that lie ahead. I did the "see, look, I'm fine" method of healing. And *mostly* I was—I didn't give myself a chance to fully feel and grasp what had happened.

May 21, 1994

The past week has been an emotional roller coaster for me. But as I write inside of you now, everything is wonderful. My love (Will) is sleeping peacefully next to me . . . his chest slowly rising up and down with each breath and we are in the most beautiful room. It's a corner room with an incredible view of the Baltimore skyline. It almost reminds me of the Hotel Nikko in Chicago. We stayed there after Will's Ring Dance which was so special to share with him.

Where do I begin? Will and I are doing really well together and have come a long way in a short period of time. As good as it's been with him, we've also made some big mistakes along the way . . . some BIG ones that I haven't even begun to completely process yet.

I have never ever been so scared in my life—this was definitely the most traumatic thing I've ever had to deal with. I just want to make what happened go away and to enjoy this week— I've worked so hard to be here.

A couple of days before graduation, Jay asked me to join him for dinner so that we could reconnect one more time before we went our separate ways. He took me out to a very nice Vietnamese restaurant where we easily talked about our respective lives. There were definitely undercurrents in the room with us—but I had my resolve and conviction being in what I believed to be a solid relationship with Will. We were *friends* of potential. After all that time, we had never kissed despite how intimate and connected we had been.

After our dinner, we went to a local bar called Riordan's where most midshipmen went for drinks. I had barely spent any time there—not that I let Jay know that little detail. We found ourselves on the top floor in a room all to ourselves. We stood by the windows overlooking Annapolis and he looked at me, leaned in, and said, "I have always wanted to kiss you."

He looked so very cute and I really wanted to kiss him desperately, but I could not because I was in love with Will. I moved my head to the side as he moved closer toward my lips. Jay was completely stunned. He was not used to any woman ever denying him, let alone me.

I softly said, "I've waited far too long to kiss you to have any ounce of regret. I am in love with someone right now and don't want to mess it up."

Jay wistfully accepted my position and shook his head with that famous half-smile on his face as he settled for a big hug. I wrapped my arms around his neck and he pulled me in close one last time so that I could feel his heart beat. We stood for a few moments too long, stuck in a solid state of the present surrounded by all that was and all that could be on either side of us. It was incredibly hard to stop there, but I knew myself and could not and would not take it any further since I cared enough about him to want to be able to be completely "present" with him for a moment that I had anticipated for so long.

Jay walked me back to my room and flashed me his smile one last time. He had clearly hoped for a different outcome as I think that he was finally ready for what "more" with me would have looked like.

For the first time ever, the Williamses were a part of all the June Week festivities and attended the Academy dances with us as well as the parades and actual graduation ceremony. At one of the graduation dances, I managed to run into Jay and his family. When I met his father, he seemed taken aback by me. He said, "You have really surprised me, Joanna! Jay described you as such an amazing athlete, but clearly left out how feminine and beautiful you also are."

His remarks blew me away inside and became something that I quietly filed away. I had many family members fly in for the event and we all settled into the Williamses' beautiful home. We enjoyed dinner parties and late nights playing charades and talking about what the future might hold.

I awoke graduation morning filled with anticipation and quickly jumped into the shower. I was determined to have every single last hair exactly in place as I put on my Service Dress Whites and prepared to shake President Clinton's hand for my diploma. As was traditional, I wrote a note to the lucky person who would recover my precious Naval Academy cover (hat) after we hurled it with all our might into the air. My note said: "Reach for the stars, and if you fall a little short, at least you'll have a handful of stardust."

Although we seemingly left early enough for Memorial Stadium, traffic came to a halt close to a mile away from the stadium. My heart began beating faster as I anxiously looked at all of my other classmates in the cars around me. I decided that I couldn't take the risk and opened my car door and made a run for it in my high heels toward the stadium some three-quarters of a mile away. Seeing me make a dash, many other doors flung open and soon all of the

'94 stragglers were running together to make it to our own graduation ceremony in time.

Because our names were next to each other alphabetically, I got to sit next to my roommate, Mikki, during the graduation ceremony. It was the best thing ever to be able to sit next to Mikki on such a monumental day in our lives. As our classmates' names began to be called out, she and I very quietly whispered back and forth until the row just before us was summoned to stand. My heart began to beat rapidly and my palms began to sweat as the moment had really arrived for me to hear my name called out and for me to have my turn to walk across the stage and finally get my diploma and commission from our Commander in Chief, President Bill Clinton, and the Commandant of Midshipmen. I could hear my mom's and dad's voices faintly in the background as I carefully made my way down the stairs.

Will gave me my very first real salute and I gave him my silver dollar in return. I think that he honestly felt uncomfortable with the salute, given the fact that we were dating and it was a symbol of rank. I remember that when all the guests finally left, I was overcome with much emotion and was worried that Ben would forget me when I headed to the West Coast for my temporary duty assignment of Navy Upward Bound and then onto Surface Warfare School. It was the first time in my life that I had genuinely felt love for a small child and enjoyed being a part of his life. Having grown up an only child, I didn't have any brothers or sisters and always felt close to the kids I babysat, but this was different. Ben felt like family to me and I hoped that the closeness we all felt together wouldn't go away with me leaving. Will held me as I sobbed and assured me that it wasn't possible for them to forget me.

The afternoon my parents and family left, Will and I went to the HFStival concert in DC and got to see Counting Crows and James live. So many of my classmates were at that concert blowing off much needed steam—and some of them were having an unforgettable moment. Among them were three of my friends from my company and the water polo team. One of their friends ended up losing his commission and his fight to stay in the Navy. I observed as they shared their last fleeting moments in Annapolis and all scattered in different directions.

The EE scandal took many of my classmates down in its wake. As cruel as this may sound, many of the final determinations were not made until just before our graduation—my classmates had been kept in a state of limbo for over a year fighting to stay in the Navy, fighting for a chance to become an officer, and fighting to finish what they had started. For many, finishing wasn't an option.

The EE cheating scandal touched every part of my class: from the football team, to the smartest members of my class, to the dirt bags and the slackers and everyone in between. It was heartbreaking to watch these grown men cling onto their dear friend who would not be continuing the journey with them.

After our incident, Will struggled with his lack of reaction and beat himself up over what he did and didn't do. When I really peeled the onion back on what had transpired, I couldn't respect him the way that I had before for not fighting for me or standing up for me. And he couldn't forgive himself either. I was terribly stubborn though and still wanted the relationship to work and to last beyond this event. It did for a little while longer, but neither of us could ultimately move past what had happened. We did a good job of pretending to be OK and of wanting to be OK. We spent our summer in San Diego having tremendous amounts of amazing sex, going out to eat, surfing and playing in the ocean on his family's boat, and dreaming of a future together. We both had begun to imagine a life together, but in the end, neither of us could really get past the Pig incident and, quite frankly, he didn't feel as though he deserved me anymore (regardless of how I felt).

After I had finished the Navy Upward Bound program in late August of 1994, my dad flew out to help me drive from San Diego to Chicago. When we finally made it home to Berwyn, Illinois, it was an incredibly hot and sticky day. I was having a particularly bad hair day and decided to get a short haircut. I was going for the Linda Evangelista cut of the early '90s. When I sat down to get the major cut—over twelve inches of my hair was about to be chopped off—I had no idea what I was in for. The hairdresser clearly didn't know what she was doing. She ended up chopping off an inch more than I had even asked for. When she was finally finished, I couldn't even recognize myself in the mirror. Only a couple of days later, I left my parents early in order to head back East to spend the weekend with Will and report in to Surface Warfare School in Newport, RI.

I had this spectacularly romantic weekend planned for us since the Williamses were out of town and allowing us to use their beautiful home on the Magothy River. I had bought a sexy dress and had plenty of special presents all lined up for Will. Yes, my hair was dramatically different, but I was still the same girl!

As soon as I picked him up, I knew that something was terribly wrong. And when I asked him what was wrong, all he could muster was a "*Nothing!*" We didn't say another word the rest of the twenty-minute drive to their house. The whole way there, he held my hand tightly. *Too tightly.* It was tense, not violent. I had to yank it out to change the radio station.

The bad feeling was so strong that by the time we pulled into the driveway of Nora and Clay's house, I couldn't hold my tears back anymore and he hadn't even said anything yet. I was openly crying at this point because he was cold and detached. He was "stone man."

We walked into the kitchen and I sat on the counter of one end and he stood on the complete opposite end looking at the floor. I couldn't stop crying and had begun shaking. I thought he would hold me and that somehow we would work this out. But instead it just got worse and worse as I watched him just stand there, frozen. I threw up that afternoon and he didn't even get up. I felt as though I could be lying dead on the ground and he wouldn't even be able to pick me up and take me to the hospital.

I *loved* him. What the hell am I talking about? Love doesn't just go away like that. It's like extra weight, it comes on a lot easier than it comes off.

Basically, he could not "stay for himself." He felt that he was not enough for me. That he didn't love me enough. That he couldn't treat me as he felt I deserved. Apparently, every time I did something "terrific," he felt even worse—as if he didn't do enough and couldn't be enough for me. I never felt that way about him, but once someone goes there in their head, there is no way back.

I knew then that my spectacularly romantic weekend was never going to happen and that something very different was in front of me. At the time, I thought that some of it had to do with my new hairstyle—as if he couldn't see me anymore in there. My eyes looked bigger with all of my hair gone, but I was definitely still me. Oddly, I thought it made it easier for him to end us because he could no longer see me.

So, with swollen eyes and a very heavy heart, I got in the car the next day and forced myself to drive the 400 miles north toward my new life in Newport, Rhode Island. There were times that I had to pull over because I was crying too much—and I am quite the messy crier. The good news is that I finally felt like I was coming home when I got to my new place at 353 Gibbs, just off the Cliff Walk.

Surface Warfare School (SWOS)

It's not the years in your life that count. It's the life in your years.
—Abraham Lincoln

I was slated to live with two female classmates (Academy grads) who were friends: Jamey, a red-headed, very tall rower; and Mary-Ellen, an Oklahoma girl. We rented this *gorgeous* modern home that Jamey had found for us about a half block from the Cliff Walk. It was such an amazing time in my life. Because Mary-Ellen was the only one with a serious boyfriend, she got the huge master suite on the top. Mary-Ellen's room had a magnificent view of the beach right off the Cliff Walk and the largest, most spectacular closet that I had ever seen. We all decided to share the closet!

The ironic thing was that I never did get to meet Mary-Ellen's *serious boyfriend.* This was all of our first experience with having our own place. And what a place it was! We could finally live like young adults: cook our own meals, buy what we pleased to cat, have sex if we so desired in our rooms—you know, be real people and wear our own clothes whenever we weren't required to be in uniform.

Surface Warfare School (SWOS) in many ways was just a refresher for all the information we had already learned at the Naval Academy. It *should have been* a breeze and a big party for all of the Academy grads because it was really just review, whereas for our ROTC peers, it was the first time they were learning much of the material. It should have been completely easy considering that not only had we been learning it for four years, but we had also been practicing it each and every summer and during the school year driving around the Academy's YPs to practice many shipping maneuvers.

SWOS was easy for me too until I finally allowed myself to really think about what had happened with Pig and what my responsibility was as a new Junior Officer. Apparently I have this delayed reaction when it comes to big things that rock my world. I found myself focused on the fact that Pig was *junior to me* and had still tried to flagrantly take advantage of the situation! What in the world would he have done with a young seventeen-year-old Seaman Recruit that was junior to him and taught to always accept the direct orders of their superiors? Pig in a position of power over those young, impressionable women was a very scary thought.

It didn't help that I met this class of '91 jet pilot, JJ, whom I had begun seeing—he was crazy about me at the time and it felt nice to be wanted and took my mind off missing Will and dealing with the Pig incident, until he started to make suggestions. He was a very good-looking guy with incredibly high principles, ideals, and beliefs. I transferred all of my feelings for Will into him briefly and did the "see, look, I'm fine" thing. (I wasn't fine at all!) He was going through a short Navy Legal course and was noble about how easy it would be for me to have justice be served in my grossly egregious situation. He promised to "stand by me," and completely believed that it was the right thing to do.

Although likely the right thing to do, it wasn't the right thing to do for me personally. I couldn't handle what it would have taken for me to come forward and expose the entire incident. The thought began to eat me alive and I started failing tests that should have been completely easy. I was great at moboards (maneuvering boards—a tool used by Surface Warfare Officers to figure out the Closest Point of Approach (CPA) of other ships) at the Academy, but I began making stupid errors on the exams. I became angry with myself on top of it all for doing poorly on something that I had excelled at before.

One evening, my dear friend Sante came over to study with me. Sante and I had been very close friends throughout the entire Academy experience—we were both English majors and both really got each other on an emotional level. On top of that, we had and have an incredible level of respect for each other—he truly is one of my favorite people ever. Up until that point, I really hadn't shared the experience with many people because I probably felt somewhat responsible considering that Will *was* in my room when he wasn't supposed to be.

Sante took one look at me and softly said, "Joanna, what's going on with you? This isn't you! I know you know this stuff . . ." We had studied moboards together the first time around!

I fearfully looked at him and tears began to well up in my eyes. I told him the entire story. He sat there and held me as I sobbed. He listened and considered the options that I was facing without judging me. I couldn't wrap my head around going back to the Academy and pressing charges against Pig because I knew that my entire love/ sex life would have been dragged through the mud and I would have been made to look like a slut—which I am not. I was still raw from the Dion Debacle and knew what I would be facing in a case of this magnitude. Sante gave me the permission that I needed to be able to move ahead without pressing charges.

In his deep, sincere voice he said, "Joanna, I don't think any less of you for not moving ahead with a big lawsuit. I care about *you!* And want you to be happy and OK. I love and respect *you* as a person." I felt so much better after talking to Sante.

I was finally able to let go of all the pain that I had attached to Pig and my final days at USNA and let myself fall in love with Newport, Rhode Island, and the very moment that I was living in. I developed some amazing friendships and finally began to be comfortable in my own skin.

> *September 25, 1994*
>
> *Today is a beautiful day. I have just biked out to this incredible place. I have never seen anything like it before in my life. It's a small cove just off the ocean with tropical fish and rocks. Wild birds peacefully cascading over the surface of the water. Boats languidly nestled just beneath the rocks. I'm so glad that I've decided to come here. It is like nothing that I have ever seen before. Peaceful. Nestled away. Surrounded by huge beautiful New England homes. I suppose that it's something to work toward. A dream. A goal.*
>
> *I look at the swirling water against the pitch of a rock on a tendril of seaweed. I could really love it here. I can hear the faint*

crashes of a wave off in the distance and the cry of a bird in search of its mate.

It may not be rugged nature, perhaps not completely untouched, but still beautiful for what it's worth. I think that this street is called Ocean Drive. Flocks of birds preparing for their imminent journey south. Yes, I could love this place! Several people don't believe me, or rather do not agree and are unable to see the quiet beauty here. But I do. Perhaps that's all that matters.

This special place that I happened to bike past and stopped to admire became my special place—I would go there specifically to let my thoughts out and put pen to paper. I still go there in my head when I need something beautiful and peaceful to wistfully be in my alternate universe. I fell in love with Newport by bike, foot, and word. I regularly ran the Cliff Walk and imagined the many famous big money families of our country's past: Vanderbilt, Duke, Oliver Hazard Perry, fabled plantation owners, and other New York elite millionaires. The backdrop was spectacularly haunting with rugged cliffs and waves crashing below—a supreme example of complete opulence, grandeur, and beauty. Sometimes it even scared me to run in the early morning hours before the sun came up—there was this feeling that you weren't alone. I could imagine ghost stories coming to life there.

My roommates and I got along well enough, but we definitely weren't besties. Jamey's room was in a constant state of cyclone—as my dad put it so eloquently during a visit, "a tornado came in and swept up every single item that that she owned, suspended and spun it in the air until dropping it to her floor." I realized just how different we all were with regards to cleanliness standards—away from the confines of the Academy and someone constantly inspecting your room and space. We were not cut from the same cloth when it came to the manner with which we lived. I found myself anticipating a space that was truly all my own.

For Halloween, my roommates and I threw the best Halloween party of Newport in 1994. We pulled out all the stops and threw a *huge* costume party with elegant homemade invitations sealed by hand-dripped wax and a special moon stamp. We had fun unleashing our creativity. The highlight was the large scavenger hunt that we put on at the start of the party. Cars of four set out in a race around Newport to gather all fifty items and make it to the crashing waves of the Cliff Walk beach right below our home. With radio blasting "What's the Frequency Kenneth," the winning car pulled in, earning bragging rights and cash prizes. The Hunt was a hit and a very memorable experience.

Belknap Decommissioning

A couple of days before Thanksgiving, Cody reached out to me after many silent months. Cody was a third-generation Academy guy—his great-grandfather and great-great-grandfather as well as an uncle had been Surface Warfare Admirals and Marine Corps Generals. In fact, his great-grandfather was Admiral Belknap, *the* Admiral Belknap that the entire class of Cruisers was named after. The US Navy was decommissioning the USS *Belknap* and bringing her home to Cody's grandmother, Rowan Howard, in Newport, Rhode Island. He invited me to be a part of the festivities and to spend Thanksgiving with him and his family.

Cody had unexpectedly called me the Monday before Thanksgiving after I got back from my classes and invited me to dinner with his family. I had already met his father, stepmother, and sister years ago, but I had never met his grandmother, Rowan. She was such a classy lady. I got the impression from Cody that he never felt quite comfortable around her or in her home because she was such a dignified, strong, classy lady. Their home was all "old Newport" and almost felt like a museum because they had so many proud family historical relics. Although she might have thrown many people off-guard, Grandma Howard and I really connected and I loved her. She and I became very close throughout my time in Newport and I hoped to someday be a lot like her.

When I met them that first evening at dinner, they all carefully peppered me with questions to see just what kind of person I was. Being questioned didn't bother me or make me feel uneasy, because I at least had enough confidence in myself to know that I could hold my own in most social situations. It was really because they had never met any of Cody's past girlfriends, and I think that they could tell that what we had was a little different.

That evening, Cody and I made our way back to my room and reconnected . . . again and again and again. We had always worked that way together and in many ways, it was comforting to be together.

Apparently, I did quite well, because Grandma Howard invited me to attend all of their decommissioning festivities, including a large cocktail party at the Officer's Club, a special family ship tour where the red carpet was rolled out, and their Thanksgiving celebration attended by the top-ranking officers of the base. I felt so honored to be included in such a private, important family moment, not to mention historical moment in US Naval History.

Prior to seeing Cody again, I wondered what would still be "there" between us and if we would still be attracted to each other. So much had happened in the year that had passed since we were last together that spontaneous weekend 1/c year when I flew out to see him and we loved. I had fallen hard for Will, graduated from the Academy, gotten my heart broken by Will, moved to my very first place, and was finally becoming my own person while he had also graduated from Washington State University and was fighting to get into vet school.

That soft question mark was unnecessary as it was better than it had ever been before. He looked amazing when he came to pick me up for that first dinner and we were able to talk easily about all sorts of things that we couldn't have gone near before—hard things, big things, real things. We had a wonderful time together for those five days that he was on the East Coast with his family and with me. And then, just as quickly as he was there, he was gone.

November 29, 1995

Cody's come and gone. Like my emotions—but they are in the opposite direction. They are very real . . . very true. They came back. I didn't think they would after . . . everything.

I am alone in my big house. I can hear it tremble as the wind hits it. That cold, harsh Atlantic wind. Sometimes it goes right through you. I feel so much sometimes. It can be overwhelming.

We've sure come a long way . . . together . . . apart. It's hard when we walk in and out of each other's lives so quickly. It seems unfair. In fact, I hate it! At least I know that it doesn't always have to be this way.

Even though Cody headed back to the West Coast, Grandma Howard adopted me. I regularly went to visit her and talk to her—I loved to hear her old stories spoken with grit and her contagious zest for life. I made it a point to see her at least twice a week and she wouldn't hear of me convalescing anywhere but in her home when I had all four of my wisdom teeth pulled. Grandma Howard put me in Cody's old boyhood bed under their colorful family quilts and made me chicken soup. It was very nice to be taken care of when my mouth hurt so badly and to feel the warmth of family—even if I had borrowed Cody's for a while. Ironically, he never could find the warm part of Grandma Howard as I could.

> *February 16, 1995*
> *I hurt inside. Not because I am sick. Perhaps too emotional though. I've been thinking about things. I'm looking forward to actually getting to a point where I may begin "living."*
> *Jamey has all of the stray bits and pieces of her life stacked around the kitchen. She's preparing for the movers to come. She's leaving Newport in about two weeks. Seeing all of the odd pieces of her life neatly (neat is not a word that I would ever consciously put next to Jamey) stacked up in piles is almost sort of sad in a final kinda way. We used to be such good friends a year ago. In fact, we flew to Chicago a year ago and really had a fantastic time together.*

Moves are always a cathartic time—time for reflecting on your life as you go through everything that you've accumulated throughout the years. I was saddened to see Jamey leave and excited at the prospect of following behind a couple of weeks later and moving on and out of Newport.

After I finished all of my schools—SWOS, CBRD, DCA school, etc.—I headed back to the West Coast to meet my ship. I swung through Annapolis on my way west and literally ran into Will on the street downtown. I was walking by the window of a small bar and peered inside when I noticed Will. My pulse quickened and I almost stumbled all over myself waiting for him to look up and notice me. When he saw me, his flashed his big familiar smile and immediately walked out to meet me. We quickly made plans to meet up for real.

Running into him was pleasantly unexpected and something that I had hoped for. We still had quite a bit of unfinished business and had danced around the remains of us on and off for most of the fall and spring.

It was nice and intense and bittersweet and sad. I wondered if he'd still be attracted to me, and he was. When we finally had a chance to talk, he said, "I guess one of our problems was that we never could say no to each other. I never wanted to fight with you or to hurt you."

When you really got down to it, that's what we did in the end— hurt each other. We still very much loved each other, but couldn't be together anymore. It was terribly confusing for me and I didn't know where to put it or place it in my head. I didn't know if I could trust him again or if I should even try.

As I spent my last few nights in Annapolis with the Williamses, I wanted to be with Will badly—to not have to say "what if" any-more. After that chance meeting on the street, we were left hungry and wanting each other.

I often felt like I was spoon-feeding Will, trying to get him to say what I wanted to hear from him—that he couldn't wait to see me. I suppose that was asking a lot from someone who was afraid of what he felt—he wasn't prepared to deal with the fact that his feelings for me were still very much alive. It was some-what comical for me to watch him fight himself and what he still felt for me.

On my last night on the East Coast, he caved in and invited me over for dinner to the small apartment that he and his classmates had rented to spend their off-time in. I enjoyed watching him be very self-conscious and excited to make me dinner—almost as if it were a date with me. He made us spaghetti with a little bit too much pepper. It was very hot for me, but I ate it anyway because that wasn't the point. It was so sweet of him to make it for me.

We talked easily about all of the things that we could never talk about before. There was this newfound maturity between us as we were both tentatively stepping into our own new grown-up spaces and lives. We ended up in a small closet with a massive American flag hanging on the wall—it covered the entire wall. A small closet would not be that big of a deal until you realize that Will was six-foot-five-inches tall! There was what appeared to be an Academy blue and white striped mattress on the floor of the closet and not much else. We ended up in that small closet all night long. I didn't care that I had a 750-mile drive ahead of me in a few hours; all that mattered to me was the time that we shared in that small damn closet.

We held. We kissed. We loved. We were two people pulling at everything to be one, to somehow be closer. We clung onto each other so tightly through it all with an intensity reserved for the last fleeting moments of a great love. We must have been together five or six times in those hours. I felt so full of emotion and so close to him. I felt everything as if it was the last time, and it was.

That night, I felt as though he really saw all of me. It was such a raw, naked sensation to have someone know every inch of you: your body; how you think and what you believe and when you're trying to convince yourself of something and when you're afraid of what you feel; all of your hidden spots and what makes you tick and what pisses you off. I was overwhelmed with everything. Somehow we finally fell asleep curled into that small uncomfortable closet floor together for not long enough.

When my alarm finally went off at 4:45 a.m., I startled awake and quickly moved into my efficient Officer alter ego and managed to get myself out the door and on the road within ten minutes. I never had time to take a shower to wash off our mixed fluids. I didn't want to wash them away. I mechanically made the long drive in about eleven and a half or twelve hours, lost in thought about what I was driving away from and toward. I didn't think about the lack of shower detail until I got home.

Sitting in a car for twelve hours after massive amounts of good-bye sex without any attempt of cleaning up caught up with me. When I walked into the door and got my hellos out of the way, I jumped into the shower to freshen up and threw my stinky clothes into the hamper. It didn't occur to me that I needed to be worried about their smell—I had been basking in it for the last twelve hours and couldn't smell it anymore. I was happily oblivious, but my mother was not!

As soon as I got out of the shower, my mom walked in and said, "What the hell did you do, Jo? Your clothes reek!"

I couldn't answer her—I just shot her a look and back-pedaled with an excuse about "what a long drive it was." Somehow she had managed to find the tact to leave it at that—if you were to know my mom, you would realize that this was a rare occasion.

I was only passing through Chicago and could stay for two nights before beginning the next leg of my cross-country journey. My mom drove with me from Chicago and helped me to set up my very first apartment in Long Beach, California.

Mom was the best car passenger ever! Although she didn't feel comfortable helping with any of the driving (she abhorred highway driving), she worked extra hard to be the most pleasant and helpful co-pilot possible. She would stock the cooler with healthy and tasty snacks and readily hand you things at any hour, wash your windows and pump the gas at every stop, and talk to you through the *whole* trip—especially through the boring parts when it's easy to get tired and drift off.

We made our way cross-country and managed to celebrate her birthday in the Grand Canyon via a helicopter. We drank in the visual feast and marveled at our country's beauty together. She helped me to pick and set up my very first apartment in Long Beach and left just before my household goods were delivered and I officially began my first job.

USS *Paul F. Foster*

The most difficult thing is the decision to act, the rest is merely tenacity.

—Amelia Earhart

I arrived aboard the USS *Paul F. Foster* (DD-964), a Spruance Class Destroyer, in mid-April of 1995 as a very young and green twenty-two-year-old officer ready to cut her teeth on the fleet. One thing that I was not lacking was enthusiasm. I was the fifth woman to report aboard the *Foster* within the past six months since Combat Exclusion had been lifted and was assigned to the Repair ("R") Division of the ship. The Senior Junior Officers (JOs) onboard were two ROTC SWOs (Surface Warfare Officers)—LT Aspire and LTJG Uduck. Two other female Academy classmates had arrived about six weeks ahead of me—Ensign Evergreen and Ensign Bird. Unlike many other wardrooms, the *Foster* wardroom was a very cutthroat environment where we all felt the intense pressure to get our pins (the equivalent of wings for a pilot) as quickly as possible and at any cost. Throwing three female Academy Ensigns in to go head-to-head made for a very competitive environment, not to mention that many of the men felt that we women were invading their ships.

One other important detail to mention was that when I reported aboard, the ship was in dry dock. She was the last ship to go through the yards in Long Beach before the base closed in 1995. When a ship goes into dry dock, she is completely out of the water resting on blocks and entirely taken apart only to be put back together piece by piece stronger. Dry dock is a very stressful time for the crew in a ship's work-up cycle, not to mention three young female Ensigns fighting to get their pins and erase the feeling of being behind all their peers who reported to ships that were deployed and underway. Getting warfare qualifications underway is impossible when the ship isn't even in the water!

Although I earned a Bachelor of Science Degree, I was an English Major in college and was much more of a creative spirit than a hard-core engineer. Being assigned as the Repair Division Officer (with the expectation that I would become the Damage Control Assistant (DCA) within the next six to nine months) in the Engineering Department was a stretch for me and a major challenge. I was slated to lead the toughest division onboard— Repair Division. These guys—my guys—were the firefighters, plumbers, and machinery repairmen of the ship—they were a tough crew that were not used to taking orders from anyone, let alone a young (younger than most of them!), short, energetic female fireball who didn't have much practical experience fighting fires, shoring up leaks, fixing toilets, or even in *really* being an officer. Quite simply, I was a round peg fiercely pounded with a mallet into a square hole.

The officer that I relieved, LTJG Malleable, was a very weak leader and was not able to make the tough calls necessary to have R Division reach its potential. He had just gotten married and, while a good guy, he had several opportunity areas. LTJG M was inefficient and lacked the respect of the other officers in the wardroom and of his division who had been running wild. The plan was for LTJG M to keep the DCA position for drills and in the event of an emergency, but for me to run the division until I would accept that critical role. There was no Chief Petty Officer in Repair Division when I got there—this turned out to be a very critical point. In the Navy, one of a Chief's largest jobs is to be a liaison between the enlisted community and the officer community and to help train their young Junior Officers to become good leaders and officers. I didn't have the luxury of having a Chief when I first got to the *Foster*.

R Division comprised nineteen men—most of whom wondered who the hell this young enthusiastic officer thought she was. Many of them had never worked with women before and certainly not someone like me! In lieu of having a Chief Petty Officer, my Leading Petty Officer (LPO) and senior enlisted person was HT1 Claus, an older smart-ass of a guy who looked like he was eight months pregnant with a beer belly. HT1 was an advocate of trying to get away with as much as humanly possible, took more frequent smoke breaks than I had ever imagined possible, and could always be counted on for a wisecrack. He was not a good example of how I wanted to run my division and within a week, I knew that I needed to fire him and replace him with someone more capable and more in tune with my leadership style and what I was hoping to accomplish in the division.

When I first got there, most of R Division was embarrassed to be a part of it. If asked which division they were a part of, they would turn their heads and mumble almost inaudibly, "R Division." On a ship, there is a lot of esprit de corps not only among shipmates, but also among the other divisions—there are several different small competitions and opportunities for a division and sailor to shine on a ship—everything from having the cleanest spaces, to the winner of the Sailor of the Quarter, or the most 1/c Petty Officers selected for Chief Petty Officer. My biggest goal became changing the mindset of my division and inspiring them to set goals for themselves to become the best versions of themselves possible. I yearned for them to be proud of their work, themselves, and their division.

Firing HT1 was quite a ballsy move for a twenty-two-year-old Ensign—female *or* male. He had a very strong (and loud!) personality and was one of the oldest enlisted guys on the ship—he had been repeatedly passed over for (promotion to) Chief Petty Officer and had a terrible attitude. If there was a way to get out of doing something, HT1 would readily find the loophole. The younger members of my division weren't sure what to make of the change. I decided that the end result of achieving my goal was worth the stinky situation I had gotten myself into.

I selected a younger DC1 who had been happy to stand in the shadows of HT1 Claus until I ignited the fire that lay deep within him. I could see immense potential and knew that he was capable of rising to the challenge ahead of him—even if he didn't believe it at first. Part of my job was to help all of the people in my division to grow beyond themselves—not a small order for someone younger than ninety percent of them all. In order to do that, I needed to earn their respect and their trust.

My strategy for gaining instant respect centered around blowing everyone away in the semi-annual Physical Readiness Test (PRT) and "hitting the deck-plates running," which to me meant:

- Never saying "no" to any task that was asked of me—even if it would be incredibly difficult to complete along with all the other things I was already juggling.
- *Always* arriving before or as my boss got to work and leaving after him—even if that meant regularly leaving at 8:30 or 9:00 p.m.
- Making it my mission to completely know the ship and all required professional material.
- Becoming a strong officer who earned the respect of her division and people.
- Showing an upbeat, positive attitude.
- Never ever letting them see me cry, ever—even if that meant racing to my stateroom before the tears began to fall.

This inability to say no would be a recurring theme for quite a while. The PRT came easy for me and I regularly recorded the best scores of anyone—man or woman—on the ships. The test consisted of as many push-ups and sit-ups as one could do in two minutes and either a 1.5-mile run or a 500-yard swim. PRT was easy for me and getting a perfect score was a minimum requirement for me personally. I honestly believe that this was a defense mechanism to try to capitalize on my strengths versus my weaknesses.

Because I enjoyed all of my collateral duties more than my actual hard job, I gladly accepted the opportunity to be the Public Affairs Officer and the Physical Fitness Officer in addition to trying to turn my division around. I thought that it showed how strong I was and how much I could handle—just how many balls could I keep moving through the air without dropping any of them? The truth was that I was completely out of my comfort zone in my division and grasped at anything that could help me feel more in control of my destiny. What I hadn't accounted for was the fact that first and foremost, my division was the most important job that I had. *Shitty Little Jobs Officer* (SLJO) was not really something to be proud of and in reality was a major pain in my ass.

Emergency Surgery

Within the first three weeks onboard, they had me tasked to go to Morale Welfare and Recreation (MWR) school at the base in Long Beach. At that time, I was in impeccable shape. I could run over five miles at a 7:00 pace (I ran a 5.2-mile race averaging 7:02-minute miles), crank out twelve pull-ups, do 100 push-ups in two minutes and 135 sit-ups, and could still swim a 500 below 5:25. I was planning on trying out for the American Gladiators the weekend following the MWR class and was excited about seeing if I could hack it.

I didn't count on my body rebelling. The first day of class, I ran at lunchtime and experienced a very sharp pain literally in my ass. It started out feeling like a burning ice pick in the fleshy part of my inner cheek. The next day when I tried to run, it hurt even worse and I instead went to medical during my lunch hour. Looking at me, they were convinced that I had just pulled a muscle and gave me a couple of Advil. As I slowly made my way back to class, my condition declined further. I went to the bathroom and sat down on a 1970s orange couch and eyed the winter coats hanging above me. I couldn't resist putting the warmest one that I could find on as I had the chills, which was odd considering May temperatures in Los Angeles. As I sat on the couch in the warm borrowed coat, time escaped me. Soon, two hours had passed. By the time I returned to class, it was almost over. Nobody said anything to me about my . . . absence, but I felt bad about it. That evening, I planned on rollerblading the pier with friends, but by the time I made it home, I could barely move. I called my mom as I lay in bed bemoaning my situation.

Sounding weak, I said, "Mom, I feel like such a sack—I had all of these plans to be active today and I have done none of them. I really do have a sharp pain in my ass."

Concerned, she said, "Oh honey, it's OK to take a day off when you don't feel well. Be good to yourself! Don't be so hard on yourself, OK? Promise me you'll go to the doctor tomorrow if this thing isn't better?"

Rolling my eyes—as I could barely move my body—I reluctantly said, "Sure, Mom." The truth was that I had never felt such a sharp pain *there* before.

By the next morning, I could feel that the skin around my inner left butt cheek felt different and I became worried that there was something very wrong with me. Driving felt almost impossible as I made my way back to the ship. I could barely make the long walk up the pier to find my boss. I checked in with my Department Head and immediately went to medical. When I got there, they immediately took my temperature and were surprised to see that it was 104 degrees. They immediately sent me to the VA hospital in Long Beach via an ambulance. First, an Indian doctor looked at me and with his very thick accent told me that I "had a dermatological problem" and he was going to prescribe something topical to take care of issue. I sat on a gurney shivering beneath four blankets and couldn't seem to get warm enough no matter what I did.

Finally, a surgeon quickly came in and saw me. He reprimanded the other doctor and said that I "needed surgery immediately." Almost in a blur, the dark mask was put over my mouth and I looked up at the nurse whose hands were close to my face. She looked down and gently said, "Slowly now, count backwards from ten."

Without any time to be scared, I began "Ten . . . nine . . . eight . . ." Blackness ensued. I woke up feeling slightly chilled and felt a little uncovered. As I opened eyes, harsh light blinded me along with the feeling of being watched. As I drowsily moved my arms, I realized that I was essentially naked in a room with other people coming out of anesthesia and one of my more senior officers from the ship. The Weapons Officer from the ship had come to see me and was standing above me looking down at me.

When the surgeon came in to see me, he explained that I had had an abscess, essentially an infectious ball that was beginning to take over my body. Without the emergency surgery, I could have died! It is now my understanding that after any surgery down there they pump your stomach up with air. I felt as though I were six months pregnant and had to toot it all out.

My hospital roommate was a nice Vietnam-era veteran who had lost her breasts due to cancer. One of the things I had to do in order to heal was to try to do laps around my recovery floor. Being an athlete, I was good conquering those kinds of tasks. I got to know the other veterans doing their physical tasking. After three days, I was released to the care of my mom who flew out for two weeks. I honestly don't know what I would have done without her help.

> *May 20th, 1995*
>
> *Right now, I am in the Long Beach VA Hospital. I had my first surgery yesterday. God what a hellish week this has been for me!*
>
> *I've been onboard for about a month now and feel completely overwhelmed with everything. It's been really difficult trying to balance the professional side with my sanity. I felt as though I'd gone to a smorgasbord and just ordered way too much. I am the Public Affairs Officer, the MWR Rep, and the Command Fitness Coordinator . . . as well as the R Division Officer. I have a ton to learn and several different PQS books to get signed off. I just want to be a good officer! Sometimes I think it'd be easier to be a civilian—even the hourly wage person that cleans the toilets.*

Perhaps the hardest part of the recovery revolved around the dreaded packing. Anytime there is a gaping wound, tissue needs to heal from the inside out. The best way to facilitate that was to pack it with sterile packing material, and, over time, have less and less of it go in. The first time they changed my packing, it felt like there was a fire in my butt cheek. I grabbed onto the metal side railings of my bed and screamed the full amount that my swimmer lungs would allow. Invariably, the only way to remove the packing was to also remove a small amount of the tissue that had healed. I dreaded each and every packing change.

My mom learned how to do it for me and religiously changed my packing *on time* twice a day. In the beginning, I would grasp at the sides of my bed with every ounce of strength that I had and scream at the top of my lungs. It was hard for her to see me in so much pain, but she knew that it was just something we had to do. I got better at swallowing the pain and she got better at making light of our situation—what a pain in the literal ass I was! She was such a blessing. Within two weeks, I was close to being healed, which made my mom feel better about needing to leave me and return home.

Resurrecting R Division

The surgery, although quite painful and scary, gave me the opportunity to really look at what I wanted to achieve and how I needed to adjust my personal course a little bit in order to make sure that I could get there. My mom helped me to gain the resolve to focus on the important things and the courage to dive into the most important task at hand—resurrecting R Division.

Because I hadn't been able to complete the required MWR class, the Captain decided to relieve me of that duty, which was a completely welcome surprise. It freed me up to focus on really digging into my division.

When I returned from surgery and showed up at Morning Quarters Formation all shined up with my spit-shined steel-toed boots and white hard hat, they looked at me like I had three heads when I explained the vision that I had for the division. I told them that I required them all to literally write down their short, medium, and long-range goals for themselves personally, professionally, and athletically. Reluctantly, they took out their tiny little pocket notebooks (not the digital kind that we are all accustomed to these days) and scribbled down some thoughts. My division wasn't prepared to have someone actually hold them all accountable and track their progress. At first, they resisted the exercise, but then began to embrace it as they could see progress and change not only in our divisional spaces, but also in themselves. We began to make serious progress on everything—we had a vision for how we wanted to operate and run, a plan for execution, and were beginning to gain traction.

That summer was a blur of walking my spaces (and the entire ship daily with the MPA) regularly, checking everyone's goals and helping them to reach them (including my own), force-feeding professional information into every spare inch of my brain, and then somehow finding a little respite for myself. For me, that respite came in the form of a quick run or a swim—not unheard of to get that run in at 10:30 p.m. when I finally got home. By the middle of the summer, we got a new Damage Control Chief (DCC) who was very instrumental in helping me to grow into myself. He was completely onboard with our direction and we worked really well together. Yet, it still was incredibly stressful and we were under the microscope.

The other divisions on the ship began to take notice of our transformation and my guys began to have more spring in their step and no longer mumbled which division they were a part of. We were completely focused on getting our fire systems back up and running and passing all of our impending major inspections before the ship could get back into the water.

Around that same time, Cody started to call me more often and seemed to flow into the most attentive version of himself that I had ever known. We had come into and out of each other's lives so many times over the past four years that in many ways it was familiar and easy to just pick back up in this new mature state that we were in. We had both grown literally and figuratively and were more ready for something real. At least, that's what I thought.

Cody flew into Long Beach just to see me for the Fourth of July weekend and gave me something tangible to look forward to in the midst of my almost-unbearable hell. We played at the beach, we played at home, and I thought we had a real chance. We made plans for our next visit and, quite frankly, the time was fleeting.

Ninety-six hours later, I was back in the shipyards with sweat rolling down my back and cortisol coursing through my veins at unthinkable levels. My guys had teased me that what I really needed that weekend was to "loosen up" because I appeared to be wrapped too tightly. In other words, they were joking that Miss Sprtel really just needed to get laid.

Honestly, they were probably right. But it really only gave me a short respite from the pressure-cooker pre-inspection ship environment and constantly feeling as though someone were watching and evaluating me. That feeling wasn't just a figment of my imagination; it was a complete reality. The Chief Engineer was a prior enlisted guy who was married with two children. I swear, he would waste time all morning reading every single page of the newspaper, paying particular attention to the baseball scores across the country. But when it came time to leave so that we could all eat a decent dinner at a decent time, he would insist that he had so much work to do that

he couldn't possibly leave until after 8:00 or 8:30 p.m. and sometimes 9:00 p.m. Which in Navy-speak meant that I couldn't leave
earlier either. I believed that he was secretly avoiding spending time
with his family when he could have been having a great dinner with
them. The unwritten rule was that, no matter what, you always left
after your boss unless he expressly told you not to worry about such
displays of supreme dedication.

When I wasn't trying to push R Division up the proverbial hill,
I was trying to force-feed myself every bit of professional knowledge possible. I shadowed the Main Propulsion Assistant (MPA)
every day as he walked all of the main engine rooms (four total) and
began to slowly retain all of the information that he was sharing..
I tried to be an information sponge and would have done anything
to earn their respect and my EOOW letter, my OOD, letter and
eventually my SWO pin. I began to know the inner workings of an
LM2500 gas turbine engine and how to be a molecule of air going
through the entire engine, what the flow rates were of our lube oil
pumps, the intricacies of all of our engineering systems. He would
quiz me nightly as we did our rounds and soon, all of our hard work
began to show.

Although the MPA was married, he was always flirty with me.
I steadfastly pretended not to notice and never acted upon his
harmless innuendos and comments. I pretended not to notice his
eyes wander up and down my blue coveralls and center on the pool
of sweat beginning to show through the space between my breasts.
I did, however, follow him around all of the sweaty engine-rooms
whenever he was willing to take me, which always seemed to be
when most of the ship was asleep and we were alone in the quiet
spaces. I drank in virtually everything that he said until I could
regurgitate it verbatim.

July 19, 1995
   I am at LA Stadium with the entire wardroom of the
Paul F. Foster. *We're here for the "wetting down" of our new
LTJGs (it's a time when the wardroom celebrates its officers'
promotion). They've really put together a class act. We were all*

picked up with limos at the ship, had lunch at the famous Dodger lounge—which I thought was really good (except for the dessert) and then spent the day at the ballpark.

This has been quite the month, quite the year—especially in terms of responsibility. Sometimes I feel like my knowledge level is a little on the low end. I have difficulty remembering parameters and exact numbers because there are so many different systems to remember. I get frustrated a lot with things: with my job and my situation. I've got so much to learn. Our fire-main system comes up online tomorrow. That's a REALLY BIG DEAL!

Although it felt as though this required an almost Herculean effort to get R Division ready for our ever-important inspection, we ended up performing extremely well and triumphing. The *Foster* was ready to come out of dry dock and to get underway again. Yippee!

As the last ship to go through the Long Beach shipyards, the base was soon closing. We would be shifting home ports up to Everett, Washington, in the beautiful Pacific Northwest. I was very excited about the move and believed that it symbolized a new chapter of my life and an end to the hot, sweaty stress of Long Beach.

Underway . . . at Last

After surviving close to six months of extreme stress trying to put the ship back together *and* make sure that she was safe to get underway, my real job was about to begin. Once we brought the ship back into the water, she had to pass Sea Trials, where all of her equipment was tested to make sure that she and the crew would be safe on long deployments around the world. During Sea Trials, the ship's entire engineering plant was pushed to its limits—this is the one time you get to see just how fast she can go; how quickly she can stop; how fast the rudder shifts from right full rudder to left full rudder, etc.

All of the unqualified JOs were vying for the coveted Conning Officer ("Conn") position in front of the captain to get the ship underway for the first time. It takes quite a bit of skill to drive a 563-foot naval warship and get her underway properly from a pier. Aside from plebe ship-handling classes and my very first six-week summer (YP) cruise, I had very little experience with conning a ship. In other words, I was as green as they come!

I was not selected to take the *Foster* out of the yards back to sea in front of the captain, but I did stand many hours of watch with him. Our captain was an Academy Grad 150s football athlete who had a very quiet intensity about him. He would ask penetrating questions that you were expected to answer immediately and would make his determination quickly regarding your level of professionalism and your potential as an officer. One of the toughest questions to answer as a young JO is the dreaded, "What's the target angle of that ship?"

The concept is not that difficult to master, but when you are put on the spot in front of someone that you are always trying to impress, it becomes a little more challenging. The idea is to imagine that you are standing on the bridge of the other ship and what angle you appear to be at relative to them—you *never* want to be 000, which would mean that the other ship was coming directly toward you (as in head-on), also known as constant bearing, decreasing range (CBDR).

As I stood my first real watch underway, I was self-conscious of my presence on the bridge and anticipated every command that I needed to say, practicing it silently in my head before actually opening my mouth to give it. "Attention in the Pilot House, this is Ensign Sprtel and I have the conn."

Because the ship needed to come right to stay on target, I needed to adjust our course. I double checked the new course change and said "Right standard rudder, steady on course 120." Although I thought my command was strong and to the point, the Helmsman didn't agree and barked back loudly, "Orders to the Helm!" which meant that he couldn't clearly decipher my command.

I dug deep within and confidently yelled out, "RIGHT STAND-ARD RUDDER, STEADY ON COURSE 120." This time, the Helmsman repeated my order and executed the command. The truth was that I had been afraid to hear my own voice—afraid of failure. I wasn't completely confident in the commands that I was giving due to my limited experience out at sea. They came out like soft question marks instead of the hard and fast commands that they needed to be and eventually would become.

I quickly found my voice and learned to go with it even if I wasn't a hundred percent sure about what I was saying. I figured that if I had made the wrong course decision, all we had to do was alter course again to get back to where we wanted to go. This concept is something that I have taken along with me throughout the rest of my professional career. One of the worst things that people can do is nothing at all and remain frozen.

It took me a while to develop a command presence on the bridge and with my people. I had to work very hard at it and did so with every opportunity. I attacked my professional studies and worked hard to pre-empt any question that the Captain might have. I had the target angle of contacts at the ready should the Captain ask. I became good friends with the senior female onboard and she sort of took me under her wing. I helped her get back into shape (physically) and she helped me to begin to hear my own voice. It became a very healthy friendship. We would run together in the mornings at 0600 before our professional day began, and one of us would bring lunch. There's no motivation like the knowledge of someone tapping their toe on the deck at 6:00 a.m. waiting for you to show up for a run.

I thought that I was really turning things around and improving my position within the wardroom. I was completely blindsided when the decision was made to fire Malleable, the current DCA, and to bring the old DCA back down for a couple of months until he departed the ship. The original plan had been for me to fleet up to DCA upon Malleable's departure since I had already been running the division for over six months.

This personnel move sent a ripple of doubt through the wardroom as people questioned the Captain's move as if it somehow indicated a lack of confidence in me. I felt the sting of his decision and the burning desire to prove myself.

In retrospect, I am not sure of how much of this decision had to do with me personally versus the stereotypes of women in particular jobs. The Damage Control Assistant (DCA) acts under the most extreme circumstances, keeping the ship afloat in times of desperation such a fire, flooding, major oil leaks, etc. DCA equals manly job. Although I was not *manly*, I could out-PT virtually anyone on the ship!

My Chief tried hard to help me improve my status—he was very loyal to me and was proud of all that we had accomplished in the Division together that last hot summer in Long Beach. Our Division passed all inspections with flying colors, won two Sailor of the Quarter Awards, and boasted the most advancements of any division on the ship. We hoped to be able to enjoy the fruits of our labor together and run a smooth division.

At the end of October, the ship was scheduled to shift home ports from Long Beach to Everett, Washington. The crew was feverishly preparing their families for the move and I was again getting ready to pack my life in boxes.

> *October 22, 1995*
>
> *I really want to be a good officer! I really do! This whole experience has been very valuable. I have learned what's important to me and exactly how I want to get there. I just hope it's not too late . . .*
>
> *I am moving out in about nine days, so I've begun packing my stuff. I reread some of my old letters from Will. They still make me cry when I read them. I really loved that man and can honestly say that I learned a lot from the experience. (see my theme here?!—learning)*
>
> *I thought of something rather profound today. The world is comprised of several different social circles and we each could find somebody we like in any given circle if the necessity arose. But finding your other half—finding the missing ingredient to completeness requires you to be in the correct circle when you are ready to make such a choice.*

I worked very hard foolishly hoping that I could change their (the Captain and Chief Engineer) minds about me and my ability to do the DCA job. They (wardroom) watched me put up a valiant fight to win over the DCA position as I professionally swung in limbo, when in reality the decision had been made before Malleable was even fired. Not knowing ate away at me and my Chief daily as I over-analyzed everything that was said and prepared to be under a constant microscope that put plebe year to shame.

November 14, 1995

   Oh dear book of mine, what are we going to do with me? I feel so utterly emotional when I should not be. When I have no real reason to doubt or second-guess myself or to feel this way. I wish that I had answers or that I had that inherent knowledge that one day I would be able to look back at this confusingly miserable time in my life and know that I had the strength to get through it all—that I would survive this somehow. I wonder what I will be like when I can remember the USS Paul F. Foster. This may sound quite callous and bad, but the truth is . . . that I am having a difficult 22nd year.

They had almost broken my spirit, which had always been one of my biggest assets—my positive attitude and grit and strength to get through any difficult situation.

   I think . . . that I want to get out of the Navy as soon as I possibly can. I think that I really can't wait until I am off this ship. I sincerely HATE it. I find it extremely difficult to maintain a positive attitude when things seem so bleak for me.

   Everyone in the wardroom is out for glory. Everyone wants a NAM (Navy Achievement Medal)—who the hell doesn't want a NAM? But that is not the sole reason for wanting to do a good job. I am still not the DCA and probably never will be. I almost don't care anymore. I just wish they'd be honest with me and tell me the truth instead of smile tacitly like vultures and zero in on me when I turn my back. It hurts. To be honest, it REALLY hurts.

Ironically, I thought that this was what I really wanted—to finally know the truth about their intentions for me. Regardless of how prepared you may think that you are for the truth, it still hurts something awful when it actually happens.

   I've never met a group of people so greedy and downright vicious. I know that this job could be really fun and adventurous and that I could really love it. It's hard to love it here when I feel like someone snuck up behind me, put a rope around my neck and gently nudged me to the edge of a cliff. NOT when I feel like that.

Maybe someday I'll have some relatively fond memories of this. Maybe I'll really look back on this growth / learning phase, but I highly doubt it. I know that I am going through a lot, but I'm not so sure that I like the direction that I'm going—the sarcastic, negative blob that I see sometimes when I look in the mirror.

When the ship got underway to change home ports, there was excitement in the air as everyone anticipated the move and the upcoming Thanksgiving holiday. Though unfounded, I still had hope that I would ultimately become the DCA and worked toward that goal daily.

The morning before the ship pulled into Everett, my boss, the Chief Engineer (CHENG), held an impromptu meeting with all of the officers and chiefs of the Engineering Department. I had no idea what was coming and was completely thrown off-guard when he began the meeting by saying in his flippant Southern drawl, "We've made a decision about who the next DCA will be."

I held my breath as I was hoping that the last month's show was not just a farce to avoid telling me the truth—that I really did still have a chance to be the DCA. The CHENG then turned to me, bugged his eyes out, and said, "Joanna, you will turn over with ENS Bird as the new Electrical Officer and she will become the Auxiliaries Officer. You are not going to be the DCA. I don't think that you are asshole enough to be the DCA *and* in order to be ass-hole enough, you need to have some type of knowledge! And you, Joanna, just don't have any."

My eyes began to sting as I processed what he said to me—in front of all of my peers and the senior enlisted in the department. It was very difficult to keep my composure together in front of them all and to handle this humiliating blow with grace.

CHENG continued on by saying "Furthermore, you only want to become a Public Affairs Officer, so what does it matter to you anyway?" There was nothing that I could say to defend myself and nowhere that I could hide to lick my wounds in private. I'm not sure really how much longer the meeting went on since I couldn't hear anything else. I just stared solidly at the papers in my hand and willed my eyes not to allow them to see how deeply this affected me. I had always been taught to "praise in public and reprimand in private." My boss completely stripped me in front of not only my peers, but all of my other counterparts in the department.

I couldn't escape that room fast enough. I literally bumped into my DCC (Chief) in the hallway outside and he looked at me with tears in his eyes and said, "Ma'am, I'm so sorry that this happened. For what it's worth, I think you would have been a great DCA and I wish that you were still my DivO. We built this Division together and this just isn't right! I have never ever in my career seen a Division Officer treated so badly." With that, he put his big hand on my shoulder and stood between me and the steel ladder so that nobody else could see my face. I was grateful for his shield—even for a moment.

Hearing his words pushed me over the edge and the tears began to roll down my cheeks. Somehow I made my way back to my stateroom to regain my composure. I had one more day to survive onboard before we would be in our new home port of Everett and I would get to see my parents for the Thanksgiving holiday leave period. I began to count down the hours to our arrival.

November 22, 1995

I found out yesterday that I will not be the DCA. I had had a sinking suspicion for quite some time, but just didn't want to believe it. The thing that bothers me the most is the way in which my boss told me . . . and HUMILIATED me in front of everyone.

On the November 22, 1995, the ship pulled into her new home port of Everett, Washington. I had anticipated the move for months and had had this dumb romantic vision in my head of someone waiting for me on the pier with open arms and a big smile. That morning, I was alone as we pulled into port and could not get off of the ship fast enough. As soon as the liberty bell rang, I beelined for the safety of my car and drove to my new home as fast as possible. There was no way that I would allow them to see how deeply I was hurting inside. As soon as I opened the door and was within its safe walls, tears rolled down my cheeks and I began to uncontrollably cry.

> *Finally in Everett. Funny, it doesn't feel as good as I thought it would. Last night, I pondered the feelings/thoughts of a man overboard. I wondered exactly how it would feel to be immersed in the cold, dark North Pacific saltwater. Could it possibly be any worse than being on here? I wondered . . . I touched the damp circles beneath my eyes trying to hide my pain.*
>
> *It's hard to conceal a pain so deep when it feels as though there's a damn knife spinning around in your stomach. Maybe I just have this incredible knack for making things more difficult for myself—creating more challenges.*
>
> *I wondered today how much money it would cost for me to be able to get out of the Navy now. How many hundreds of thousands of dollars would it cost? I still wonder. But that'd mean that I'd need to have a better alternative, and I don't.*
>
> *I feel so stripped, so ALONE and so vulnerable. And to think that I would let these idiot people affect me like this, HURT me like this. WHY? WHY does it matter at all? I'm just putting in my time now.*

But the truth was that I could never really just "put my time in" even if I fantasized about it. I cared too much about my Division and wanted to do a good job, not to mention the "good girl" factor that was rooted deep within me.

> *It's kind of sad because I didn't always have this type of attitude. I really used to give a damn. I hate when things don't work out the way that you planned or the way that you want them to. It hurts. I am finally here (in Everett)—Cody and I are nothing anymore.*

I think that what really bothers me is that I have never been one of those people that was discounted/discarded as I am now. Rather, I have always fought not to be. I am tired of the fight— at least this particular fight. I am tired of hurting. I'm tired of walking around with that bad taste in my mouth. I want to wash it out. Rinse it out and hurl it into their faces, cover them all with the bile that they created in the pit of my stomach, in my very being.

Perhaps someday I will have the last laugh. I will be the one to make a difference. Maybe not in this field, but definitely in something.

I met my parents the next day and we went up into the mountains and stayed together in a cute little cabin—what I needed most was to be surrounded by people who loved me and cared for me no matter what. I spent a lot of time licking my wounds, crying, soul searching, and getting my head in the right space to tackle the challenge that lay ahead with becoming the Electrical Officer. More importantly, I was trying to wrap my head around how to swallow my pride and accept exactly where I was and let go of how bad I felt about the way I was treated.

I allowed myself to settle into the seemingly easier role of a smaller division and focus more on my professional qualifications. I finally gave myself some space to breathe and found many mountains to hike up and ski down, as well as cute Seattle boys to date. My friendship with my new running buddy became one of the healthiest that I had experienced. Things began to fall into place and I began to see glimmers of light and hope through the Seattle grayness and the Navy gray that surrounded me.

Men—I dated some pretty unique Seattle men! I dated the professional skier who sold me my skis (two different times with a large break in between); a guide on Mount Rainier who was personal friends with Scott Fischer of *Into Thin Air* fame and was subsequently crushed by the 1997 Everest accident that led to Scott's death and the end of our short-lived relationship; reconnected with a Navy SEAL who rocked my world and had me seriously questioning the possibility of a future; got my first taste of traditional rock climbing and mountain biking with a '93 grad and shared some great times with him; had a passionate couple of weeks with a troubled artist with longer hair than my own and a complete abhorrence for any schedule whatsoever (which I couldn't grasp because my entire existence revolved around a schedule). The artist inspired me to write again and finally the words just flowed.

March 16, 1996

I write to you from the USS Paul F. Foster—patiently moored in the quiet waters of the San Francisco Bay at Pier 2, Naval Air Station Alameda.

I cannot sleep yet because I need to make sure that I record my thoughts on life today. San Francisco is AMAZING. Talk about a dramatic back-drop of rolling hills, ocean, sky scrapers, lights, country within fifty miles, versatility . . . I LOVED it . . . I truly felt alive yesterday—so full of life. So full of energy and so happy to be alive. I had no set schedule or anyone to tell me what I HAD to do. In the morning, I went for a run and then LT Aspire and I took the bus into town and the Bay Area Rapid Transit (BART) into San Francisco. I wore that little dress I made last summer—the one that I drew on the fabric, cut out, and sewed together in less than three hours (one of my more creative jobs, I must admit). Anyway, we were dressed to spend the day, tied a big blue guy shirt around my waist and off we went on our adventure.

We tromped around the entire city. Walked through China-town, ate at an authentic little restaurant. We both bought backpacks and by the end of the day, we'd filled one completely and took a ton of pictures.

The thing I liked most was the pace of the day which seemed to progress with sheer abandonment. It was so spontaneous and full. I felt FULL from it. It got cold, so we went to a thrift store and bought used jeans. We must have walked around ten miles yesterday! I can see how people get attached to this town. It is very beautiful.

My favorite kind of day is one filled with *everything* and that particular day really hit the mark perfectly for me. It was filled with so much good that whatever bad things from before were quickly forgotten. It was my slice of goodness in such stressful environment.

The next several months were pretty much a blur for me with ship operations underway and enjoying the Pacific Northwest. I did thoroughly enjoy attending the Portland Rose Festival in late May in Portland, Oregon, where it felt as though the city and its people really embraced us. It was such a colorful town and I got to have another one of those full days with my friend. I particularly remember an overnight stop we took in a small town on the mouth of the Columbia River called Astoria. While most of my shipmates raced off the boat, heading to the nearest bar for a cold refreshment, I put on my running shoes and went out for the most amazing adventure. The beauty of this place was such a sharp contrast to the grayness of the ship that was my home. I devoured all of the colors of the rugged scenery—the waves violently crashing below the cliffs and the quaint sea village homes with beautiful voluptuous roses and green grass. I was so visually stimulated that I could have run for miles and miles without stopping—and that's exactly what I did.

Shortly after the Portland Rose Festival, we did another underway to San Diego where we were to be in port for a few days. As was my norm, as soon as liberty was called, I put on my running shoes and headed off the brow to run the trail right alongside the beach. It was a hot day and I was about halfway through my five-mile run when I heard someone come up from behind me and tentatively say:

"Jo, is that you? I'd recognize those legs anywhere . . ."

Quite startled, I craned my neck around to see who it was. To my surprise, Jay was riding right up behind me with a smile on his face. I hadn't seen him since we had dinner at that quaint little Vietnamese restaurant days before our graduation—before he went to BUDS and I went to SWOs—that night when I didn't kiss him, when maybe should have . . .

We quickly made plans for him to pick me up at Dick's Last Resort after the wardroom's early "Hail and Farewell" (going-away party) for LT Aspire. Sadly, my best friend on the ship was leaving for shore duty where she was slated to be a coveted Admiral's Aide. I was beyond excited to see Jay and could barely contain myself imagining what could possibly lie ahead.

Everything became a blur for me as our time was filled with . . . so much of everything. Jay taught me how to surf that afternoon in the smaller Coronado waves and watched as I stubbornly stood up on my board before toppling into the foam, encouraging me every step of the way. We ate and walked and talked until we finally ended up back at his place. He was such a gentleman that he offered to sleep on the floor—but as soon as the words tumbled out of his mouth we both laughed and wrapped our arms around each other falling into his bed. We did all of the things that we had never had the chance to do, with no regrets, with complete abandon and desire. In fact, we were together the entire evening and into the morning—even in our sleep. It was the type of connection where I awoke wondering if I had dreamed making love while asleep or if our bodies had really found their way back together (they had). We rode long trails together, met friends for drinks, and even ended up at the top of a hotel with sweeping views of San Diego Harbor our last evening as I tentatively mentioned that "I was up for orders soon . . . and could pick something closer for us to have a real shot." But, at that point, Jay was just coming into his own as a new SEAL and couldn't wrap his mind around what was in the room with us. We laughed and loved and lived those three days together—and were at a real crossroads even though we both didn't realize it at the time.

July 3, 1996
I write to you from Hawaii where I met my parents to cel-
ebrate their 25th wedding anniversary. Before I left, I saw the
man that I wrote the published "gun" poem about—Jay. I lit-
erally ran into him by chance, but it completely blew me away.
I wasn't expecting to have such deeply passionate feelings for
him . . . still. I wasn't expecting it at all. He was always spooked
by me before—probably still is—and our timing was never right.
I didn't know where to put the whole weekend emotionally and
still probably don't know quite where to place it. I felt as if the

entire ordeal picked me up and spun me around. As if I'd been swept up by a big wave only to be dropped a little disoriented.

He told me that there are certain things about different women that attract him to them. Sometimes their looks, the way the laugh, etc. But, with me, it was the entire feeling of being with me—the way that I make him FEEL. That made my heart skip a beat . . .

Jay said that he had "gotten used to me" and wouldn't it be odd the next evening without me there with him. Why would this man say these things—seemingly so sincerely and then not act accordingly or even call. I don't get it.

It's almost as if it's easier for him to pretend that I don't exist and that none of this ever happened. It's mind-boggling because my reaction is the direct opposite—I feel that when you find and have something as powerful as this, you need to accept it and embrace it for whatever it is and be GRATEFUL for it. So . . . that's what leads me to believe that it's going to just be one of those memories that I'll never forget. Like the way that he looked at me. The lingering scent of the ocean on his skin. How it felt to be that close to him after all that time of wondering what it would be like to feel his warm breath on my back and his chest easily rise next to mine. Waking up next to him . . . not wanting to get out of bed. It saddens me to think that that's all it'll ever be—a wonderfully sweet "isn't it pretty to think so."

We had an incredible conversation Sunday evening before I headed westward to Hawaii—almost unparalleled for me. We talked into the morning hours. It was as if the two of us were writing a story intertwining thoughts and paragraphs and feelings together. I felt as if he were right next to me the whole time. And we talked about each other's feelings regarding our time together. It was so abrupt and unexpected. He said that it was "like a dream" for him. At the end of it, he said that he didn't want to have to say goodbye to me again and how bad he was at it . . ."

Jay was about to deploy to Guam and I was still focused on my pin. The time was fleeting and we both ended up going in different directions, but it was powerful nonetheless.

Immediately afterwards, I missed being with Jay something awful as it was very easy to get used to being with him—we were such good playmates and lovers. I was saddened that we didn't try harder to get on the same path together, but, in all honesty, I really didn't have much time to lament the situation. I quickly re-immersed myself in pursuit of my pin. I managed to get my CICWO (Command Information Center Watch Officer) letter and (after several rescheduled boards) my Officer of the Deck letter finally on November 12, 1996. The last qualification necessary for me was my SWO (Surface Warfare—my water "wings" like those that pilots wear) pin. Officer of the Deck was a very big job—essentially, you are responsible for the entire ship in the absence of the captain. Although he's never all that far away, it is a very big responsibility.

The *Foster* was in the last phase of our pre-deployment workups with one last underway before we were to deploy to the Persian Gulf for six months.

> *January 12, 1997*
>
> *I am currently on my way down to SoCAL (Southern CA—San Diego). Such a tease it is. As I sat in the wardroom listening to the Nav Brief, I was overcome with all of these memories from my time in Long Beach. I looked at the chart and my eyes were transfixed by the area where I once lived . . . to the beach and boardwalk that I used to run frequently and the Mole Pier.*
>
> *It's gotta be those rose-colored glasses I tell you! They make it all seem better in retrospect than it really was while I was living it.*
>
> *I was also thinking about LTJG Uduck—how she and I were so close throughout my time in California and how now, if there were a temperature scale for relationships, we'd be at 40 below. I wonder what I'll say to her when I leave in May— when I go down the line of supposed friends/commanders and get bonged off the ship for good. Maybe I would like to say "thank you" to her in spite of everything—for making my Long Beach time such fun. I don't know if she's sincere enough to accept that. It's always a shame when friendships shift. And such a dramatic shift this has been, too.*

I spoke to the detailer the other day—before we got underway for fifteen days. I put in for either San Diego or Hawaii, but managed to land Okinawa, Japan. The part that disturbs me most about it is the fact that I will not be able to talk to my parents or see them as much since it's halfway around the world. BUT, I will get to see a part of the world and explore an area that I otherwise would not be able to . . . extra $$$$ and my friend Dan is there. We could explore together—that's the best part of it.

For me personally, this last underway meant that I would go head to head with LTJG Bird for my pin. LTJG Evergreen earned her pin about a month beforehand. We were expected to have our SWO boards shortly after this last very tenuous week-long underway. The plan was for Bird and me to go "six on, six off" for the week under the strict observation of the Captain and all senior officers on the ship. "Six on and six off" was particularly difficult because I had to maintain the following schedule while still doing my day job of running my division of twenty guys: I was on the bridge from midnight to 6:00 a.m.; slept from 6:00 a.m. to around 9:00 a.m., then did division work; on watch again from noon to 6:00 p.m.; ate dinner, unwound and slept until 11:30 p.m. before going back on watch. This particular schedule is very taxing for anyone, because you never are able to get more than four hours of consecutive sleep at a time and are always "on"—especially with a SWO board looming. They would be evaluating us not only on our ship-handling skills, but also could ask us anything that was considered standard SWO knowledge—which really meant that no topic was off-limits.

January 17, 1997
Today we pulled both into and out of San Diego in a matter of hours. It was such a short-lived nicety.

I was supposed to stand the 12-18, but since Sea & Anchor went so long, my watch only would have been twenty or thirty minutes tops. Really, it shouldn't have been that big of a deal. But, it was the WORST short watch I've ever had. Let's put it this way, I have total indigestion right now.

I relieved LTJG Uduck rather rapidly as I understood that she had to quickly eat and be back down in combat as quickly as possible. I shouldn't have relieved her without having a COMPLETE understanding of where all of our contacts (ships) were.

Within a matter of about ten minutes, the SHIT hit the fan. ALL OF IT DID! All of a sudden, in a matter of six minutes or so, I had the Cimarron *(the Commanding Officer of the USS* Cimarron*) calling us on Bridge to Bridge telling us that our CPA (Closest Point of Approach) would be 1.5 nm (nautical miles) and asking us to come Right. Uduck didn't even tell me that* Cimarron *was even out there! COMBAT seemed to be comatose. They weren't giving us any contact information, CPAs or ANYTHING despite the fact that I demanded the information as the OOD (Officer of the Deck). And, in the middle of it all, the Captain came up on the bridge. It was so ugly.*

And this is what crossed my mind: what an extremely stressful, important job this is. At that point, throughout the entire ordeal, I was responsible for this ship and its safety and when it all hit the fan, I had some difficulty pulling the picture together. No wonder most of the men lose their hair and look twenty years older than they really are. This job is insane! Tomorrow will be better, I promise. You see, I'm already making an effort to improve this whole attitude thing I've got going on.

In one week, I get to see the Roberstons and to meet Eric's brother, Kenny. I am REALLY looking forward to the weekend.

That watch was the worst watch that I had ever stood—ever. I managed to recover from it somehow and even had some strong watches afterwards, but the sting from that one still stung deep within me as I could feel the soft question mark.

I somehow survived that underway only to come home to an empty, dark, lonely apartment without food in it. There is *nothing* worse than an empty, dark apartment with no food *and* no car in order to purchase groceries in a Seattle January. Of course, I just completely glossed over the fact that there was nobody there to wrap their arms around me and hold me through the night either after such a stressful time underway. I vowed that no matter what, I would not be in the same position the next evening. My Acura Legend had been in the shop after my very first car accident and was due back shortly. My insurance promised me a rental car for the following day so that I could remedy my situation.

I managed to make it through my next work day unscathed and anxiously awaited my rental car so that I could go and buy some food to make my place feel more like home. I stood at the end of pier where they were supposed to meet me with the rental as the rain started to fall. If you've ever spent any time in Seattle, you are acutely aware of the very pleasant thirty-five-degree rain that happens in the wintertime. I watched as many of my peers walked by me that early evening without even looking up or asking if I needed help. I felt practically invisible to them. Close to forty-five minutes had passed and I was beginning to shiver as the cold went through to my bones. I was tired, discouraged, and wet—and that only touched how I felt about the car, not about how things were going with Operation SWO Pin.

Finally, an enlisted guy on my ship noticed the soaking wet young junior officer at the end of the pier (me), rolled down his window and casually asked with a smile, "Hey! Do you need help? It's awfully cold and wet out there!" It was such a kind gesture exactly when I needed it most.

My face brightened as I looked at the warm face in the open car window and said "That would be *really* great! Would you by any chance mind taking me to the grocery store on the way home? I haven't been able to get anything since our underway."

"Hop in!"

His name was Spencer Verde and he was a 2/c Petty Officer on my ship—in the Navigation Department. I had never spoken to him before on a personal level, had apparently (I didn't really remember) stood several watches with him at arms-length on a strictly professional level and once borrowed his hat to run an impromptu Turkey Trot that took place immediately upon the ship's return to Everett in November. About the only thing I remembered about that Turkey Trot was how insanely red from cold my legs were after I ran the 5k in shorts in twenty-degree weather. I did however manage to get top three overall, was the top woman, and won the turkey for our dinner!

What happened next was a seemingly small, easy decision that sent me onto a completely different course. Because he had been so great and helped me when nobody else would even stop, I spontaneously decided that the least I could do was to cook him dinner.

As we pulled into the parking lot of the grocery store, I said, "Thank you so much for the ride today! Since you've been so great, would you like to stay for dinner? I can cook something up!"

Spence smiled and quickly replied, "Sounds good!"

Earning "Teflon Woman"

When everything seems to be going against you, remember that the airplane takes off against the wind, not with it.
—Henry Ford

I have completely glossed over the fact that interacting with Spence on a personal level was completely unacceptable in the eyes of the Navy and was considered to be "fraternization." Fraternization was illegal under the Uniform Code of Military Justice:

> *The Navy's policies on fraternization are contained in OPNAV Instruction 5370.2B, Navy Fraternization Policy.*
>
> **Policy.** *Personal relationships between officer and enlisted members that are unduly familiar and that do not respect differences in rank and grade are prohibited, and violate long-standing custom and tradition of the naval service. Similar relationships that are unduly familiar between officers or between enlisted members of different rank or grade may also be prejudicial to good order and discipline or of a nature to bring discredit on the naval service and are prohibited. Commands are expected to take administrative and disciplinary action as necessary to correct such inappropriate behavior. The policies listed here are lawful general orders. Violation of these policies subject the involved members to disciplinary action under the Uniform Code of Military Justice (UCMJ).*[5]

---

[5] http://usmilitary.about.com/od/navy/a/fraternization.uqE.htm

Fraternization was a complete no-no and grounds for the "Big Chicken Dinner"—in other words, a bad conduct discharge out of the Navy, not to mention the shame involved with getting into such *massive* trouble *and* the possible monetary implications of paying back the Navy for my Academy education. In other words, the risk was very great for me.

Alas, I was not thinking about fraternization when I invited Spence to have dinner with me after his kind gesture. I was thinking about the complete humaneness of what he had done for me and had the desire to do something nice for him. Prior to that moment, I hadn't even allowed myself to notice that he was pretty darn cute until I really took a good look at him.

We meandered through the food aisles and I hand-selected a basketful of fresh ingredients to craft our dinner and subsist me through the week. The cart was filled with colorful tomatoes, red and yellow peppers, onions, fresh herbs, chicken, spinach, French bread, and lots of fresh fruit. By the time we got home, I became acutely aware of the mutual attraction that was beginning to form between us. I watched him easily move through my kitchen and cut things up for our dinner and decided that it'd be OK to get to know him better—much better. He was kind *and* funny *and* genuine *and* real. Spence was one of the most athletic men on the ship and was one of our Search And Rescue (SAR) swimmers and had also been sponsored as a professional mountain biker—he was completely my type of guy and I was in trouble! But, more importantly, he saw me, not just some figment of me. I had been starved for affection and quite frankly for anything that remotely felt good after being onboard the cutthroat social incubator that the *Foster* had been for me. It was nice to be able to smile my wide smile and to laugh freely as who I am without being afraid of what anyone thought.

It was with that abandon that I allowed myself to look at him as a man instead of a 2/c Petty Officer that was on my ship and allowed myself to break this very real law. Realistically, the "*Danger Danger Danger*" alarm should have been sounding off loud and clear in my head. But instead, the only thing that I could do was move toward this wonderful thing that was in front of me and embrace the goodness that was there amid all the other shit. Spence felt like a safe haven from the rest of what my life had become.

Ironically, when we had met, I was about to fly out to Santa Cruz where I was to be set up with a good friend's brother-in-law, Kenny. I was spending a long weekend with them in Santa Cruz while Kenny was driving in from the Lake Tahoe area—my friends were convinced that we would be a very good fit for each other and looked forward to making a love connection. I had been excited about the weekend . . . until . . . I met Spence.

I had been open with Spence about exactly why I was heading to Santa Cruz—this didn't deter him at all. When it's on, it's on, and there's no hiding it or denying it. It was on with Spence even though everything else seemed to be against us.

> *January 26, 1997*
>
> *I think the airplane theme is always constant in most of my books. So be it. I am currently on my way back from seeing the Robertsons. I had a wonderful time—they were right about Kenny and thinking we'd get along well. He'd be good for me. Probably too good for me. We're going in the same direction, you know. Yet, I am CONFUSED because just before I left Seattle, I met this wonderful man who made me feel like I haven't felt in years. I've only known him for a short time, yet I already know that I could love him—that I could support and believe in this man. Yet, there are so many things against us. Like our jobs and the whole timing thing. I just want to chase this one into the wind. Spencer G. Verde. That's his name. He looked at me with his heart in his eyes. I felt like we were looking into each other. And he's genuinely sweet too.*
>
> *I was telling him about my amazing trip to Lake Louise, Canada with the Williamses for New Years—God it was so spectacularly gorgeous there. I said, "You have to see it someday."*
>
> *And he said, "Then, go with me!"*
>
> *I was so completely shocked and in awe of his open-ness and fearless honesty—I would have been afraid to say something like that even though I would have thought it and felt it.*
>
> *Spence looked deep into my eyes and said, "Don't question this anymore. Just accept it and enjoy the time we have."*

Before I left for the airport, he helped me to pack my things and drove me to Sea-Tac. I was late as usual (like arrived at the airport ten minutes before my flight was to take off), but that didn't deter him from quickly getting out of the car at departures, picking up my bag, and depositing me at the ticket counter. He gave me this wonderful, soft, passionate kiss and encouraged me on my run to the gate. As I was leaving he said to me, "Our first weekend together and you have to fly away . . . Next weekend you're ALL MINE!"

It was with Spence in my mind that I headed to Santa Cruz to try and meet Kenny with an open heart. I had a nice time with the Robertsons and did hit it off with Kenny. He was twenty-nine and already very stable in a way that I wouldn't be for quite some time. We liked the same sort of things and were both very athletic and adrenaline junkies of sorts. He was very giving with his family and on paper we worked well. But he honestly didn't stand a chance when stacked up against the picture that was Spence.

When Kenny dropped me off at the airport, he quickly leaned across the front seat of his red truck, kissed me goodbye, and told me that he'd like to fly up and see me before I deployed to the Persian Gulf. He couldn't even be troubled to get out of the truck to properly kiss me goodbye and hug me. This contrast did not go unnoticed. As I exited the airplane and headed down the escalator, I knew that I was done with doubting whatever was growing between Spence and me—I decided then and there that I was in for whatever was in store for us. I was practically giddy with excitement as I headed to the airport exit and into his arms.

January 26, 1997
Lots of thoughts running through my head today. I need to put these conflicts inside my mind down on paper and sort and sift and figure things out somehow.

Where to even begin is another question. I haven't exactly been the most popular officer onboard the Foster. *Some of it, I suppose I've caused myself—by being different.*

Unfortunately, I've cultivated some really nice friendships with people that I am legally not supposed to. I never used to give it a thought before. Nor would I have even opened myself up to that. But, with only 4.5 months left on the ship, I am sickened by the wardroom and the way that they treat each other. Many times I feel alone on this ship.

Last night was a wonderful, unforgettable night with Spence. We were both so happy and into each other. It scares me in a way. I don't want to be a firecracker anymore. I'd rather be a glowing star. I don't doubt him or his feelings . . . I trust him.

But realistically, as good as this has potential to become, it has the same opposite bad/negative/horrible possibility as well. I could, worst-case scenario, be put in jail for loving the wrong man. Lose my job—granted, I want out of this particular organization as soon as I can—but getting out that way, I don't know if I could ever forgive myself. It would be a blemish that would be extremely difficult to heal and recover from. And yes, there is life after the Navy, but I want to be the one to make that decision. I don't think that I could live with myself if that ever ended up happening to me. With all of these big things in mind, I need to make sure that Spence understands this and the importance of being careful. I wonder if THIS is worth the uphill risk involved. My heart says yes, my rationale says maybe not quite so. I am wholeheartedly confused.

When away from here, I see this wonderful, caring, big-hearted man with insurmountable potential that I want to explore with . . . WOE is me . . .

Although I was aware of the risks and what could possibly happen, I decided that the reward was worth the risk. The empty feeling that I had had for so long sharply contrasted with what I hoped for and needed—what Spence represented. Things began to move rapidly as we allowed ourselves to completely fall for each other. I sucked the marrow out of each and every night with him and hungrily looked forward to the next. I swept the apparent risk under the proverbial rug and went with the strong wave of emotion that had become us.

February 1, 1997
  It's a Saturday morning and I'm lying here feeling like a per-
fect ninety-degree angle because I think that I have finally found
my complement. It sounds so . . . trite, but I mean it.
  Last night Spence said the most amazing thing to me: "You
are what I want and what I didn't even know that I wanted."

It didn't take Spence and me long to become very serious and
to begin imagining a life together even though the path would be
tumultuous. "It" was in the room with us from the beginning and
was very hard to deny. He was the one safe thing in my life where I
felt OK to really just be . . . be who I was without fear of judgment
or trying to compete. We genuinely enjoyed each other's company
and went skiing and let our imaginations run wild with all of the
places we'd like to someday explore together.

Just before the weekend, I finally got my Acura Legend back
from the shop after my very first accident. Spence and I were very
excited too as we intended to get away into the mountains for the
weekend. We settled on a small Bavarian village deep in the mountains called Leavenworth and left Everett with the excitement of
two young lovers off on an adventure.

We talked easily on the two-hour drive and marveled at the fresh
snow coupled with a rare blue-sky Washington day. The snow drifts
in some places were three feet high. When we finally got into Leavenworth, it was like nothing I had ever seen before. I felt as though
we'd stepped in to another time period in another land—it really did
look European to me.

We stayed in a small bed & breakfast off the beaten path and
basically fell hopelessly in love. That afternoon, we went ice skating
and walked around the small, quaint town, window shopping. When
we finally came up for air and decided that we needed to eat dinner,
the kitchen had already closed and all that was left was soup, bread,
salad, and dessert, which was perfect for me. After dinner, a small
mountain band began to play and we danced together easily—even
in our big clunky snow boots. It was like a dream that I didn't want
to wake up from.

Our last morning there, we split up on a romantic mission to surprise each other. The mission was to find some very special things for each other in an hour—all the while remaining completely hidden from the other until it was time exchange little presents. Although this doesn't seem like such a difficult task, it is in a small town. I enjoyed ducking below the cashier of a small boutique as Spence excitedly purchased me a blown glass decanter with delicate, passionate hearts swirled across the top. The cashier was in on my secret and managed to let me go unnoticed. She seemed to think that we were pretty damn romantic and wished me the best of everything.

I found him an original watercolor of a frog that I intended to mat and frame myself, a small Toblerone chocolate bar (my favorite chocolate bar), and a fresh Linzer cookie from a local bakery complete with a hand-drawn Valentine on the paper plate expressing just how much I adored him. It was new for me to allow myself to be unabashedly romantic and sappy with someone and to know that they would accept it with gratitude—I hadn't had that since my first love, Adam.

The weather began to turn and was incredibly cold. We intended to then cross-country ski for the afternoon. The sky was deceptively blue with the crispness of the air. It was so cold that I needed to stop and get some new wool socks to keep my toes warm enough.

We rented our skis and went off exploring the trails together. Spence was a natural athlete—definitely my type of guy—and we seemed to feed off of each other's energy through the day running on fumes. We met this nice couple that was also "forbidden." She was married and he was "Dan the Sausageman" (a prominent sausage dealer in Seattle)—they seemed to be in love and very happy together even with the crumbs of their stolen moments—much like we had felt. Spence and I exchanged information with the fun couple and promised to keep in touch as we headed off in different directions. On our way back to the car, we ran into a woman who had badly injured her knee. Spence and I immediately went into rescue mode and proceeded to carry her out (close to a mile) to a safe location where she could get help. We felt good about the day and about how well we worked together as a team.

We made a quick stop at a local brewery called Gustav's and ordered something small to eat. I got to practice my Spanish skills with the server and proceeded to have about a quarter of my beer before I had had enough. My face became crimson red and I knew that I had reached my miniscule alcohol quota—which didn't go unnoticed by Spence. He teased me for my low tolerance level and offered to drive us home.

As we wound our way down the mountain with daylight waning, all of the ice that had melted in the sunny afternoon had quickly begun to freeze back over. I had put my seat back and fallen asleep soundly after all of the fresh air and the day's activities. We went over a bridge and wound around a slow left-hand turn when Spence had just enough time to wake me quickly and tell me to brace for impact and decide in a split second which vehicle to hit! Directly in front of us there was a truck in the ditch to the right, a white mini-van in the left ditch, and a car in the middle of the road. People were everywhere except for the car that was dead ahead. Spence squared up on the car's bumper around the minivan and we both braced for impact. The airbag went off in Spence's face, smashing his wrist in the process. Immediately after we hit the car, we were rear-ended by two more vehicles that had come around the curve. Everything began to move in that slow motion state of a high-stress event. We both jumped out of the car and he looked at me with a fear that I had never seen before in his eyes as he explained that his license had expired and that he had let his insurance lapse.

I had seconds to figure out what to do next and immediately made the choice to take credit for the accident even though I hadn't been the one driving. It seemed to be the only option available in my clouded state of consciousness. All six cars ended up receiving tickets for the ice-induced pile-up.

Somehow, Spence and I managed to limp home in a car that would soon be totaled. He drove the two hours home with no align-ment, very rough steering, and an air bag that had blown, as a somber cloud hung over us in the car. I didn't blame him for the accident—it truly was an accident, but I was concerned about my car now being totaled after I had just received it back two days beforehand. I had no idea that this was a precursor for what lay ahead.

The next day, we both went into work as if nothing had happened. But *something had happened*—in fact, *lots* had happened: (1) we had fallen completely in love; (2) my car was totaled; (3) we both had a difficult time not sharing our happiness with others—even in a generic sense because it felt so much bigger than either of us alone. It was just a matter of time before people on the ship found out.

When discussing the weekend's activities with our co-workers, we both casually mentioned our trip to the mountains with someone special and the car accident. Spence told one of his friends that he had "wrecked his girl's car" and was pretty bummed about it. Although he never specifically mentioned my name, it wasn't difficult to piece the story together once a few details had been dropped—all it took was someone who had heard both stories to begin to compare the pieces of the puzzle.

The next evening, we went shopping for groceries at the local Safeway together to gather supplies for our next feast. We had always been careful to not be seen together and most definitely to not act as we normally would have acted if we were free of the UCMJ. But this evening, we had let our guard down and walked around in a daze of sorts, not quite touching but very much together. As we were making our way toward the checkout line, I stopped to pick up the latest *People* magazine with a smiling picture of Gwyneth Paltrow and Brad Pitt all happy in love and recently engaged on the cover.

I teasingly looked up at Spence with my hair covering my right eye and said in my most sultry voice, "I'll be your Gwyneth Paltrow if you'll be my Brad Pitt." It wasn't just the voice that I used, but it was also the look in my eyes and my body language that screamed "I am completely into this man."

Spence kind of smiled and softly said, "He he, yes, of course."

I moved my attention from the magazine and Spence to the checkout line and immediately noticed that one of the officers from my ship was just pulling out his credit card to pay his bill. My stomach immediately dropped out, my palms began to sweat, and I tried to put on my game face as best as I could. I had no idea if

LT Tublier had seen and heard my foolish attempt at flirtiness with Spence.

In the most commandingly cold, monotone voice that I could muster, I very quietly and efficiently said, *"Leave. Now,"* to Spence and hoped that he would hear the alarm in my barely audible voice.

He put his hands into his pockets, slumped his head down below his baseball cap, and walked away from me through and out the store.

I decided that my best course of action was to pretend as though nothing had happened and brightly said, "Hey Tube!" to LT Tublier.

Tublier looked at me with a half smirk and said, "Hey, Joanna. How's it going?"

I grasped at small talk as if my life depended upon it and in some ways, it did. I knew that Tublier was headed to another female officer's apartment that was in my complex—LT Uduck who absolutely hated me. The rumor in the wardroom was that Tublier and Uduck were sleeping together and had crossed the friend boundary even though he was married with five children. He spent many of his nights at her place and they were always laughing and joking together throughout the day.

Tublier had been prior enlisted and seemed to be relatively cool, but if he went home and told Uduck, all bets were off. Uduck would have loved to see me perish and this was her chance to really stick it to me.

I managed to catch up with Spence about fifteen minutes after I was sure that Tublier had completely left the area. We lay in bed that evening, afraid of what the next day might hold, speculating if he would spill the beans and change the course of our future.

The day began as any other did, with morning quarters formation and setting my division on course. In the afternoon, I had a meeting with the Operations Officer to discuss my upcoming SWO board. Things eerily progressed as they always had without too many fires to put out. That is, until I went to my meeting with the Operations Officer. As soon as I went into his stateroom, he told me to lock the door behind me and to take a seat. As I sat across from him, I noticed that his tone had changed and that he was extremely serious. He chose to dive immediately into what the meeting was really about and said, "We are conducting a formal investigation into the possible fraternization between you and PO2 Verde."

Ops then said that I was "to immediately begin the turn-over process of my division" and would be leaving the ship by the end of the week, within two weeks of our impending deployment to the Persian Gulf.

I sat in the cold steel chair in complete disbelief and didn't know what to say or how to react. I didn't say much to Ops—I neither confirmed nor denied it. I tried to not admit to anything, but was also not feeding him more information either. This was a lot to digest. My entire life swung in the balance as I sat in that damn chair for those long five minutes.

As soon as I walked out of his stateroom, I felt that everyone looked at me differently—as if they all knew the trouble that I was in and were secretly laughing at me for my stupidity. When an officer gets into trouble in a wardroom, most people don't quite know how to react to that officer and choose to do nothing at all. In fact, the wardroom pretends as if they never knew you at all or as if you had somehow contracted a highly contagious, deadly disease such as the Ebola virus where interacting with you at all could mean that some of your shit could rub off on them and cause apparent career suicide. I tried to hide in the shadows of the ship, as I felt as if I were the gum on the bottom of someone's shoe. I can't exactly tell you why I cared so much about what those people thought about me, but I did. I cared way too much for my own good.

About the only humane thing that the *Foster* did was to temporarily reassign me to Naval Station Everett's staff where I was to work on the staff of (then) Captain Angela Brownley, an extremely accomplished female staff officer. Captain Brownley was an amazing role model to me as she exhibited a quiet strength about her and the ability to clearly see actions necessary to achieve the desired outcome. She was a Surface Warfare qualified staff officer on her way to eventually earning two stars in the Navy. Captain Brownley treated me as if I added value to her staff and allowed me to join her wardroom without prejudice and included me in all wardroom activities. Because of my prior experience and strong interest level, it was decided that I would work with the base's Public Affairs Officer,

Joan Potts. Joan was a civilian contractor who handled the image of the base to the outside world—and coincidentally did the job that I had always *thought* that I wanted to do. Joan and I became very close—she was like a fairy godmother to me who gave me the soft place to land that I needed at that time in my life.

I think that you can always tell when someone is teetering on the edge of just too damn much. Joan saw that in my face one day when she made the most absolute heartfelt gesture—she handed me a tiny golden angel pin and told me that I was not alone and never would be alone. Joan said that this angel would guide me through the worst of times. I put that little angel underneath the front pocket of my uniform, discreetly hidden from everyone and very close to my heart. I proceeded to wear it there for close to two years until it was time for me to pass the angel along. There were many days that it took everything that I had to still be breathing in and out by the time the sun went down—where I would catch my finger subconsciously reaching up to touch my magic angel for a little boost of secret strength. I will never forget the generous kindness that Joan and the entire staff at Naval Station Everett showed me.

On February 7, I received formal notification of my impending Captain's Mast. It is *extremely* rare for an officer to ever go to Captain's Mast. Having always been a "good girl" of sorts, I never imagined that this would be my story. I took the entire ordeal very personally and struggled each day to live with myself for what I had done. Of course, there was the other side of me that was finally thrilled to have someone special in my life which made the entire ordeal nearly impossible for me to handle.

February 10, 1997

Nine days later and my life has dramatically changed. This is an extremely difficult time for me. I have been kicked off the ship and am currently waiting to move on with my life. I have to begin the turnover process immediately.

I have been written up for fraternization—that "worst case" thing that I was referring to earlier. Well, it has happened. I was completely dumbfounded. I do not know the extent of what they know about Spence and me, but am confident that they don't know that we love each other and that we intend to get married someday. I have to see a lawyer today to figure out what my options are. The whole direction of my life has changed—no more Okinawa or Hawaii and no SWO pin . . .

It's amazing to be able to feel such intense happiness amidst such a painful experience. It's just so ironic because there had been this sense of foreboding over our relationship: the first time that I told him that I loved him, I said, "No matter how difficult things get—and they may get ugly sometime—never forget that I love you." Last night, we were together for probably the last time in months and he asked me to marry him. We don't know when or how or where. In fact, we're not even going to tell anyone yet because I don't think they'll understand right now. But I do.

I've lost weight over this. I haven't been able to eat or sleep very well. My clothes have started to hang over my body and have become loose. I just wish that it were due to a good, healthy reason.

Spence was summoned to Captain's Mast before I was—he got to go to see the Captain, Commander Martin, to receive his punishment for dating me. Captain's Mast is a very serious occurrence where the enlisted sailors come before the Captain, much like someone would come before a judge in the civilian court. Spence received:

- a punitive letter of reprimand that would stay in his until-now pristine record
- loss of one pay grade, from SM2 busted down to SM3
- loss of his SAR (Search And Rescue) rating and all the extra pay and bragging rights that went along with it
- loss of half a month's pay for two months
- fifteen days of extra duty.

During Mast, the Captain told Spence that he "had to live with himself for ruining my credibility." Because of the lost SAR designation and punitive letter of reprimand, he was no longer eligible for shore duty and had to finish his time in the Navy on the USS

Lincoln after he left the *Foster*. One of the harder things for Spence was the fact that his stellar reputation became tarnished by our breaking the code and he was given every shitty job possible for the six-month deployment and also had to fight for his ESWS pin in an hour-and-a-half board where most other boards in the past were less than thirty minutes long. He truly had received preferential treatment—and not in a good way!

Hitting Bottom

I went to Captain's Mast on February 12, 1997. It is a very rare occasion for an Officer to ever go to Captain's Mast, period. Although in the very beginning of the investigation I tried to deny being involved with Spence, I quickly realized that it was a lost cause to continue denying it. I chose to do whatever it took to protect myself and admitted to only what I knew they could prove. In other words, I never admitted to having fallen in love or the extent of what I felt for him or him for me.

I was numb as I stood at attention on the Bridge in my Service Dress Blues and watched the Captain read through the formal findings of my investigation. I did not contest the charges and stoically accepted my fate without contest as the Captain very sternly informed that I would be charged with a punitive letter of reprimand that would stay in my service record unless set aside or expunged by a higher authority. I was informed that I had the right to appeal the charges within five business days or a "reasonable amount of time" if I so desired and that I would have to show cause for promotion. In other words, I would not get promoted to O3 (Lieutenant) in my current status without a significant amount of effort.

A punitive letter of reprimand is a very serious, career-ending charge in a young Junior Officer's record where the Navy must decide to retain the individual or separate them from service. Very rarely can someone recover from a punitive letter left in their record.

This was *no* joking matter. Everything began to spiral out of control for me as my entire life became completely uncertain. I sought legal counsel and tried to come up with a plan of how to proceed. I honestly have no idea how I survived this entire ordeal and how

I managed to stop the complete tailspin from ruining me and my career.

The next day, CDR Martin sent out his official findings to the Commander of Naval Personnel along with his recommendations regarding the future of my career. This became very real and very official very fast.

After spending about a week with the wardroom of NavSta Everett, the Commanding Officer of the base and her Executive Officer had stuck their necks out for me and reached out to Commander Martin asking him to give me the opportunity to earn my SWO pin and have some chance to salvage my career. If I were able to earn my SWO pin, I could at least keep my orders to the staff position in Pearl Harbor—the pin was a necessity in this next job and I would not be able to keep the orders without it.

At 0800 on the morning of February 13, I received a call from the XO of the *Foster* asking me to please come in for my SWO board—he explained that they would allow me to sit the board and have a shot at earning my SWO pin. The Executive Officer of the base had called him and asked for a personal favor to give me one shot at earning my pin since I was so close to earning it. When I had gotten caught with Spence, I was expecting instead to be told that they were scheduling my final SWO board, *not* that they were investigating me for fraternization.

Regardless of how difficult my time had been on the *Foster*, earning my SWO pin was one of my biggest goals—something that I had devoted two years of very hard work to and an accomplishment that I craved. Being given barely an hour's notice didn't deter me from trying to put my best foot forward. I went into the Commanding Officer's stateroom where all five of the ship's Department Heads, Commanding Officer, and Executive Officer sat waiting for me like a pack of hungry wolves. They each took turns firing questions away at me—some simple, some tactical, and some very technical and challenging. For a SWO board, any subject was fair game and the young Junior Officer was expected to know it or know how to find it. Even more than a Trivial Pursuit game, this was a supreme example of someone's ability to perform in a high-stress environment, a la plebe year rates on steroids. I did my best to maintain my composure and to not let them see how difficult it was for me to be in that small room with them all since I had barely spoken to anyone in over a week.

I came out of the board feeling as though I had done pretty well—well enough to earn my pin. But, in all honesty, who was I kidding? There's no way that these guys would give me a fair shot after having just kicked me off the ship. Despite finding out about the board an hour beforehand, I did my best and my best just wasn't good enough in this instance. The ten minutes that I sat outside his stateroom waiting for my results felt like five hours. When he came out into the hallway, CDR Martin looked at me with a very serious face and said that he was sorry, but I just wasn't ready for my SWO pin and that he would be filing a non-attainment letter on my behalf. He wished me the best and dismissed me.

My impromptu board results stung in a way that I didn't think possible. I had spent months convincing myself that I didn't want this life and how much I hated Surface Warfare—I took the pin for granted and knew that I would earn mine someday. It was when my pin became an impossibility and something just outside of my grasp that I realized how important it was to me. I hated feeling like a failure and being labeled as a "non-attainment" story not to mention that "similar but not the same" feeling I had just before graduation where everything that I had worked for was again slipping through my fingertips. Prior to this board, I could have kept my orders to Pearl Harbor and my impending personal goods move—movers were scheduled to come within the week to pick up my life's belongings and ship them off to Pearl Harbor. Failing the board meant that I could no longer keep those orders and my future became even more uncertain.

After the board's blue ball experience, I sullenly drove back to my apartment and immediately went to the rental office to tell Linzy, the girl working the front desk, that I would need to delay my move since everything was so uncertain. It was in that same breath that I had asked her for more time in my apartment that she had told me that they had already rented my place and that I needed to be out within two weeks. I looked at her, with my notice in hand, and began to cry . . . really cry for everything that I had just been through. I had reached my own personal bottom, my "1," in this scenario. I completely lost it in her office and she didn't know what to do with me. The rest was a blur.

To add to my fun that day, I also got word from the mechanics that my car was definitely totaled and also heard from USAA that they were going to review my rates. At the time, they expected to still keep me on and insure me and had assured me of this as I began to search for a new vehicle. While I knew that my rates would likely go up after two costly accidents in such a short period of time, I had no idea that within the month, after I would lease a new Honda Prelude, USAA would drop me completely and that I would have to earn my way back into their auto insurance group.

When I finally walked back into my apartment, there was a message waiting for me on my machine that Spence was in the hospital. I couldn't call him directly and had to get his father on the phone and do a three-way call to the hospital to find out exactly what had happened. While Spence was working on putting up all of the ship's ceremonial flags just days prior to deploying to the Persian Gulf, he was using a chain-fall to finish rigging up 150 flags on over 200 feet of cable connecting the ship's mast to the bow and stern. A cleat gave way bringing 500-plus pounds of force down on his mouth, shattering his front four teeth and giving him a mild concussion. Because the dentist on the base was not equipped to handle such an emergency, he was rushed to a civilian dentist and hospital to try and receive some sort of temporary solution that would work through the six-month month deployment. After being pumped up with painkillers and a temporary bridge, Spence took off on his bike and rode the twelve miles to my little apartment in the rain just to be with me. I took care of him as best as I could as we clung to each other through the night, uncertain about what lay ahead. The temporary bridge turned out to be way more temporary than anyone anticipated and lasted a mere month in his mouth. Sadly, Spence spent that memorable deployment without his four front teeth. Now, his bridge is a reminder of that time of his life that we shared.

I felt that this day was my bottom of the entire incident—my "1." I finally allowed myself to feel everything that I needed to feel, to cry as much as I needed to and to even gasp for air. Prior to this, I held it all in and stuffed it trying to appear strong and OK when inside I was hurting something unimaginable.

The *Foster* deployed within days of that terrifying accident. I managed to quickly turn over all of my Officer duties. I quietly slipped off the ship with barely a goodbye to any of the other officers onboard.

I was very ashamed to be leaving in that manner and many of the other JOs (Junior Officers) didn't quite know what to say or how to say it . . . so, they said nothing. *That* is what I remember of my last days aboard the USS *Paul F. Foster*—feeling even more alone than I had before, which was no small feat.

Light Creeping Through My Dark Tunnel

Once the *Foster* left Everett and deployed, I started to really dig in to myself and did some serious soul searching about what I wanted in this "next" chapter of my life. The Captain and XO of Naval Station Everett renewed my faith in the Navy and I honestly enjoyed being a part of their wardroom for the short time that I spent there. Captain Brownley inspired me to fight to get another chance out at sea and suggested that I appeal the NJP (Non Judicial Punishment) and take it up the Chain of Command. Once the appeal was submitted up the Chain of Command, they reviewed it at a level above the *Paul F. Foster*. The staff of Commander of Naval Station Seattle, Rear Admiral Lower Half Sinter (a one-star Admiral), contacted me and scheduled a meeting for me to see the Admiral as soon as possible. Although this wasn't an "Admiral's Mast" per se, it was my one opportunity to impress the Admiral and dramatically change my fate.

On March 4, 1997, I made my way up to Whidbey Island, a gorgeous base about two hours northwest of Everett, to see the Admiral. I was dressed in my best set of Service Dress Blues and had my angel hidden close to my heart. I will never forget how I felt walking through the long corridor to his office. With each step, I could literally hear my heart beating and feel the sweat begin to form in my palms. As I made my way to his office, each step was purposeful. I stood at his door, confidently knocked, and waited for his permission to come in.

"Good morning, sir. LT Sprtel reporting as ordered," I said as strongly and confidently as I possibly could.

Admiral Sinter had been moving papers around his full desk and looked up for a moment, taking me in with his eyes. He sat down slowly and considered his words thoughtfully. "LT Sprtel, what do you have to say for yourself?"

I gathered every bit of strength that I had and with as much conviction as I could muster, said, "Sir, I realize that I have made a grave mistake—one that I have and will pay dearly for the rest of my life. However . . ."

Admiral Sinter interrupted me and said, "Wait a second there, LT Sprtel. How old are you?"

In my normal voice I replied, "I'm twenty-four, sir!"

Admiral Sinter then said, "You are wrong. You made a mistake, yes. But not a grave mistake. Please continue."

"The most disheartening thing to me is that I will never get to wear my Surface Warfare pin. It means the world to me."

Admiral Sinter grabbed his pen and then looked at me from across his desk and seriously asked, "What would you say if I could get you back on a ship quickly—knowing that it would be an uphill battle for you?"

Without hesitation and with as much excitement as I could muster, I replied, "I would do it in a heartbeat, sir."

The meeting ended rather quickly with Admiral Sinter recommending that I be given a second chance in the Surface Warfare community and that I get back out to sea as quickly as possible. As I drove the two hours back to Everett, I was flooded with emotion and the realization that I would be given an unprecedented second chance to get back out to sea. I hadn't realized just how important it was to me until what I had taken for granted was taken away from me. It had become what I wanted and needed most in order to feel like I was not a failure.

I secretly hoped to be assigned to something in the Pacific Fleet—I thought that San Diego would be the most attractive geographically to me, considering that I was trying to still foolishly keep the possibility of Spence and me alive. I went so far as to follow up my initial meeting with the Admiral with a memorandum peppered with ship suggestions to show how serious I was about getting back out to sea.

Captain Brownley also wrote up an endorsement on my behalf that trailed my original letter to the Admiral. Her endorsement helped to strengthen my case and was greatly appreciated.

Within a week, I had orders to become the first woman onboard the USS *La Moure County* (LST-1194), an amphibious ship in Little Creek, Virginia. The ship was in the middle of a six-month overhaul in the yards and she was to be retrofitted with new modifications so that she could accommodate female sailors more comfortably. I was scheduled to be the senior female on board as well as the first woman and only woman on board until the integration was complete.

I didn't really allow myself to think about exactly what a challenge this task ahead of me would be—I just gathered myself together and went for it. Being the first woman on board and only woman would have been challenging enough for anyone, but given my situation where I would be arriving without my SWO pin on my second tour—all eyes would surely be on me. The expectation is that everyone receives their pin on their first ship. The fact that I would be arriving without mine would mean that everyone would know that something had happened, just not exactly what had happened. It was up to me to share or not to share what had transpired. It was with resolve that I spent my last week in Everett and waited for my father to arrive to drive the first half of my cross-country journey back to the East Coast via a short stop at home in LaGrange Park, Illinois.

March 12, 1997

I am currently at the shore—Pacific Beach, Washington, at a women's leadership symposium through the wardroom of Naval Station Everett. This has been quite a week for me. Today, I was summoned out of the symposium to take a call. It was Captain Riley from Bupers 4 (the Bureau of Naval Personnel) telling me of my impending orders to the USS La

Moure County *(LST-1194) in Little Creek, Virginia. The ship is currently going through the female retrofit. I will be one of if not THE first female on board and the senior female on board too. TALK ABOUT A CHALLENGE FOR ME! And an opportunity! I will be moving as soon as possible to the East Coast. It will be a challenge for me that I want to succeed at more than anything.*

This conference has inspired me so much. I feel like that twelve-year-old again—the perfect chocolate covered strawberry waiting to be picked. However, I am no longer waiting to be picked, but rather am going to work toward becoming the Joanna Lynn Sprtel that I have aspired to become. I own me and who I am!

I listened to this speaker today, Judy Ford, who told me that "the world had a broken heart." Such a simple concept but so sadly true. I thirst for profound thoughts and am hungry for them again.

It was during one of our last fleeting conversations when Spence joked that I was "'Teflon Woman'—a woman who walked through a complete shit storm and managed to reach the other end of it with nothing sticking to her." I laughed at his remark, but often marveled at how remarkable my new outcome was.

La Moure County

There's nothing as exciting as a comeback — seeing someone with dreams, watching them fail, and then getting a second chance.
                                                                    —Rachel Griffiths

A s soon as I arrived back from the women's conference on the shore, I fell into *Ms. Make It Happen* mode and quickly scheduled my move and began the arduous task of packing up my life and preparing for the movers. My dad flew out to help me drive from Everett, Washington, to our home in the Chicago-land area where we would stay for a short period of time before my mom would resume the next leg of the trip with me from Chicago to Little Creek, Virginia.

We needed to drive the northern route back toward Chicago as I still had the traffic ticket from the accident with Spence to attend to. On our way across, we ended up stopping at the courthouse so that I could make my appearance in Service Dress Blues in front of the judge. She dropped the ticket for me and wished me well.

It was on that trip that I felt so much gratitude for the relationship that I have with my father. We enjoyed the beautiful landscape of our country together and had many wonderful conversations as well as a new affliction called "Honda Butt," which is where your butt hurts immensely from sitting in a small Prelude bucket seat for twelve hours at a time. I was filled with hope and inspiration as I made my way eastward and truly felt grateful for this opportunity to get to transcend the father-daughter relationship toward friendship too.

After a short few days at home, my mom and I began the next leg of our journey to the East Coast. True to form, my mom was again a model passenger. She could always be counted on for thought-provoking conversation after hundreds of miles of seemingly endless roads. My mom's help didn't stop there—she was also fantastic at setting up a house and finding the path of least resistance.

With my mom by my side, I made my way to Little Creek and prepared to check aboard the USS *La Moure County*. We managed to find a great little apartment just off of Chick's Beach—it was the back side of a back-to-back duplex that my landlord had just built about a half a block from the beach. It was spectacular and although a little out of my price range, I knew that I could make the numbers work and imagined all of my future runs along the beach and swims in the ocean, not to mention all of the great meals that I would cook in my new kitchen.

The morning that I reported aboard, I put on my best set of Service Dress Blues and affixed my angel hidden below my left breast pocket. Although I knew I was up for this challenge, it was still very scary for me. Again, I could hear my heart beating in my ears as I made my way up the brow. I was careful to make sure that my hand didn't shake as I crisply saluted the ensign and then again as I saluted the Officer of the Deck and "Requested permission to come aboard."

My mom waited anxiously in my little Prelude parked on the pier. She saw me salute and walk onboard and she also saw the crew's reaction to me—apparently all eyes were on me, as I was the first woman to ever show up. I met with the Captain, CDR B.J. Dubloon, and was given my assignment as Auxiliaries (A) Division Officer and then eventually as Main Propulsion Assistant (MPA), the premier Engineering Division Officer job. I had already successfully been through the very first Light Off Assessment of the Pacific Fleet and had a lot to offer the Chief Engineer and the entire Engineering Department.

That first day, I only stayed onboard long enough to check in and would not begin my real job for another week. They had given me the time to get my house in order and also get my dear mom back on a plane to Chicago.

The Captain was a class of 1980 USNA graduate as was the Chief Engineer. He believed in taking the path of least resistance while still allowing the crew to have fun at sea and perform well. CDR Dubloon reminded me of a different generation of Surface Warfare Officers (SWOs)—one that I could have embraced from the get-go.

April 13, 1997

I have reported aboard and things are OK. I have a lot to do and sincerely enjoy the wardroom. These words do not even scratch the surface of all that has happened and my thoughts. The first woman onboard the USS La Moure County! *Quite a challenge this is!*

Within a month of reporting aboard, I was again given a shot to sit for my SWO board on May 8, 1997. Instead of feeling under the microscope, I had a newfound confidence in myself and in my abilities—it showed through in my performance during the board. I completely rocked it! It also didn't hurt that I had gotten along extremely well with all of the officers in the wardroom and that they all respected me and my abilities. Unlike the wardroom of the *Foster*, we all played together well on the *La Moure County* and often hung out on the weekends too. I rocked that board and earned my pin in one try within a month of being onboard, which was a huge accomplishment for me and helped to fuel my confidence and performance.

That evening, the entire wardroom went out to a small dive-bar in Hampton Rhodes, Virginia, to celebrate the Supply Officer's wife's new pregnancy and my pin. The bar was about half an hour away from my place. I didn't think anything of it until they made me drink a massive Long Island iced tea to get to my newly earned pin. The drink was extremely tall by anyone's standards and for me—a real lightweight—it was massive. At the cheers of my peers and fellow wardroom members, I chugged the drink not knowing any better and seemed to be fine until . . . the room began to spin. All of a sudden I knew that I was not OK to drive and had to get a ride home. I was happier than I could remember to finally have my pin proudly on my chest—it sat right above my left breast pocket (and my hidden angel).

June 15, 1997

Very early in the morning I write to you. There are so many thoughts going through my head. Sometimes in the confusion of my day, I almost lose myself. I could never truly lose myself, but sometimes I forget about the importance of having and making time for me.

I looked at and finished another photo album today. God, what a year this 1997 thing has become. I had essentially lost everything that I had worked toward and had to fight to keep it all or somehow get it back. It's a scary feeling to watch it all slip away and to not be in control anymore. I never want to feel that way again. Things still feel raw sometimes deep inside of me. I never imagined.

I got my pin May 8, 1997. It was one of the best feelings for me—right up there with graduating from the Academy. Perhaps because I thought that I would never have the chance to get it. Maybe that's why it meant more to me.

CDR Dubloon took a completely different approach with the stressful shipyard environment then my previous Commanding Officers had. Instead of the entire crew working insane hours— often from 7:00 a.m. to 8:00 or 9:00 p.m. as at my past command, CDR Dubloon inspired his crew to figure out how to work as smart as possible and offered us all the opportunity to have a different work day. Our new proposed day began at 6:00 a.m. and finished at 1:00 p.m. with no smoke breaks or lunch breaks. The crew was free after 1:00 p.m. providing that they could completely finish their work and that the ship would be ready for our impending Light Off Assessment. Most days, it worked really well for everyone, as we were all motivated to get home early. I found this to be complete boost to morale and a nice motivational tool.

While the ship was in the yards and going through the modifications necessary for females, there was no specific head (bathroom) dedicated to me. The solution became a Flip Head, where we were required to flip the sign to say if there was a male or female occupying the space. One particular morning, the Supply Officer forgot to change the sign and went in to read his morning . . . ummm . . . paper. I got into the stall and immediately noticed a pair of massive steel-toed boots right next to me and could see the newspaper dipping below the metal stall doors. As chipper and happy as could be, the Supply Officer sang out, "Good morning, Joanna!"

I was completely dumb-founded and managed to blurt out a quick "Hi, Suppo."

I was careful not to pass gas or do anything other than pee. The good news is that I didn't need to do anything else. Whew! I averted a very embarrassing situation, but was still a little shocked. Good thing I had relatively thick skin.

I spent that summer hanging out with a few officers from my ship, mainly Bobby Burns, the MPA, and his friends on other Norfolk ships. They all became part of my inner circle of friends as well as my neighbors. We often could be found wakeboarding in Lynnhaven Bay on the weekends, having barbecues or dinner parties. It was such a change for me compared to what I had experienced onboard the *Foster*. I also picked a fantastic place to live and was surrounded by many active people my age to hang out with. Most of my neighbors were part of SEAL Teams 2 and 4 and we all got along quite well. They took me under their wing and together we worked out, kayaked, swapped dinners, went out for sushi and drinks at the Hot Tuna, spent Friday nights at the Duck Inn, and tried to figure out the meaning of life. We were all young, successful Generation Xers trying to figure it all out and grow into ourselves.

I spent the Fourth of July with my old roommate Mikki and her husband, Bran. Together we went to the Norfolk fireworks display. Bran laughed at the saps that Mikki and I were when the fireworks went off and Lee Greenwood's "Proud to be an American" flooded the area . . . and our hearts as we remembered our very first Army-Navy game together, clutching that field-sized flag as it billowed in the breeze. It was such a powerful and heartfelt memory for both Mikki and me that neither one of us could contain the tears as they shamelessly rolled down our cheeks—and Bran just looked down at the two of us, shaking his head at what a study in contradiction we both were. Here we were, two strong and successful female Surface Warfare Officers crying during a fireworks display song. I think that it hit both of us—to see how far we had both come together and what we had both respectively gone through to get to that point. Mikki and I are like family and always will be.

Toward the end of July, all the pressure associated with Spence started to really take its toll on me. While I completely cared for him and desperately wanted to be able to grow the seeds we had planted, I couldn't live with myself for what I was doing. I struggled with having to lie about who I loved and feeling as though I was letting down the very people who had given me this unprecedented second chance. Every time that I came into contact with another Academy grad, I was secretly worried that they somehow knew of the trouble that I had gotten into and always felt a little guarded and reserved (which is very unlike me).

Ironically, I had been living for August when he would be back from deployment and we could spend a couple of weeks together. But as it got closer and closer, some very big cracks began to form in our relationship.

> *July 25, 1997*
>
> *Almost to August . . . all of a sudden—to my dismay, all of the wonderful, warm thoughts that consumed me are replaced by this turbulent ocean. I don't know what I feel or think about this whole thing.*
>
> *Lately—since Monday—I've been questioning everything. Feeling as if I actually do need to make out that "list." The infamous PRO & CON list that helped me choose the Naval Academy and to realize that Will was not for me no matter how in love with him I was.*
>
> *I don't understand exactly what's going on inside of me. The entire time that we have been going through all of this, I had no doubts. I didn't really question . . . even when everything else was falling apart around me. Now, I am wondering <u>what</u> I was thinking?! If our decision was driven by what it's supposed to be driven by or if everything was just amplified.*
>
> *USAA (my insurance company) has decided to drop me. My insurance will not be renewed. I don't know what I'm going to do. Also, I can't afford to pay more for insurance. I almost feel numb. I don't know what I feel anymore. I used to look at my watch and figure out how many days until I'd be able to see him. I haven't done that in a while.*
>
> *What I didn't tell you is that I don't <u>feel</u> engaged. This doesn't feel the way I've always imagined it would. I always thought that*

I'd be excited and happy and ebullient. Instead, I have to lie about it and don't feel excited about it right now at all. It doesn't feel real to me anymore. Almost as if there are too many hurdles for me to jump through first and way too much at risk which could inadvertently lead to way too much pain. I know that I CAN'T deal with this again.

It makes my head hurt. And I don't know if he even understands all the things that I have gone through in the past six months alone. I have made many sacrifices and put A LOT into this—both literally and figuratively. I have been the one to lose everything (almost) and then to fight to keep it and hold onto it. Funny thing is that the Navy was never something that I intended to make a career out of or that I ever intended to have interfere with who I am and what I believe in.

I just don't understand how such warm, wonderful thoughts could be replaced by such cold uncertainty. I wish that I knew the answer to that question. Honestly. (NO SHIT!)

I hurt. I wish that I had better thoughts to put inside of you. I wish that I didn't feel this way. Part of me wants to say that we should relax things. That he should come and find me someday once his life is together and we can actually approach this thing correctly—without having to lie or hide or for things to be so dramatic. Right now, it's all so turbulent still. And risky. Very very risky with the ability to pretty much ruin my life. I'm not so sure that I'm still willing to risk that anymore.

Spence and I didn't survive much past that last conversation—it was just too much for each of us to handle. We were both young, stubborn and very headstrong. This doesn't even take into account the extreme amount of stress that our relationship had withstood and what we had both sacrificed individually. In my mind, I broke up with him while in his, he broke up with me. Regardless, neither one of us could stomach continuing in the manner with which we had. The only way that I could cope was to do the whole "see, look, I'm fine" thing by pretending to be OK when in reality I was really hurting.

Right around this time, all of my neighbors and I threw a massive beach party bash and invited all of our friends. It was the largest party that I have ever been a part of. We grilled fresh chicken and steak kabobs, had several different healthy salads prepared, and also many kegs to keep the mounds of SEALs and other Navy testosterone men happy. My roommate Mikki and her husband, Bran, joined us as well as all of my friends from the wardroom. It was quite a nice diversion, but still my heart was heavy as I danced with abandon by myself.

I looked up and noticed a man smiling at me—he had warm brown eyes and looked kind. His name was Bryce and he had just graduated from the US Coast Guard Academy and came to our party as a friend of a friend—apparently word had really spread about our little bash. Bryce was completely legal and it was easy to rationalize why being with him was such a better option than the relationship that I had nursed for so long—he *had* to be better as an Academy grad and all, right? I made sure that I couldn't think about Spence by planning things with Bryce and even bringing him home to Chicago with me during the time that I was supposed to be there with Spence. In retrospect, I had just boomeranged into him and transferred all of my feelings for Spence to him unwittingly.

Although on paper, Bryce seemed to be a much better fit for me, he had a couple of major flaws that were not apparent on the surface:

- He had racked up thousands of dollars in credit card debt that he had no idea how to handle. His bills sat in a rat's nest pile that he refused to go near and the envelopes remained unopened until I personally opened them. I helped him to devise an aggressive payment plan to manage his bills and personally paid off one of his $800 bills that had an obscenely high interest rate.
- He had no real plan following the Academy since he wasn't able to receive his commission. The Academy allowed him to graduate, but found him to be "Not Physically Qualified" (NPQ) due to a recent diagnosis of Type I diabetes. Bryce was loosely contemplating grad school, but had no real direction since what he thought he was going to be doing completely changed at the last moment.
- He did not have full control of his emotions due to a very difficult relationship with his mother when he was young.

Obviously, these were all very large red flags that I chose to overlook briefly in my crazed "see, look, I'm fine" method of healing. Within mere weeks of knowing each other, Bryce asked me to marry him. Even though I knew that the answer was "NO," I couldn't bring myself to just say no and weakly accepted. We bumped along for several weeks as my family and friends began to hold their breath for me to land. It cost me $800 and took me about two months to realize that I was making a major mistake while he had hopelessly fallen for me and clung to me like a life raft. I had no business trying to start any type of relationship with anyone given where I was in my mind and in my heart.

The *La Moure County* began her pre-deployment work-up cycle after successfully coming through the yards in early September. We spent many weeks out at sea doing operations up and down the East Coast and even navigated up the tight Savannah River en route to Savannah, Georgia, where we would stay for four days in-port.

I loved my time in Savannah and lost myself in the wisteria trees that gently flowed in the early fall breeze. I wrote a lot while I was there and ran through the quaint southern town. On one particular occasion, I found myself tucked away in the back of a church and anonymously watched a young couple get married.

> *November 15, 1997*
> *In Savannah, Georgia, I sit in a beautiful Lutheran church watching two strangers pledge their hearts away to each other.*
>
> *Being inside a church brings tears to my eyes. It has been so long and I have been through so much . . . I listened as the priest said that they are "equal people allowing nothing to come between them . . . not in front of or behind" and went on to say that "no marriage is an island." This priest seems to be quite a wise man! He advised the couple to "never allow people to come between you, but to remain a part of you."*
>
> *I think it's going to take me a long time to heal . . . Their names are Carl and Natalie. Taking a huge step together today. Someday, it'll happen to me too—I have faith in that. I just don't know when . . . hopefully someday before I'm sixty!!!*

By the time the ship was ready to pull back into Little Creek I knew that I needed to immediately break up with Bryce and do some soul searching. As I stood my watch on the bridge as the Officer of the Deck I easily talked with the Captain. We made our way back into Little Creek smoothly and as we began our approach into the pier, standing there with a perma-grin was Bryce, rigidly holding a bunch of flowers in his hand. As if he somehow could sense that I was drifting away from him, he tried the best he could to hold onto me with as much force as he had. All of my officer buddies on the bridge shot me funny looks and began to rib me for the sole guy on the pier waiting for our arrival. They knew that I intended to move in another direction—a direction away from Bryce, and joked that I should really be gentle with the poor guy.

I was as gentle as possible while still standing firm on my point. I tried to get him to pay me back the money ($800) that he owed me, but deep down knew that I had just made a very generous contribution to the Bryce Enrichment Fund and that he would never repay me anything that he owed me. In the end, I was happy to be willfully free and out of the relationship and the emotional mess that he represented. In a last-ditch effort to recover some of my funds, my parents drove up with me when they visited during Thanksgiving to try and persuade him to do the right thing. His brother answered the door and two grown men began screaming at my father and slammed the door in our faces. Good thing I side-stepped anything further with that family and got out for the low, low cost of $800.

Show Down with Senior Chief

One of the only remaining qualifications that I had yet to earn was my Engineering Officer of the Watch (EOOW) letter. During my time onboard the USS *La Moure County*, I had run all the big divisions in the Engineering Department—Main Propulsion Assistant (MPA), Auxiliaries/Electrical (A & E)—and knew our plant inside and out. This also doesn't take into account my two years of experience in the Engineering Department onboard the *Foster*. I had a great working relationship with the guys in the hole (my engineers working in the plant day in and day out) and thought that I was prepared for my EOOW board. I believed that at this point, earning my EOOW letter would just be a formality, since I had proven myself in the Department and onboard the ship.

The Captain and Chief Engineer leaned heavily on my Senior Chief, ENCS D, Senior in the Engineering Department. Senior was the Senior Enlisted guy in my division and had over twenty years of experience in the Navy. He was a very good person and a valuable member of our Engineering Team. We had a good working relationship and often joked around with each other. He invited me to his family's picnics and gave me advice when I needed it. All in all, I believed the relationship to be healthy one. So, it was with this knowledge that I prepared for my board.

A typical EOOW board would have two parts:

- A classical board (much like a SWO board) where the Captain, Chief Engineer, and senior Enlisted Engineers would quiz you on different parts of the Engineering plant.
- A Casualty Control Drill where "they" evaluate how you perform all Casualty Control procedures in a highly stressful environment. Onboard the *La Moure County*, Casualty Control Drills consisted of three or four drills run over the course of a forty-five-minute period. Prior to this day, we had *never* done cascading drills *ever*.

I completed the first part of my EOOW board and flew through all of their questions very easily. Perhaps too easily because they clearly had something else in mind for the practical Casualty Control Drill showdown in the Central Control Station (CCS)—the heart of the Engineering Plant where all direct orders come from.

Running Casualty Control Drills is a complete adrenaline rush because the EOOW needs to react immediately with the correct response to any possible given complication in the Engineering Plant in order to keep the ship afloat and making way, not to mention keeping all of the people alive. In order to elicit confidence in your orders and immediate action, a leader must come across as strong, confident, and not questioning the order but rather giving it directly and with enthusiasm. The bible of Casualty Control Drills is a series of large manuals with a red plastic cover called the Engineering Operational Casualty Control (EOCC) within the Engineering Operational Sequencing System (EOSS). In order to successfully complete a Casualty Control Drill, the EOOW must be able to completely know his or her way around the EOCC and be able to quickly anticipate the necessary steps from the engine-rooms and the right sequencing of events to save the ship.

After having completed several slower-paced drills, I felt that I was ready for this final step to earning my EOOW letter. I was a little nervous as I made my way down into CCS and saw my Senior Chief. The moment I saw Senior Chief, I noticed a sly look on his face. But what came out of his mouth was even more astounding.

I looked at him and said "Good morning, Senior!"

He looked down at me and said as strongly as he possibly could, "You're going down, ma'am! No fucking broad is going to be EOOW on my ship!!!"

I thought that surely I must have just imagined that snide comment and looked back up at him. What I saw was a hardened face and decided that it was time I dig in and show them all what I was made of. *Game on!*

I stubbornly retaliated, dug my heels in, sucked in a deep breath, and looked up at him and spat back, "FUCK YOU, Senior Chief! I KNOW MY SHIT. Bring it!"

I think that everyone in CCS was completely stunned at what had just happened. I was the senior woman onboard and highly respected—it was unheard of for a Senior Chief to speak to someone like that at such a crucial moment. I didn't have time to really digest it at all because within seconds, all hell broke loose in the Drill Set.

The Chief Engineer, Senior Chief, and Captain all had headsets on and began running the drills in a *cascading* fashion. Where in the past, we would run four or five casualties in forty-five minutes, they proceeded to throw twelve casualties at me in a cascading fashion in less than thirty minutes. We had never run a drill set like that before. At first, they called a lube oil leak in Engineroom #1 followed by a fire in Engineroom #3 and flooding somewhere else. This is a very high-stress environment and would be easy for anyone to crack under the pressure of so much going on.

It never occurred to me that I couldn't do it—failure wasn't an option! I just dug in and stubbornly barked out my commands per the EOCC as fast and strong as I could. It was hard to keep everything straight in my mind since there were multiple issues in each Engineroom, but somehow I managed to maintain my focus. I could barely catch my breath as the next casualty appeared until finally the set came to an end. While my evaluators were deliberating over my performance and if my performance was good enough to warrant a new EOOW letter, my senior Engineman, EN1, ran out of the main engineroom and gave me a hearty high-five. He had sweat dripping down his cheek and a big smile across his face as he enthusiastically slapped my back and told me, "That was fucking awesome, ma'am."

Regardless of the outcome, his praise meant the world to me—I had finally completely earned the respect of all of my guys and we had worked well as a team during the most challenging drill set they had ever seen. Although there was room for improvement, we did pretty damn well considering. I have knots in my stomach even remembering it now.

After about fifteen excruciating minutes, the Captain and Chief Engineer pulled me aside in a little huddle and very seriously told me of my opportunity areas. I stood there nodding at them and accepting all of their constructive criticism and prepared for what I believed to be a very lengthy let-down. At the end of the list of all the things that I could have done a little better, the Captain and Chief Engineer both cracked a smile and said that despite my short-comings, I was now a fully qualified EOOW!

I think that the respect of my EN1 and all of my guys trumped the EOOW letter. I've always been about being a good leader first and foremost. They all seemed to look at me differently for standing up to Senior Chief when he talked to me that way right before the drill.

Working Up to UNITAS 1998

The ship was set to deploy in mid-June 1998 for a cruise around South America called UNITAS. Although I thought that I would get out of the Navy as soon as I possibly could, I still struggled with the decision, as a shore tour is really considered one of the perks of being in the Navy—a chance where you get to regroup and not be out to sea so much. I felt that I had earned that perk and struggled with the decision immensely. The fact that I even thought twice about it surprised me.

> *February 5, 1998*
>
> *Quite a heightened emotional state for me today . . . for Virginia Beach as well. We have been hit by a nor'eastern storm. I watched the Chesapeake Bay churn with a force I didn't know was in her. It really puts us humans in check and makes us realize how small we really are. If it had gotten much worse, we would have been called in to get underway as quickly as possible to save the ship. We were all on high alert. Everyone in town worried about the safety of their homes—I noticed that many didn't make it as I finally ventured out to do my five-mile beach run. It was devastating! I've had a lot on my mind. This month, I'm up for orders and am at a point where I need to decide whether I want to accept shore duty orders or to get out. I've completed my infamous pros and cons list detailing my thoughts on the issue. As I look at the "stay in" side, I see no compelling reason to stay in—fear and safety are not enough for me. Amazing that I've even had to actually contemplate this.*

Stay In	Get Out
It's safer: decent $ / benefits; easy	I do not want to live my life "safely." I yearn to chase my dreams as far as they'll take me.
Fear of the unknown	I'm only 25—by then, I'll be 26 and will be able to bounce back from mistakes.
Relatively practical: opportunity to get MBA while on shore duty	I believe in my goals and plan.
Shore duty is one of the Navy's "perks" I feel that I deserve.	No ROTC billets in Chicago
Possibility of getting stationed near Elise	3 GREAT grad school programs in Chicago
The new $50,000 bonus sounds very appealing.	Could finally begin to establish roots
I'm scared of the unknown.	I don't like being "owned" by the Navy. I want to be able to see whomever I choose and run my own life.
Chance to meet the SEAL guy—the fiercely athletic man that I always thought I'd end up with.	I don't find my job very fulfilling. Although I have great guys, I could honestly care less about oil filters!
I'm a little scared . . . this is what I know.	Why prolong the inevitable?
	I could get a corporate job and go to grad school and likely make more then I am now.

Stay In	Get Out
	I have a good support network in place to help me with the transition.
	Tainted views on the Navy. I'm a little jaded after everything.
	I know that the Navy isn't "it" for me. I am capable of much much more.
	I never know exactly when/ where I'll be reminded of my past mistakes and exactly who knows about it. It will always be over my head dangling just within reach no matter how far away in my past it has become.
	I have done things for someone else/something else for the last eight years now. It's time for me to take a chane on me—however good or bad that may be.
	I'd like to put the past behind me and become HER.
	Maybe I've gotten what I'm going to get out of the Navy?

Even though the "get out" side seemed to be quite compelling in terms of the volume of information placed there, the "stay in" side still oddly appealed to me for a shore tour.

In March, I flew out to spend a week with Elise in Laguna Beach, California, and we had a wonderful time together. She was exactly the reset button that I needed to gain clarity and help me navigate this tough decision.

In an effort to keep my options open, I diligently contacted the detailer weekly to try to get a plum assignment that would allow me to go to grad school while serving on shore duty. I called the detailer two or three times per week and emailed him for over six weeks waiting for the ROTC list to come out.

April 7, 1998

Today was an extremely rough day. It shook me to the core. Funny how the past always has a way of coming back and haunting you when you least expect it. If only we'd all receive mandatory training on how to prevent the growth and insurgence of skeletons. But, then our lives would be void of . . . life . . . of trials and tribulations. It's not as if I enjoy pain and suffering and crying from my toes—I'm just used to it. As you can tell, I'm licking my wounds today.

A brief synopsis you would like?! OK! Here goes: I still have not completely decided whether I would like to stay in for a shore duty tour or get out. The only thing that'd keep me in is an ROTC instructor duty position which would enable me to get my MBA for free and do something I enjoy—teaching/ training and trying to make a difference. Anyway, I, in a way, sort of feel that the Navy owes me this tour. Maybe I owe it to myself to take a chance on me for once and forget the whole "path of least resistance" which on the surface appears to be a shore tour. Bear with me as I am tangent queen this evening.

Anyway, I have been calling the detailers now for about six weeks: two or three times per week plus emailing them waiting for the ROTC list to come out. I called him (my detailer) today and he mentioned that the list had finally come out. He asked me for my SSN number and then said that "with significant problems" I would "not be eligible" and basically refused to tell me anything further. My original fitrep (fitness report = semi-annual formal evaluation) from CDR Martin and the Paul F. Foster had not been expunged! Not only that, but they also did not have any of my last two stellar fitreps from the USS La Moure County. Case closed. Door shut. PERIOD.

I felt kicked—as if the rug had been ripped from beneath my bare feet. A year ago, the CO (Commanding Officer) assured me that it was all taken care of and now . . . I am fucked! My CO, whom before I had held in the highest level of respect, is now an unsympathetic prick.

I faxed all of my last fitreps to the CDR who fucked it up in the first place. I don't know what will happen next nor what I really want to happen. I just HURT. It's me and Sarah McLachlan tonight—she soothes me.

Talking to the detailer that afternoon was a major blow for me. I had believed that my past mistakes had been "expunged" per the Admiral and my Commanding Officer. When I found out that that was not the case, it literally crushed me and immediately brought me back to that bad place filled with shame and questioning my future. Shortly after that, I submitted my Letter of Resignation to the Secretary of the Navy, mere weeks before our impending deployment.

May 18, 1998

Somewhere off the coast of North Carolina we are right now. You have caught me in perhaps one of the most exciting times of my life (which is currently in a major state of flux). I've recently made some BIG life decisions. Things I've been wrestling with for months, but finally had the courage to be decisive about.

Last week, I submitted my letter of resignation from the Navy (something I've been a part of for eight years now). Funny how we arrive at certain decisions . . . only to find ourselves back where we started from. At the very beginning of this ride— I knew instinctively that this wouldn't be for me forever. Then somehow, "you" just get molded. Go through the maze and become accustomed to its safety and forget to take a chance on what brought you there in the first place—yourself. But, not me! I am going to chase my dreams into the sunset—as far as they'll take me!

Despite this major blow and the Navy virtually making my choice for me, I was personally firing on all cylinders and had achieved many of the goals that I set for myself going into 1998.

- I got into all-around excellent shape physically—better shape than I had been in for years. I completed my first triathlon and had even turned down an invitation to be the female leg of a local Beast of the East Adventure Race Team (this particular race was a grueling 250 mile "as the crow flies" Adventure Race through the Virginia mountains about two weeks before our six-month deployment). I often trained hard with my SEAL neighbors and could regularly pump out twelve pull-ups and could run consecutive seven-minute miles.
- I sold my Honda Prelude, saving myself from the $500/month payment over deployment when I would not even be in the states to drive it.
- I sub-leased my apartment for six months while I was gone on deployment to a young lady, which saved me another $1200 per month.
- Ferociously attacked gathering all the professional books I thought would help me grow personally while on the deployment: investment strategy books, real estate investing books, and even entrepreneurial books to help me craft my business plan and create my own future.

Perhaps one of the biggest accomplishments was actually putting on Lieutenant (LT-O3) on June 1, 1998. My parents flew out to surprise me and pin on my new railroad track insignia. For me, this was a major accomplishment considering that the likelihood that I would make LT just over a year before was minimal at best. Becoming a LT was a big step for me and included a lot more responsibility and respect. I embraced it completely.

In order to make my stateroom more fun, I painted the walls a deep cobalt/teal blue and sewed up bright red star curtains to hide our racks. Suddenly, my stateroom became a safe haven for me from the grayness of life out at sea. My roommate during the UNITAS deployment was scheduled to be the Navy dentist, LCDR Patricia Villalobos. She was a very short, fiery Latino woman with Columbian roots. We picked up Patricia in Puerto Rico and got along quite well in the beginning. She supplied our room with a TV and radio so that we could be more comfortable during the six months.

I was able to go home on leave to visit my family for ten days just prior to leaving for South America on July 6, 1998. I saw everyone that I loved and was able to also interview prospective MBA programs. I really liked DePaul's program and seemed to connect well with the adviser that I met with, Felicia Richardson-McGee, but still was unsure about which school I would apply to or if I would enroll in a full-time or part-time program.

UNITAS 1998

*Twenty years from now you will be more disappointed by the
things that you didn't do than by the ones you did do, so throw
off the bowlines, sail away from safe harbor, catch the trade
winds in your sails. Explore, dream, discover.*

—*Mark Twain*

I deployed with the USS *La Moure County* (LST-1194) for the
annual UNITAS deployment around South America. Basically,
it's a humanitarian mission that allows the United States to work
with all of the Navies of the Southern Hemisphere and complete
many humanitarian missions. Specifically, UNITAS is:

*The annual UNITAS deployment is a primary means of sup-
porting regional stability in the Western Hemisphere. Five months
each year, regular and reserve surface combatants and P-3C aircraft, a submarine and Marines embarked on an amphibious
ship, circumnavigate South America. The largest annual field
exercise south of the U.S. border, UNITAS has been conducted
for nearly half a century. In the early years of UNITAS, a single U.S. Task Group would circumnavigate South America and
conduct bilateral exercises as it steamed from country to country.
Some called it a "cocktail cruise" because it was highlighted by
Navy band concerts and never-ending social events. But today's
new UNITAS is not your father's UNITAS—it is about
building multinational coalitions and defending the Americas.
The social events have not gone entirely away, but the training is
more intense, challenging and relevant than ever before.*

Held each year since 1959, UNITAS is a multi-lateral Naval operation including traditional at-sea exercises and in port training activities with participating Naval forces in support of the U.S. policy of engagement in the region. It presents an unequaled opportunity to build capabilities and cooperative relations among U.S. and south and central American Naval forces while promoting hemispheric coalition, and two-way cooperation resulting in mutual benefit.

In 1998, Canada, Germany, the United Kingdom, South Africa and the Netherlands also participated during certain phases. At each Latin American stop, US naval forces exercise with the host nation's air, sea and land forces. These exercises generally provide the only opportunity each year for many of these Latin American nations to operate with US and other foreign forces.[6]

July 6, 1998

Today was a monumental day from the standpoint that we left on deployment. I have much to say on this subject as so much has gone through my mind in the past week. It's almost crazy.

First of all, my parents and I have bought an investment property together and I am very excited about it. That's something that I've always wanted to do and now we're doing it! It's about two doors down from my parents' place, but needs a lot of work. We bought it for $155k and should be able to sell it for around $210k.

I spent my last day in the States pretty much alone. It was as I never would have imagined my last day to be. I was a little sad—in my mind, I had always conjured up a romantic image of someone spending my last moments with me and missing me deeply. And yesterday, there was no one. Maybe that was just my own choice, I don't know. That part of it did suck though . . .

This is a huge adventure for me. I wonder what these pages will hold . . . my own personal perennial question. I must get some rest right now as I have the rev watch this morning (from 0345–0745).

---

[6] http://www.globalsecurity.org/military/ops/unitas.htm

The very first part of the deployment involved embarking our SEAL Team in Virginia Beach, picking up 200-plus Marines and all their Amphibious Assault Vehicles (AAVs), and the medical complement of our crew in Puerto Rico.

Our first official stop was Puerto Rico, where I was to meet my new roommate and we were to pick up the rest of our crew and supplies for the humanitarian efforts. We spent about five days in Puerto Rico and I had the opportunity to meet up with some old friends off of my first ship, a couple with a new four-month-old baby.

> *July 21, 1998*
>
> *On Saturday evening, we got all dressed up and went out to San Juan to a little discotheque called Alejandros. My friends got a babysitter for the evening so that we could really have some fun. It was such a culture shock to me. All of the women were EXTREMELY dressed up in VERY sexy clothes—as if you could almost pour them into their dresses. This also does not even come close to describing the amount of makeup on their faces. They were all perfectly done up. It was different for me to see that. I danced with a sexy guy from Chile with long curly black hair, but arms smaller than mine, and another Puerto Rican man. I've decided that my mission on this trip is to learn salsa and meringue.*
>
> *I think that I am very lucky to have a chance to see these places. My work is still taxing—extremely—since it doesn't really interest me so much. But exploring and seeing this part of the world does, so I guess that it's all a part of it.*

On July 22, we pulled into Puerto La Cruz, Venezuela. Puerto La Cruz is a nice coastal city nestled on the edge of the coastal mountains in the very southern shores of the Caribbean Sea. The wardroom celebrated a wetting down (promotion party) at a nice resort where our LTJGs were all celebrating their new promotion. One of the SEAL Team guys also got in on the action as he too had just been promoted. We all piled into small taxis and drove through the town to the beautiful hotel which starkly contrasted its surroundings. When I was there, there seemed to be a lot of poverty, but the children all had beautiful smiles on their faces and, although different than the way we live in the States, the homes seemed warm to me. Although we were in striking distance of the world-renowned Angel Falls (the largest waterfall in the world), we weren't there long enough for me to enjoy a visit.

Wetting downs are a time for everyone to blow off some steam and for the wardroom to have fun together. Typically, much drinking is involved, but in this particular case what I remember most is the fun I had having chicken fights in the resort pool with the SEALs and then going out dancing together. I finally danced with a man who knew how to lead me! I hadn't danced like that in a long time, if ever. It was the way I always wanted to move with someone and was nice to be in sync like that. Dancing with him was like being able to catch a whiff of the best meal ever . . . to even see it, but not to be able to ever taste it—and to want to taste it very badly.

As the senior female officer onboard, I was very visible and often held under a microscope—a difficult position to be in for someone counting down the days to getting out of the Navy. I had longed to be a carefree twenty-five-year-old on the trip of a lifetime, not a stuffy LT. Sometimes I made choices that were not congruent with my position and my judgment lapsed, while other times, people were unreasonably critical. The Navy in general can be very unforgiving to women, but a shipboard environment even more so—there's no hiding beneath your uniform. Even a two-pound weight gain is noticeable and the male crew will often make sure you're aware that *they* have noticed a change in your physique.

> *July 28, 1998*
>
> *I thought that yesterday was a bad day, but today was even worse! And it's only 0857! I am filled with all these different thoughts—things zipping through my mind because I've allowed them to.*
>
> *Makes me wonder how much I've caused versus how many things are virtual reactions to me. THAT'S an interesting one to ponder. I think it's a mixture of both, to be honest.*
>
> *Yesterday, I had something very bad happen while I was on watch. A BM2 (Boatswain's Mate 2/c), in front of the*

entire watch team, belligerently and disrespectfully asked me why I was allowed to wear shirts with spaghetti straps and Birken- stock shoes when no one else was allowed to wear them. I stood there—THE OOD—frozen. I didn't know what to say, which was the completely wrong reaction.

Then, this Ensign, who was a prior-enlisted Chief Petty Officer, pulled him onto the bridge wing reprimanding him and telling that he was completely out of line. And then I talked to him about it as well. It was just very bad. I felt undermined being questioned like that in front of my entire watch team. Clearly a lesson that I needed to learn.

The more I thought about it, the more I realized that I may have been wrong. I knew that I was stretching the boundaries with that even when I was wearing the shirts and Birkenstocks. And then when nobody said anything to me, I just assumed that it was OK, which isn't the right answer. I think what he said hurt me so much because I knew that deep down, he was right. Somehow I need to make the next 243 days the very best possible and do things FOR ME.

Last night when I was trying to get some rest before my mid watch (1145pm–0345am), the Ensign knocked on my door to talk to me. She told me that she had taken the liberty to go and talk to my boss, the CHENG (Chief Engineer) about what had happened on the bridge. I felt betrayed by her and thought that she should have talked to me about it before going to my boss. I would have talked to him! And was even thinking that it was better he hear it from me than from anyone else. So . . . that's what happened.

Then, this morning, I was pulled aside by one of my old First Class Petty Officers and he proceeded to tell me that some of the guys were thinking that I "was going to crack" on this deployment. I had no idea what the hell he meant! When I asked him, he said SEXUALLY. He told me that they were discuss- ing my supposed sex life. Or rather, in my case, my apparent lack of it. What really bothered me was that he based it on the fact that when I was in the gym, I had a pair of compression shorts on—the kind that I normally wear when I go running. I had on a tee shirt and never wore just my sports bra alone with it. I can't wait to hear the next rumor about me. That one is ALMOST funny.

I talked to Patricia about it for a long time. She urged me to work on getting a thicker skin and to not take things so personally. I feel lucky to have a roommate who's become a sympathetic friend and a sounding board.

I clearly still had some growing and maturing to do—especially in order to continue to grow into my position as a more senior officer and accept the ultimate responsibility that came along with it. In retrospect, I needed that wake-up call in order to clean up my proverbial act regardless of how much hearing it hurt.

After Venezuela, we continued to head south inching our way closer to the equator and the inevitable "Crossing the Line" rite of passage. This initiation process is different on every ship, but one thing is completely certain—it's an unforgettable life event. "The tradition may have originated with ceremonies when passing headlands, and become a 'folly' sanctioned as a boost to morale, or have been created as a test for seasoned sailors to ensure their new shipmates were capable of handling long rough times at sea. Sailors who have already crossed the Equator are nicknamed (Trusty/ Honorable) **Shellbacks**, often referred to as **Sons of Neptune**; those who have not are nicknamed (Slimy) **Pollywogs**."[7] Since I had never been south of the equator on a Navy ship, I was a "slimy pollywog" and would have to pay the hefty initiation price set by the salty "Shellbacks." The ceremony is a fun day anticipated by all and is a nice break from the daily grind while out at sea. Specifically:

The two-day event (evening and day) is a ritual in which previously indoctrinated crew members (Trusty Shellbacks) are organized into a "Court of Neptune" to indoctrinate the Slimy Pollywogs into "the mysteries of the Deep". Physical hardship, in keeping with the spirit of the initiation, are tolerated, and each Pollywog is expected to endure a standard initiation rite in

---

[7] http://en.wikipedia.org/wiki/Line-crossing_ceremony

order to become a Shellback. Depending on the Ocean or Fleet AOR, there can be variations in the rite. Some rites have discussed a role reversal as follows, but this is not always a normal feature, and may be dependent on whether a small number of Shellbacks exist to conduct the initiation.

The transition flows from established order to the controlled "chaos" of the Pollywog Revolt, the beginnings of re-order in the initiation rite as the fewer but experienced enlisted crew converts the Wogs through physical tests, then back to, and thereby affirming, the pre-established order of officers and enlisted.

The eve of the equatorial crossing is called Wog Day and, as with many other night-before rituals, is a mild type of reversal of the day to come. Wogs—all of the uninitiated—are allowed to capture and interrogate any shellbacks they can find (e.g., tying them up, cracking eggs or pouring aftershave lotion on their heads). The wogs are made very aware of the fact that it will be much harder on them if they do anything like this.

*After crossing the line, Pollywogs receive subpoenas to appear before **King Neptune and his court** (usually including his first assistant* Davy Jones *and her Highness* Amphitrite *and often various dignitaries, who are all represented by the highest ranking seamen), who officiate at the ceremony, which is often preceded by a beauty contest of men dressing up as women, each department of the ship being required to introduce one contestant in swimsuit drag. Afterwards, some wogs may be "interrogated" by King Neptune and his entourage, and the use of "truth serum" (hot sauce plus after shave) and whole uncooked eggs put in the mouth. During the ceremony, the Pollywogs undergo a number of increasingly embarrassing ordeals (wearing clothing inside out and backwards; crawling on hands and knees on non-skid-coated decks; being swatted with short lengths of firehose; being locked in stocks and pillories and pelted with mushy fruit; being locked in a water coffin of salt-water and bright green sea dye (fluorescent sodium salt); crawling through chutes or large tubs of rotting garbage; kissing the Royal Baby's belly coated with axle grease, hair chopping, etc.), largely for the entertainment of the Shellbacks.*

> *Once the ceremony is complete, a Pollywog receives a certificate declaring his new status. Another rare status is the* **Golden Shellback**, *a person who has crossed the* Equator *at the* 180th meridian (International Date Line). *The rarest Shellback status is that of the* **Emerald Shellback** *(USA), or* **Royal Diamond Shellback** *(Commonwealth), which is received after crossing the Equator at the prime meridian. When a ship must cross the Equator reasonably close to one of these meridians, the ship's captain will typically plot a course across the* **Golden X** *so that the ship's crew can be initiated as Golden or Emerald/Royal Diamond Shellbacks.*[8]

On the *La Moure County*, the day began with all Slimy (and did we ever get slimy!) Pollywogs being required to wear their uniforms inside out and backwards. Our MPA thought it would be funny to see me wear our Chief Engineer's (my boss) pants. In retrospect, it wasn't the kindest of gestures and I'm very sorry for having done it. At the time, it was quite amusing for everyone except for him. CHENG was an ex-Navy football star and was a rather large man six-foot-five-inches tall and also a little hefty. In order for me to be able to wear his pants, I had to use a bungee cord to hold them up. The worst part is that for a short while, I had stuffed a pillow down there too. He was not happy with me for my antics and I deserved whatever ill will he had for me. In retrospect, I was cruel and mean and feel bad about it.

There was a disgusting obstacle course set up on the flight deck which we were all required to go through. I remember a gloppy red food-like substance stuck in my hair, smeared onto my face, and all over my body, and being required to drink the grog held captive by King Neptune (played by one of our Senior Chiefs in costume). In the finale, we were required to eat the truth serum, lick Neptune's gross pot belly, and were eventually cleaned up by the very strong stream of water from a fire-hose.

Our next stop was Fortaleza, Brazil, where we were in-port just long enough to refuel and resupply in order to continue on our way to Rio de Janeiro, Brazil. The underway was over a week long, but

---

[8] http://en.wikipedia.org/wiki/Line-crossing_ceremony

not arduous from the standpoint of terribly bad seas. That being said, we had an incident that sent ripples through our wardroom and officer community onboard.

Officer and Warrant Altercation

On August 1, 1998 one of our young Ensigns, the Deck Officer, got into an argument with his CWO3 (Chief Warrant officer) who worked for him in the Deck Department. Our CWO3 was as salty as they come, having served over thirty years in the Navy—many as a Boatswains Mate, often referred to as BOSUN X. A Warrant Officer is an unusual rank in that "Warrants" are rated as an officer above the senior-most enlisted personnel, as well as midshipmen and candidates, but below all officers of grade O-1 (Ensign) and above.

> *Warrant officers are highly skilled, single-track specialty officers. Chief Warrant Officers (W-2 to W-5) are commissioned by the President of the United States and take the same oath as regular* commissioned officers *(O-1 to O-10). Warrant officers can and do command detachments, units, activities, vessels, aircraft, and armored vehicles as well as lead, coach, train, and counsel subordinates. However, the warrant officer's primary task as a leader is to serve as a technical expert, providing valuable skills, guidance, and expertise to commanders and organizations in their particular field.*[9]

Where this gets interesting is that our young Ensign had been onboard for about eight months fresh from Newport's Surface Warfare School and was just beginning to come into his own as an officer. He was diligently working on all of his professional Surface Warfare qualifications: CICWO, OOD, and ultimately SWO. *BOSUN X worked for the Ensign.* The Ensign was a rather laid-back guy who didn't seem to make many waves in the wardroom—I liked him a lot and thought highly of him. He was not argumentative or short-fused and seemed to be very level-headed. However, the

---

[9] http://en.wikipedia.org/wiki/Warrant_officer_%28United_States%29

relationship between BOSUN and our Ensign had become quite strained during the deployment.

BOSUN was a unique individual with many years of faithful service under his belt even though he was eccentric and a bit reclusive. BOSUN lived onboard the ship all the time and only left in order to go out for an occasional meal. Although he had children from a previous marriage that were now grown, the ship and crew had become his family. BOSUN was known to eat two or three dinners at a time, but had a very high metabolism that kept him in trim shape regardless of how big his eyes were. BOSUN was always respectful to me and seemed to be a good addition to our wardroom.

During this particular underway, both men were put on the same Bridge Watch rotation together, except the tables were turned in terms of who reported in to whom. BOSUN had earned his SWO pin, just as I had, and was standing the Officer of the Deck watch while the Ensign was serving the Conning Officer watch, which reported directly into the OOD. The OOD is responsible for the navigation and *overall safety* of the ship in the Captain's absence and is assisted by the Conning Officer, who is working on earning his Officer of the Deck qualification. The Conn's responsibility is maneuvering the ship (giving the commands for all course and speed adjustments) as necessary and assisting the OOD in any way possible. OOD is a major responsibility and one not to be taken lightly.

On this particular day, BOSUN and Ensign had gotten into an argument earlier in the work day regarding the operation of their division. The argument festered throughout the day and the situation had grown to near volatility when the two had reported in to serve their mid-watch together (from 2345–0345). Somehow, the men managed to serve their entire watch without killing each other. But when they were relieved, they both stepped out onto the cool, dark bridge-wing and things got out of control. A bridge-wing is a perch-like narrow walkway off the port (left) and starboard (right) sides of the pilothouse (Bridge) affording the Captain and OOD a better view of the entire side of the ship when conducting more challenging maneuvers. What is difficult to conceptualize is that there is nothing but very deep, cold, ocean water over a hundred feet below the bridge-wing.

As soon as they got onto the dark bridge-wing, BOSUN shoved his Ensign into the life boats. The lack of sleep combined with the festering argument caused the situation to quickly escalate and spiral out of control. Fists flew and each man ended up with a black eye until BOSUN pulled out his K-Bar (large knife), shoving his opponent onto the chains of the bridge-wing. Luckily, the current OOD managed to break up the situation before someone got thrown overboard. The men were physically forced apart and escorted to their respective staterooms and held under strict supervision. Neither was allowed to walk freely throughout the ship and was only allowed to leave in order to use the bathroom or eat. Unfortunately, this argument could have cost both men their careers. Our Ensign was taken off the ship within days while the BOSUN was forced to retire almost immediately with a blemish on his otherwise strong record. We were told that our Ensign might eventually be able to come back to the ship.

As I've told you, when something like this happens in the wardroom, many of the officers have no idea how to react to the situation and choose instead to do nothing. Remember the Ebola virus syndrome that I felt? I had empathy for both men. I visited our Ensign often—I knew what he was going through and how awful lonely he felt. Probably more than almost anyone did.

> *August 2, 1998*
> *I have come full circle today. I gave my angel to someone more in need of its powers than I was. That angel was given to me over a year ago when I had that same "deer in the headlights" look. Something very very bad happened last night that is inexcusable. It's nice to know that I finally don't need my little angel as much as someone else does.*

When I went to visit our Ensign, I shared my story with him which was not something that I took lightly. I hadn't talked to anyone onboard up until that point, but felt that he needed to hear what I went through and hoped that he could grasp some hope from it. Ensign sat there and quietly listened as I shared the predicament that I managed to get myself into and out of with Spence. He didn't judge me, but instead was grateful for my gesture of humanity during such an awful time for him. Life as he knew it onboard the *La Moure County* was over and he was facing the possibility of a very different future than he had expected. I watched his pale face and red eyes as he watched me reach underneath my left breast pocket and unpin my little angel and hand it over to him.

"Please pass it onto someone else who needs it more than you do when you are ready," I said as I handed it over to him. "He gave me courage and strength through a very difficult time and I hope that he does the same for you. I want you to have him as you need him more now."

Ensign took the little angel and immediately pinned it under the left breast pocket of his uniform—completely out of sight.

> *August 15, 1998*
>
> *Things have been odd here. We had a horrible incident pummel the wardroom. An incident which no doubt changed two people's lives forever. Both of which are off the ship now.*
>
> *I've always said that it's amazing what the body does and how it reacts when under extreme stress. I completely believe that. In the brief time that I did see and talk to BOSUN, he had stopped eating. I would imagine that his whole life began to pass before his eyes.*
>
> *Two men let their anger get the best of them one night on the bridge-wing. An otherwise quiet night out at sea turned ugly in an instant. I would imagine that if they had it all to do over again, none of it would have ever happened. Such is hindsight. Whatever the outcome, I hope they will both be able to put this behind them and move forward in their lives.*
>
> *Ensign left the ship two days ago. They say that he may be back . . . I watched him leave the ship in Rio—there he stood on the pier alone with his sea bag surely leaving several things behind: friends, uniforms and eight months worth of hard work toward his pin. I hope that things will work out for the best for him. Gary the Guardian Angel is with him as long as he needs him. Someday, he'll make his way to another needy lapel.*

God, it amazes me how things seem to go full circle. I'm
twenty-five years old and have things turned out like I thought
they would? In some ways, yes. Yet, I still feel unsettled. I'm still
thirsty—thirsty for life and all that it has to offer.

Rio de Janeiro

Rio inspired me from the very first glimpse that I caught on the
bridge-wing as we navigated through the channel into port. I was
in awe as the blue sky provided the perfect backdrop for the Christ
Redeemer statue and lush green mountain peaks popping out of the
sea. We were scheduled to be in Rio for a total of close to two separate weeks (I think about twelve days) with Brazilian Navy Operations sandwiched in between our port visits to Rio. Our liberty in
Rio was very iffy and often restricted, making it difficult to spend
the night and leave very early for an exhilarating exploration.

My favorite thing to do upon liberty call was always to get my
running shoes on and explore by foot and get a much-needed workout in at the same time. Very close to the base was a 50-meter pool
nestled high atop a mountain. Reaching the pool required a stair
workout of several hundred stairs. I followed our SAR swimmer
(typically one of the best athletes on the ship) to the pool and managed to do a couple of rounds of stairs with him before getting my
first real swim under my belt in quite a while. The water was cool and
I felt pretty strong as I managed to get in close to 2000 meters—a
very paltry distance compared to what I had been used to, but nothing to sneeze at in the middle of a deployment after not swimming
for months. With every lap I swam, I started to feel as though I was
getting a part of myself back—the true and real me, not the Navy
version of me.

As soon as I put my civilian clothes on and headed out into Rio
and nearby Copacabana, the stark contrast really struck me. The city
was a unique mix of beautiful natural landscape with urban buildings, while there seemed to be a rather large prostitution culture
where women openly walked the streets and actively hunted for new
clients. It made me feel uncomfortable, as many of the women were
much younger than me. It was new for me to be in an environment

where the *art* was so openly a part of the culture. Many of the guys that I worked with *and for* definitely indulged.

>*August 15, 1998*
>   *It amazes me how many married men seem to lose their wed-ding rings on deployment and "forget" their wives at home. This job o' mine is like a death wish for a marriage I think. At least if monogamy is important to you.*

Since Rio was considered to be the semi-precious gemstone cap-ital of the world, I decided that I needed to get my own piece of that action. Instead of spending my liberty out drinking and pay-ing for love, I spent the majority of my time shopping for gem-stones by going directly to the source. I think that I must have spent an entire half of a day at a shop called Star Jewelers and quickly became friends with the owner. In the end, I purchased close to $2,000 worth of stones that I hoped to have set in Peru where the cost of gold and silver was lower and labor very, very reasonable. I bought emeralds, amethysts, rubies, tourmaline, moonstones and many other semi-precious stones. I was in gemstone heaven! My imagination had gone wild as I thought of all the amazing pieces I could create from their rich colors. It was such a different thought process compared to the monochromatic military existence that I ground through day after day. I loved the visual stimulation of all the colors and felt through them.

>*I bought several beautiful gemstone here. Really REALLY beautiful ones. I love what I got! I spent far more than I ever have in one place before—I bought $1,720 worth—all gem-stones too. I plan to slowly get them all set the way that I'd like. I'm pretty much set for life with this stuff! It was a very nice experience for me too. One in which I really enjoyed. My cheeks were rosy and my adrenaline began to climb.*
>   *The good thing is that in retrospect, I am still very happy with my purchases and feel that I made WISE choices. I don't have buyer's remorse at all!*

For special clients it's often customary for the owner to offer a special parting gift. I was taken into the back office with the owner of Star Jewelers where he opened up a hidden drawer and allowed me to pick anything that I wanted. I chose a nice pair of blue aquamarine dangly earrings in a modest setting that seemed perfect for me at the time.

One of the more memorable events of my time in Rio was the Hail and Farewell of the Commanding Officer and the Supply Officer. The Captain was scheduled to be relieved in the next month by one of the first female Commanding Officers, Commander Catherine A. Murphy. The entire wardroom was told to barely eat throughout the day because we would be heading to the Churrascaria for dinner. I was told to expect a lot of food, but this completely blew me away.

Our wardroom of twenty-plus officers took up an entire wall of the restaurant as they continued to bring out every single item on the menu over and over and over. Our Supply Officer was in heaven as he completely appreciated well-cooked and well-prepared food. Very similar, but way better than a US Brazilian steak house, every type of imaginable meat possible is brought out on spits and skewers, plates and platters: sausages of all types including red, white, brown, and black; duck, chicken, goose, steak of every cut possible, pork, mutton, veal . . . pretty much if you can dream the meat, it was there and cooked to complete perfection. I could not recall ever eating more in my life and fondly remember trying a little of pretty much everything. We all laughed together and enjoyed blowing off some steam and eating our way through the Brazilian Churrascaria. The Captain passed cigars out to everyone as the dessert finale as fond stories were shared of his time onboard. It was a Hail and Farewell that I will never forget and am grateful to have attended.

My last day in Rio, I managed to finally get to the Corcovado Cristo Statue. I went with some of my Enginemen since we weren't allowed to go on liberty without a buddy. We all pitched in for a scary taxi ride through Ipanema where our driver nearly collided with several other cars as he appeared to be in race car training. Somehow we managed to get there unscathed. I climbed the stairs to the top and captured the moment with the ubiquitous arms-outstretched picture. It was such an icon and so very beautiful.

> *August 16, 1998*
> *My last day in Rio de Janeiro for now. I am sitting up at the Cristo Statue and it's amazingly beautiful up here. The only thing missing is someone special to share it with.*
>
> *I've enjoyed Rio and would someday like to explore it the "right" way. Do you think I'm far too picky to even think of a "right" or a "wrong" way and should just be grateful for the opportunity to be here?*

I spent my last couple of hours in Rio sitting at a café table watching the waves crash onto the nearby sand. I was filled with thought and hope for the future and wondered if I'd ever get to sink my toes into that sand again.

Montevideo, Uruguay

The transit between Rio and Montevideo took us about five days. I noticed the water seemed to change and turned a brackish brown as we made our sharp starboard turn toward Montevideo. Montevideo is located on the mouth of the Rio de la Plata (River Plate) and across from Buenos Aires, Argentina.

> *August 22, 1998*
> *Montevideo, Uruguay is beckoning me through her brassy-brown waters and cosmopolitan, industrialized art-laden cityscape. The water almost appears dirty to me.*
>
> *I have much to say to you today. We bombed Sudan and Afghanistan two days ago to stop a terrorist coup. Two US embassies were bombed a couple of weeks ago and we believed the terrorist camps to be located there. It's part of why our liberty has been so . . . sporadic too. It's sobering for me to think that all of my friends will be the people flying the missions, driving the ships—the people in harm's way. I guess that's the nature of the beast for us with our particular line of work. I know that it's*

what we've trained to do all these years, but training and doing are two different things! This just makes me really open up my eyes a little bit to the fact that everyone I've come into contact with in the past eight years may be involved somehow.

    As we pull in, I can see the sun diamonds dancing on the water for me! VERY BEAUTIFUL, I must say! Today was the first day that I wore my SDB's since making Lieutenant. Such a simple thing, but I was actually excited to put them on. You see, I feel that particular uniform looks best on me.

Part of the mission of UNITAS is to spread goodwill throughout the countries that we visit. In Montevideo, we had unloaded several large pallets of clothes and toys for the abandoned children living in the orphanages. I was selected to lead the tour for the children upon our arrival.

    The children were all different ages and their eyes so big and filled with awe. I saw so much potential in their faces and expectation and pain. I feel that for a short period of time, I may have been able to touch their lives. Of course we all promised to write and keep in touch—which I sincerely hope that some of them do. Anyways, my heart went out to them. It escapes me how people could abandon such children. And yet, had I been with a child at certain stages in my life, I may have done something similar or worse. Thank God that I have never been faced with the gut-wrenching question. I really enjoyed my time with the children—they touched my heart.

I was able to enjoy a couple of days of liberty in Montevideo and did some shopping. My "going to the source" theory played out well here as I found a fantastic leather shop to take advantage of amazing availability of high quality leathers. I purchase a pair of sexy black leather pants and a skirt. One of my more vivid memories was in the mall where I watched the young adults walking around with their yerba mate gourds easily tucked underneath their armpits or slung over their shoulders. I had never seen such a thing before and quickly fell in love with it. I also managed to quell my major craving for good chocolate there as I found the largest Toblerone bar I had ever seen. I must have looked like my own version of crazed woman as I lugged that under my arm!

The other thing that struck me about Montevideo was the unique mix of modernism coupled with European flair in the architecture. I enjoyed meandering her streets and shops with the time that I had.

Argentina

We embarked a Senior Argentine Officer in Montevideo to help pilot the ship through the difficult ports heading south. This also gave him the opportunity to have a little exposure to the way the US Navy operates. It was around this time that the Captain asked me to be the translator between the pilots and the Captain on the bridge during critical shipping operations. In the past, they had used native speakers who were very junior enlisted sailors who didn't necessarily have the tactical shipping experience. I felt honored to have the opportunity to work with the pilots and I was able to make some nice friendships that often translated into a *real* local experience when we pulled into port.

This was definitely the case with Commander Matesa from Argentina. I got to know him on the bridge as we were navigating through some rough waters and spent time with him in the wardroom during our meals learning about his culture and about him. When we pulled into Puerto Belgrano, Argentina, he invited me to his home for dinner and to meet his wonderfully large family. It was nice for me to have a home-cooked meal and to feel the warmth of a real family which sharply contrasted to how I often felt on the ship. Because of the duty rotation, I didn't have a lot of liberty in Argentina, but what I did see, I liked quite a bit. The economy was very agricultural with the largest amount of cattle per capita in the world.

The Matesa family opened their home and their hearts to me and I enjoyed every moment of our time together. Commander Matesa had five children ranging in age from one to twelve and I really seemed to connect with the middle youngest boy, Pichu (five) and his sister Lu Lu (three). What I remember most about the family was their warmth and generosity. CDR Matesa brought them all onboard for a ship's tour which I gladly did. It was precious to see the youngest two sit in the Captain's Chair—something that I personally had never dared to do! I'll never forget the sight of them all on the pier as the ship pulled out that gray late morning. They had brought me mate (tea) and pan (bread) for the next leg of my journey south and gave me big hugs. Little Pichu vigorously waved to me from way down below with tears in his eyes—he was very sad that I was leaving. It touched me deeply as I hoped that someday our paths would cross again.

What ensued was quite a long underway period where we continued to steam south and do operations with the Argentine Navy. Days meshed into each other as I settled back into my underway routine of standing watch, running my division, and trying to fit in any type of workout adhering to my philosophy that something is *always* better than nothing when it comes to a workout. For me, sometimes that something was just an eight-minute sprint on the treadmill or bike.

> *August 31, 1998*
>
> *I talked to my mom and dad a couple of nights ago. I really needed to hear their voices. They were on their way back home from visiting my cousin Nancy at the hospital. Her body is tired of fighting the cancer. She lost both breasts, part of her stomach, and now her brain is swelling. It's just sad. She was a bright, sarcastic woman—a little different, but still my family. She helped me out with several plane flights through the years and was always good for an endearing laugh. And so here I am, thousands of miles away, unable to say goodbye or be with my family.*
>
> *So much to say . . . I feel so many things this evening as I write to you. A female First Class Petty Officer onboard got caught having sex with a Marine onboard the ship in her office. Unbeknownst to her, she will be going to XOI and Captain's Mast today. And she'll have to face everyone. The worst part is the humiliation I'm sure she's going to feel if not already. I understand what she must be going through unfortunately. Wish I didn't! That "quiet before the storm" feeling. I sincerely hope that I don't have to feel that stripped ever again. Her situation made me feel . . . and remember how my predicament affected me.*

Clearly I would continue to feel the "this feels similar, but not the same" phenomena regularly whenever something felt even remotely similar to what I went through with my Spence ordeal. The experience gave me empathy for others who watch in horror as their lives spiral possibly out of control.

I received an AMCROSS message the next day telling me that Nancy's fight was over.

> *September 1, 1998*
>
> *Nancy left this world early this morning. I've said my good-bye and feel better as I know she's in a better place with no pain. No more pain—that's the key.*
>
> *When my time comes someday, I want to be cremated with my remains scattered on some adrenaline-filled excursion by the people that I love—after all of my usable parts are recycled, that is. That's how I want to go! And I know how my dad wants to go too. I don't understand why so many people want a funeral . . . want people to mourn their deaths in some morbid cemetery scene. And the waste of money that I think that is. I would much rather have the money go toward taking my family on an excellent trip somewhere where they can feel happy to be alive. And I'll be in the wind that blows through their hair and the sun that warms their skin. SO THERE!*
>
> *God has been good to me though. I feel blessed for what he has given me: wonderful parents and friends; the ability to see things from a different perspective; my big heart and competitive attitude coupled with a real thirst for life. Maybe that's all there is inside of me this evening as I write to you off the coast of Argentina.*

Although we didn't get much liberty time in Argentina, we sure spent a lot of time in her waters. In fact, we literally floated off of her coastline underway, not making way for days. I found it to be a crazy waste of time and money, but I'm sure that there's more going on than I was aware of. It was too deep to anchor and the only thing that we could do was shut down both shafts and drift around for over two days. It was a very different exercise for me while underway because usually there is a very distinct course and speed leading us to our desired destination. Perhaps it was more of a personal theme that I had trouble with—I've never been good at "sitting on my hands" and waiting.

We finally got the thumbs-up to begin heading toward Punta Arenas, Chile, where we were scheduled to pick up our Chilean pilots to enter the Strait of Magellan for our difficult transit.

Chile

We pulled into Punta Arenas, Chile, in order to refuel and pick up our three Chilean pilots. Punta Arenas is a small fishing village on the very tip of the Strait of Magellan. Unfortunately, I didn't get any liberty in that port as I froze my buns off on Small Boat Duty ferrying people back and forth on liberty. The transit through the Strait was perhaps one of the most picturesque that I have ever seen in my lifetime as well as one of the most navigationally demanding. We embarked three Chilean pilots: Christian Soro, Victor Zanelli, and Rojas. I found Zanelli to be funny has hell with his curly-haired antics, but got along best with Christian Soro. They were a breath of fresh air for our wardroom and lightened the mood considerably.

The 350-mile transit through the Strait took us roughly four days. At its narrowest point, the Strait is a little over one mile wide requiring very precise shipping and navigation. In the beginning, we traversed harsh, snowy, icy-cold weather and ventured where only the bravest of adventurous souls go to begin their journeys in kayaking and mountaineering her massive snow-laden peaks. The beauty of the land took my breath away as I stood my watch on the bridge gaping at her untouched coast and watched as the penguins played and slid on the ice. I felt closer to mother nature/God than I ever had before. There were no towns with the exception of a couple of very small fishing villages toward the end of the Strait.

Christian, Zanelli, and Rojas were extremely professional, yet still able to joke around and have fun on the bridge which was completely different from the perennial stick that seems to be up most of our officer's asses. It was very refreshing for me and made me smile inside every time I got to stand a watch with them.

Perhaps the most interesting part of the transit was the Golfo de Penas where we had to enter the Pacific very briefly before reentering the Strait in order to finish the transit. This part of the Strait got its name from the fact that at the turn of the century, two out of every ten ships managed to complete the transit. Literally, ships were swallowed by the vicious sea as her large waves would overtake the hull and their respective engines would drive them to the bottom of the ocean. It was scary for us too—even on a 560-foot-long US Navy vessel. Prior to entering this Gulf, we were all told to completely stow and tie down everything within our staterooms and were warned that if it wasn't tied down, it would become a missile hazard. I thought that I had been in rough seas before and could handle this. But, the truth of the matter was that I had never seen rolls like this before!

The *La Moure County* took 45-degree rolls and we all watched in horror as she almost came unhinged. We barely limped out of the Gulf that evening. I tried to get some rest in my stateroom before my rev watch (0200–0700), but the ship rolled so much that I just squeezed my eyes shut and hoped not to fall out of my rack and fly across the room. I talked to Patricia through the night as we both took turns reassuring each other. We listened as the hull creaked around us and everything within our drawers banged.

While we were transiting this section, we had several events that in and of themselves would have been a major deal:

- A Class C electrical fire.
- Almost lost our starboard anchor. One of the Boatswain's Mates had to get harnessed up to salvage the anchor (and risk his life) as it teetered on the edge.
- Lost our entire port shaft leaving only the starboard shaft available to propel us out of the Gulf when the following equipment went down: three main propulsion diesel engines, one of our three SSDGs (Diesel Generators), and a boiler all at once due to a leaky valve in our fuel oil tank which diluted the fuel oil. This fed all of our equipment bad fuel oil and caused the entire shaft to cease.

This was probably the first time that I had ever really been scared while out to sea. And, in the midst of it all, Zanelli was on the bridge that night as all hell broke loose in his colorful shower slippers, cracking jokes and keeping his eye on our navigational progress, making sure we were safe and heading in the right direction despite the worsened state of the ship. When we finally popped out of the Straits and into the mighty Pacific, the sun was out and seas had settled down.

We limped our way up to Talcahuano, Chile, the seaport very close to Concepción.

On the day we pulled in, the Navigator, Carol, and I were asked to go to lunch with Christian Soro and Victor Zanelli. They took us to their Naval Club for an exquisite lunch of their local fish called ceviche. I think it had something to do with the fact that they were in awe of us—there were no women in Chile's Navy at that time and it was very different for them to work with women and see that we could perform at the same level as men at the same jobs. After the lunch, there was a get-together for all of the Chilean and American officers to mingle and socialize. We were even allowed to wear civilian clothes!

After the social, I went out with some of the officers from our wardroom into Concepción and had a most memorable time. We ended up at this little hole in the wall bar called La Bohemia where the walls were a deep, brick red and the ceiling had hand-painted gold stars strewn across it. Black and white matted and framed pictures of Groucho Marx hung on the walls of this small pub. I loved the place! After such a rough week at sea, I wanted to dance while everyone else really just wanted to unwind with a drink. The owner of the bar moved a couple of tables, changed the music, and danced with me all night long. It was a perfect way to keep everyone happy together. I had so much fun! For once, I felt that I could completely abandon my guard and let the joy out—even among the wardroom. We didn't return to the ship until after 3:00 a.m.—and many of us had a very early wakeup call!

The next day, I signed up for the ski trip into the Chilean Andes at a volcano called Chillán. Imagine a blanket of white snow covering an inactive volcano high up in the beautiful Andes—spectacular.

As would be my luck, I couldn't just easily make my way to the bus and prepare for this great adventure in a relaxed fashion, I had to write two casualty reports on our equipment as fast as humanly possible (in like five minutes) as the entire busload of people waited for me. Although I was angry about it, I was happy that I at least still got to go and exhaled as soon as the bus pulled away.

This was considered late spring skiing at Chillán and the weather was warm enough for us to wear T-shirts. I had on my crazy rainbow tie-dyed shirt with a thermal under it and did just fine—it made for some very fun pictures. What I did forget to pack and apply was sunscreen, which I paid for the entire ensuing week as my face became a red tomato.

I always manage to run into pretty great people wherever it is that I end up and Chillán was no exception. Upon picking up my gear, I met two Americans traveling abroad. Ward was a lawyer from Texas who was between firms and about to start a new job while his traveling companion was a very bubbly and upbeat girl named Libby. The three of us hit it off famously and managed to ski together the entire day—I wish we could have had more adventures but am grateful for the time. I was sad when I had to re-board the bus and head back down to the ship. The next morning we were leaving and heading north to Valparaiso, where I would finally see my parents. I had been counting down the days to their arrival for over a month and couldn't wait to share the time with them.

Instead of being able to easily prepare for their visit, I found myself incredibly stressed as our Commanding Officer's Change of Command was happening in Valparaiso. We had to prepare briefs for the new Captain on all of our divisions and tie up any remaining loose ends with CDR Dubloon prior to his departure—it is customary for the Commanding Officer to give out awards upon his departure. Instead of being excited and already packed, I was working until the very last possible moment scrambling to put together an award for myself which turned out to be a futile effort. I had the soft hope that if I wrote up an award for myself, maybe he'd give me one. Normally, I would have at least packed already and been watching our arrival ready to start waving as we approached the pier.

My parents' trip from the airport was very hectic. They landed in Santiago and rented a car to drive the short distance to the ship in Valparaiso. Traffic was horrendous coupled with the fact that they were in a foreign country and my dad did not speak the language at all. They felt happy to be in one piece and alive by the time they arrived at the ship. When they arrived, my dad had to find somewhere to park while my mom needed to pee. She had a very hard time figuring out where the nearest bathroom was and finally some Mormon missionaries took pity on her and showed her the way, saving her much embarrassment.

My parents, being the people that they are, felt indebted to these three missionaries and offered to have me give them a tour of the ship. This only heightened my stress level. There I was, trying to pack all of my stuff for our little four-day vacation and trying to be happy to see my parents along with three Hasidic-looking men staring at me expectantly. Somehow I managed to dig deep and give them a very short tour—but what I really should have done was *just say no.*

Finally, we left the ship and checked into our hotel in Viña del Mar. It was fairly nice: a very small room with three little beds and no heat. Since we were in town during their national holiday (September 18), everything else was completely booked up and we had to make do. On the first day, we took a big carriage ride around the city to get an idea of the city and what we'd like to do. Really, the most important thing we did was just be together—I *really* needed that!

Valparaiso itself seemed to be kind of dirty and crime-ridden. But Viña del Mar is quite nice and only fifteen minutes north. I was surprised by the strong European influence evident not only in their architecture, but also their customs and the features of their people. Unlike the rest of South America, it's not unheard of to spot light-skinned, blonde-haired, blue-eyed people. Chile was settled by many immigrants from Germany, Spain, Scandinavia, Croatia, and other European countries between 1890 and 1940. Quite simply, I loved my time in Chile—the people are what made my visit spectacular.

Christian Soro invited my parents and me over for an Asado (barbecue) to celebrate their National Independence Day. It was such a nice experience for us to be included. We were able to have some very intellectual conversations and learned a lot about the culture and shared many stories and laughs. What really took me aback was their complete generosity and kindness. At one point, I complimented his wife's nail polish color as I wondered if I would be able to get away with wearing that in uniform. She immediately went into her bathroom, got the polish out, and gave it to me so that I could feel like a girl again. It was such a kind, sweet gesture.

Although I was on leave, I had to return to the ship to sign my departing fitrep from CDR Dubloon and do a turnover with the new Commanding Officer, CDR Catherine A. Murphy. The original plan was for me to be one of the first officers in with the CO so that I could get back on leave and go with Christian for a tour of their Naval Academy. Christian planned to meet us at the ship about an hour and a half later.

Because we missed the hotel's free breakfast, I didn't think it'd be a big deal to eat breakfast on the ship. When I got into the wardroom, I "requested permission to join the mess" from CDR Dubloon. CDR Dubloon just glared at me and said, "You know you have to work today?"

Of course I knew that I had to work that day—I was *in off of leave* to do just that—in a foreign country while my parents were in town no less! My blood began to boil as I wished that I could have said "no shit, asshole!"

But, instead, I respectfully said, "Where would you like for us to sit, Sir?"

He barely looked up from his messages and grunted, "I don't care." Although he'd met my parents several times, he never even said hello to them.

My parents shot me this look that said, "Don't let him see how much he's pissed you off, Jo." I did my best to swallow it and put on my happy face, even if it was forced. This set the stage for the rest of my day. The time quickly got away from us and before I knew it, Christian had arrived to take us on our excursion. I couldn't yet leave and had no idea when I'd be able to, so Christian offered to take my parents on the tour and out to lunch at the Officer's Club so that they too weren't stuck waiting in my small stateroom.

Instead of going first, I ended up being the last officer called in that day. I sat around doing nothing but waiting for over six and a half hours. As the clock ticked away, I continued to get more and more frustrated. It angered me that I had been sitting in my stateroom while on leave for several hours waiting for my name to be called and watching my shipmates come and go throughout the day. Plus, you know how much I *love* wasting time. Finally, after over six and a half hours, I had been called to meet with the new CO, CDR Murphy. I immediately liked her and respected her. She was firm, yet approachable. Somehow she figured out that I had been there off of leave to meet with her and apologized for the wasted day with my parents. There was no way for her to know of my circumstance—we had barely met before this first official meeting. I appreciated her empathy given my situation.

I was so grateful to Christian for his generosity in taking my parents off the ship on a little sightseeing excursion. They all really seemed to get along well and I felt that I had just made friends for life with the Soro family.

The next day was our last one together as a family in Chile. We drove up the coast to Rincon, ate a delicious lunch above the waves crashing below, and did some shopping. We really enjoyed each other's company—all the way around. And then, it came time for them to leave and our visit—so much anticipated—to be over. I was very sad to see them go.

When I returned to the ship, I had to sign my fitrep with CDR Dubloon. I missed his official Hail and Farewell while I was with my parents and hoped to have a moment to thank him for giving me that second chance over a year ago. Regardless of how I now felt about him, I knew that I would always be grateful for the opportunity to serve beneath him and to get back out to sea with a SWO pin. When I knocked on his door and requested permission to come aboard, he just pushed my fitrep (evaluation) into my hand and told me to "sit down and read it" while he went into the head. He had nothing to say to me except, "You realize that you're now ranked with all the Department Heads?"

CDR Dubloon took a dump while I sat in his stateroom reading my final fitrep from him. I had to yell my parting thoughts to him: "Sir, thank you for giving me a chance."

It left such a bad taste in my mouth and decimated whatever respect that I had remaining for him. I noticed that something had changed between the Captain and me in the early spring, but never knew exactly what it was. I wondered if he had found out about Spence and me, but never had the opportunity to ask and didn't honestly really want to know the answer so I just weakly accepted the change as where I now was. I had been counting down the days until I could get out of the Navy and told myself that it didn't matter anymore. The truth is that deep down it did in fact hurt quite a bit. The thing that was very hard for me to swallow was the sharp contrast of my feelings: I knew that I would always feel indebted to him for giving me a chance and used to immensely respect him and think the world of him, sharply contrasted with how I now felt as we were parting company. I felt empty as I feebly said my goodbye.

Valdivia

I had the opportunity to go on exchange with our sister ship and Chile's flagship, the *Valdivia*. Chile had purchased the *Valdivia* from the United States a couple of years beforehand. Right after they bought the *Valdivia*, she ran aground and broke in half—literally. She ended up spending over a year in the shipyards getting repaired and this operation that I was on was her very first underway, her sea trials. The *Valdivia* was a perfect fit for me since it was the exact same class of ship as ours and I knew her inside and out. The Ensign and I embarked on the *Valdivia* together and were the first women onboard—ever. It was such a tremendous honor for both of us.

They treated us extremely well and made sure that all of our needs were met, including allowing us to sleep in my same stateroom while I was embarked. We shared the head (bathroom) with the Executive Officer. It took me a little time to get used to their food schedule: they eat a very small breakfast in the morning from 0730–0830 (like toast or a small sandwich of ham and cheese) and tea; lunch goes from 1200–1300; snack/tea from 1600–1700 (a little sandwich and tea again) and dinner is from 2000–2100. Dinner being served so late was the biggest challenge for me as I fought the urge to gnaw off my arm.

September 25, 1998

I write to you from our sister ship, the Chilean LST-93 Valdivia where I have been on exchange for two days and have two more. It's been quite an interesting experience for me as we were the first women onboard—EVER. They've never had any women onboard and definitely not for four days. I think it's interesting for them to see a woman be able to do the same things that they do professionally when in the past, they thought that we were incapable of it. It's been interesting to say the least.

It's amazing, how when put in a situation like this, I realize how much I really do know—how much knowledge I have gained over the years about surface warfare, leadership, and being an officer. AND how hard it was to come by.

My Spanish has dramatically improved. I'm able to have full conversations now and they all understand me. I've also learned all of the commands in Spanish and have been able to help out quite a bit.

I hope that what we did was a positive step for women! They are/were not accustomed to having women do the same job as them and we were able to show them that it is possible to be a professional woman onboard a ship. Of course, they treated us as women first and officers second—witnessed by the kiss on the cheek. But it was their way and it wasn't bad or disrespectful. Just DIFFERENT.

When we got underway, the Captain and Chief Engineer asked me if I would like to light off (start up their entire engineering plant) their plant. I worked very hard to learn all of the proper commands in Spanish and they allowed me to go through the entire light off sequence to light off their plant. They don't seem to have anywhere near the safety programs in place that we do, yet they still seem to do OK. It is VERY RARE for a Chief Engineer to allow someone outside of his crew to light off his plant—I felt so honored and empowered. It was such an amazing opportunity and something that I will never forget.

I noticed that their Officers trained in one specialty of the ship unlike our officers where we were required to know the entire ship operation. My training had been very strong not only in the engineering plant operations, but in shipping, navigating, operations, weapons, etc. They were surprised that I could seamlessly move between the bridge, plant, and operations. It made me feel good about my Surface Warfare knowledge and about myself in general.

The Ensign and I helped their Executive Officer and Operations Officer out a lot with their briefs—they had to give two amphibious warfare briefs in English to the UNITAS Operation and wanted to make sure they were using proper grammar. It was nice to do something tangible for a change and to feel appreciated.

We got to take two helo (helicopter) rides up the coast of Chile to see the surrounding area which was amazing. The land was so rugged and serene—I wished that I had had high-end camera equipment to capture its beauty.

During some of the briefs onboard the Valdivia, *I met this absolutely gorgeous SEAL Lieutenant (you do know my attraction to SEALs). I couldn't believe that he wanted to talk to ME . . . I was flattered and even a little giddy. He was incredibly athletic, smart and accomplished—he had his masters degree as well and had started his own business on the side a few years beforehand. Obviously, he was someone that I could be into.*

When the ship pulled into Coquimbo, Chile, the Ensign and I were invited to an Asado with the wardroom of the Valdivia. *They took some formal pictures of us to send to their Naval Academy's magazine. They grilled up six different types of meat to perfection and had the alcohol flowing. The Executive Officer (#2 in Command) brought out a guitar and I danced with the Captain. It was the perfect mix of: good food, good drink, good music, good people to make a really good time!*

After the Asado, SEAL God Christian invited me out with him and a group of our SEALs. Christian made it very

*obvious to everyone that he was interested in me. When he saw
me, he gave me a massive hug and a wrapped bottle of wine with
a big red bow tied to it. I felt a little uncomfortable, but I was also
very flattered by the gesture. It never went anywhere past this, but
sure was "pretty to think so" as Earnest Hemingway once said.*

Peru

During this underway, I began standing my watches on the bridge
as Officer of the Deck instead of down in CCS (Central Control
Station) as EOOW. I always stood some bridge watches, but not all
of my watches. Now, I was exclusively standing my watches on the
bridge. The more I got to know the Captain, the more I grew to like
and respect her as well as want to emulate her. The quality of my
watch dramatically improved as it became important to me to be
viewed as the strong Surface Warfare Officer that I now believed
and knew myself to be. As my watches improved, my experience in
the wardroom also began to improve.

CDR Murphy was one of the first females in Command at Sea and
she was the first female CO of an amphibious ship. It was groundbreaking—I am lucky to have been able to serve with her and to
learn from her! She's extremely meticulous and straight as an arrow,
yet is still approachable and has warmth within her strength. Perhaps
part of her warmth comes being the mother of a ten-year-old son
and balancing a major career with a young family. CDR Murphy was
the example of "doing it better and smarter" and I really looked up
to her. I wanted and needed to change my "short-timers" perspective
of counting down the days until my release from the Navy.

On October 1, 1998, we pulled into Callao, Peru, the seaport for
Lima, and were scheduled to be in port for a total of nine days with
some operations tucked into the middle. I intended to immediately
book a trip to visit the historical sacred Inca ruins of Machu Picchu
and longed to climb up the steps of the mountain, feel the ghosts,
and drink in the lush scenery. But as we pulled in to Callao, liberty
was heavily restricted due to a bomb threat. The first day that we
were finally allowed off the ship, I went out to dinner with some
friends and then went dancing. At dinner, I discovered a native drink

called Chicha Morado made from red corn. It tasted similar to a refreshing grape juice. I loved it and drank two very large glasses of it and enjoyed every single sip until my stomach began rumbling sometime in the early morning after I had been dancing all night.

The drink knocked me on my ass for close to three days as I could keep nothing down at all. Not even half a slice of bread. I was completely incapacitated and miserable in my steel bed. I lay there thinking of my mom and wishing that she could take care of me. Instead, all that I was able to do was sleep and feebly race to the head to eliminate what remained in my stomach. I vomited and pooped for three days straight. It's absolutely no fun to be sick on a Navy ship—especially with the SWO mentality that "SWOs aren't allowed to get sick" and feeling that I was somehow slacking when in fact I was vilely ill. Finally, there was a break in the war going on in my stomach and I was able to keep a piece of bread down.

When we got back underway after our first short liberty call, we embarked a Peruvian officer named Juan Carlos Zevallos. He and I were the same rank and around the same age. We became fast friends onboard. He was funny, smart, and very kind. I often sat with him in the wardroom as we shared our meals together and I got to work on my Spanish-speaking skills. I showed him around our ship and we compared notes on the different ways in which our respective Navies operated. I learned a lot from him, but mostly it became a very healthy friendship. In the end, people are just people and we connected on that human level.

I vividly remember being out on the water with Juan Carlos doing a small boat exercise right after I was finally able to get back to work. I was completely emaciated and he looked at me and laughed at my sorry state as even the minimal waves of our small boat made my face turn green after all I'd been through. We made plans for our impending liberty in Lima and I looked forward to experiencing it with him.

After all was said and done, I only ended up with about a day and a half of liberty in Peru. The first night, J.C. took me out to eat and then to a locals-only meringue club. I had eaten bland crackers or nothing at all for so long, that I craved taste. To me, that meant a plate full of seasoned tomatoes. He watched with a small smile on his face as I enthusiastically downed an entire plate of sliced tomatoes with a little onion. After my tomato show, we went to the meringue club and proceeded to dance as I had never danced before.

Juan Carlos was such a strong dancer that it was easy to follow him and learn all of his fancy moves. I was very happy to be able to dance with someone so easy to move with. He made it easy and I felt beautiful and sexy next to him. On one occasion, we were the only two people on the dance floor which happened to be raised up like a stage where everyone could see us. I was nervous to get up there and do that, but he helped me to feel at ease and comfortable. As soon as we started moving to the beat together, I was able to lose myself in that once-in-a-lifetime moment and dance as if I knew what the hell I was doing. He made that last part easy for me. I think that my face said it all that evening—I was filled with joy.

The next day, Juan Carlos took me shopping to the best markets in Lima and patiently helped me to select gold-leafed glasses of all different types for the home and family that I someday hoped to have. He was very attentive and sweet—especially considering that I know how painful shopping is for most men. He then took me to the Centro in Lima where there are so many beautiful parks, sculptures, and water fountains. It was so picturesque—I wish I had had more time to properly explore the city and the country. It's on my list to revisit someday.

That evening, he took me out for a special dinner and then we ended up on a cliff overlooking the beach and waves crashing below. It was like an "Inspiration Point" scenario. We began to talk about our lives and he leaned in for a kiss. My body immediately responded and we kissed like high school kids drinking each other in. It's amazing how quickly your body responds after so much . . . inactivity. I knew that Juan Carlos liked me a lot and would have wanted to pursue something more with me if I had seemed more motivated to do so. But I wasn't in the right head space then to think about such a thing. I was much more focused on trying to figure out my life plan and getting my proverbial act together than something meaningful and deliberate that would be quite a challenge given our geographical challenges. When we finally had to say goodbye, I knew that I would never forget our time . . . or him.

> *October 12, 1998*
> *Got an email from the detailer to contact him ASAP. And when I did, Murphy's Cloud began to rumble for me again . . . Apparently, now there's something wrong with my Letter of Resignation and there's a very strong chance that it will get disapproved and I will have to move in December. What an emotional roller coaster this has been for me! I talked to the Commanding Officer about it—many other things too. I was able to get a lot off my chest which was refreshing for me. I really respect her a lot!*
>
> *She offered to call the detailer for me tomorrow to see what she can do to help me out. Hopefully, I'll still be able to get out. It'll either be that (I can get out) or: Italy, Iceland, or possibly Chicago. If Chicago, I can be closer to home and go to grad school right away, but Iceland sure sounds exciting.*
>
> *I'm honestly in SHOCK—I've never heard of such a thing where someone's LOR (letter of resignation) was denied. I have heard though that with the large exodus of Surface Warfare Officers and how lean our Navy has become, some letters have been denied—just never imagined that mine would be one of them. Whatever happens, I have some good options and will be OK. What a MAJOR change of plans for me.*

This was a huge life course change. As Surface Navy always goes, you need to be prepared to adjust course as necessary, be nimble and adaptable to change. At least I could get my MBA while being close to family and home while finishing up my time in the Navy. Little did I know just how important that would become.

Ecuador

The ship continued to head North toward Ecuador—this time without Juan Carlos or any guest riders. Less than a month after finding out about my cousin Nancy's death, I received another AMCROSS message announcing the death of her mother, my Aunt Jean. It was very tough for me to be so far away from my family during such a difficult time when all you want to do is be together with the ones you love.

> *October 18, 1998*
>
> *Exactly one month before we return to the States—to "home." Things are messed up for me. I find myself at the convergence of several paths and don't quite know which way to go. We are off the coast of Ecuador—Salinas to be exact.*
>
> *Everything is jumbled in my mind, so bear with me as I sift through it all. I feel as though we've had this discussion months ago when I first decided to get out of the Navy. I never imagined that there would be any sort of complication with my resignation. I had formulated a plan for myself that I was intent upon executing. It was a responsible plan that included business school and trying to start my own business before I turn thirty. Now, it's all fuzzy as if I'm trying to find my way amidst the fog.*
>
> *I haven't felt this much in a long time. I feel so damn much! It's one of the Sundays that I wish I could be at Lux in Seattle or my place on the Cliff Walk in Newport.*
>
> *Aunt Jean passed away five days ago . . . only a month after her daughter. So much pain and sadness for my family lately and also, paradoxically, the end to so much pain and sadness. My heart needs to cry. To absorb all that has happened. To feel. It's been so long since I let myself really FEEL everything. Perhaps I tried not to feel out here on this deployment. But this is just too much. I can't not feel.*

We pulled into the beach town of Salinas, Ecuador, without much fanfare. As soon as liberty was called, I went for a long run along the beach. I longed to watch the waves crash up close and to feel the wind in my free hair—not my hair in the military bun that I had to wear daily while onboard the ship. My body felt sluggish as I pounded out the miles. I hadn't run in what felt like weeks and I could definitely tell. Even so, it was exactly the attitude adjustment that I needed.

I remember Salinas as being a rather small beach town that seemed to cater to the surfer crowd. After trinket shopping the beach vendors, I ended up at the local surfer bar/dance joint with seemingly the rest of my ship. I managed to find myself a cute local surfer named Charlie to dance with. We had fun moving to the beat together and he took me back to his home, a little blue tent on the beach. I giggled as we ducked into his home—I had never been taken back home to a *tent* before! My tent experience was limited to deliberate camping events, not as a permanent home. It was a unique experience for me and really reminded me of how fortunate I am. I enjoyed dancing with Charlie and getting to know him, but that's as far as it went.

To be honest, the wind had pretty much been taken out of my sails with the recent traumatic events of my life and I was really just ready to head home and begin my next chapter. We still had about a month remaining of the deployment with a transit through the Panama Canal and our last port call in Cartagena, Colombia.

Just prior to transiting the Panama Canal, I received an acceptance letter from DePaul's MBA program and took that as a sign that I was meant to go back home to Chicago instead of taking the adventurous and fun route of a tour of Iceland or Sigonella, Italy. In place of retaking the GRE and applying to bigger-name schools such as Northwestern or the University of Chicago, I decided to begin school in January at DePaul and to take advantage of being able to at least make some positive movements in my life. At the time, DePaul was ranked second in the country in part-time entrepreneurship programs, which suited me just fine considering that that's what I wanted to do with myself anyway—start something big!

Panama Canal

After a nondescript visit to Manta, Ecuador, we continued north toward the Panama Canal. The Panama Canal connects the Pacific Ocean to the Atlantic Ocean via the Caribbean Sea and the Isthmus of Panama. This was considered to be a US territory up until 1999, mere months after I went through her locks. Locks are situated at each end to lift ships up to Gatun Lake which sits eighty-five feet above sea level. The Panama Canal is 48 miles long and 108 feet wide and is considered to be one of the seven wonders of the world. The *La Moure County* went through the Panama Canal on November 3, 1998, and all of her crew received the official "Order of the Ditch" certificate from the US Navy.

I vaguely remember standing my watch through the Panama Canal—we went through during the middle of the night and although a major shipping event, it felt pretty nondescript to me since the pilots pretty much took control of the ship throughout the operation. We did briefly stop at a base in Panama, but were not allowed to see any of the country at all due to security concerns. We were among the last US military to visit the base before it changed hands in less than two months. I did however manage to get in a long, hot, sweaty jungle run. It was so hot and sticky that I was happy to just finish and be done with it.

Cartagena, Colombia

The last big stop on our South American adventure was Cartagena, Colombia. The embarked pilot, Señor Jiménez, took a liking to me after our many hours together on the bridge navigating some tough waters and pulling into port. He invited me back to stay with his family and looked forward to introducing me to his daughter, Natalie, who happened to be around the same age as me.

Because I hadn't been able to set any of my semi-precious stones in Peru where the cost of labor and materials (gold and silver) was much less due to my chicha incident, I had the main objective of somehow managing to get all of my stones designed and set with the very short two days of liberty that we had in Cartagena.

The pilot, true to his word, brought me home to meet his family. I was touched by their warmth and complete generosity. The Jiménez family home was beautifully decorated with tile floors and lush, vibrant flowers all over the backyard. His wife surely took pride in her garden and her family. Natalie and I hit it off famously. She showed me around all of her favorite places in Cartagena as well as the historical "must sees" such as the fort. We also managed to find ourselves dancing into the early morning hours having the type of fun that girls in their mid-twenties are capable of (the good, clean kind).

Piloto Jiménez recommended a jewelry shop that he believed would be up to the task of setting all of my Brazilian stones. As soon as I was able, I made my way to the small jewelry shop and got lost in their many books getting ideas of how to design and set a lifetime's worth of gemstones: tourmalines, rubies, amethysts, and emeralds. I reveled in the creative process of designing each and every piece and must have spent five or six hours huddled over the many catalogs in their shop. The shop had never seen so much action in a day and a half—I ended up employing their entire staff around the clock to finish my order in time for the ship's departure. I arrived back at the agreed upon time the next day, 5:00 p.m., which would give me roughly two hours to make it back to the ship. They told me that they'd need close to two more hours to completely finish the job. I prepared for the worst-case scenario—leaving Cartagena without my stuff.

Because I spent so much money with them, they allowed me to pick a parting gift. By this time, my eye had become quite good at choosing the best possible stones and I immediately noticed a pair of very large, deep and clear emerald earrings. I didn't care for the setting as it reminded me of hanging bones, but the stones were amazing and free of inclusions. The owner swallowed hard and reluctantly parted with the earrings; they turned out to be one of my most valuable purchases and were appraised at over $750 in 1999.

Even with the entire staff's commitment, we almost missed our deadline and I was close to missing the cutoff to liberty and ship's movement. I was so late that Piloto Jiménez had to personally drive me out to the ship, which was anchored about a mile off shore, as I had missed the last liberty boat back. I was nervous at the thought of making such a grand entrance back on the ship—me riding in on a small speedboat with rooster tail aggressively approaching US Navy warship at night. The good news was that Piloto Jiménez was in contact with them and I didn't seem to be in hot water when I got back. The added bonus was that I somehow managed to get all of my jewelry set and was thrilled with the outcome.

The ship got underway from Colombia very early the next morning and headed north toward Puerto Rico with a purpose, the purpose of our impending homecoming in less than a week's time. Our

first stop was to debark those shipmates whose home was in Puerto
Rico—for me, that meant saying goodbye to my roommate and
our dentist, LCDR Patricia Villalobos. Navy ship's homecomings
are very exciting and special events for the families that have been
maintaining the home-front and for the sailors that have been gone
and away for so many long months. The entire crew was ready to
just head back home.

Although I didn't know what to expect with regards to our ship's
homecoming, I at the very least thought that I'd get to participate
in it and feel what it's like to come back to the states and our home
port after being gone for six months. It would be a lie to say that I
didn't have some romantic vision of pulling back into port among
the hundreds and hundreds of excited family members with bands
playing, flags waving, and homemade "Welcome Home" banners
strewn about. Although I didn't have anyone special waiting for
me at the other end, I still wanted to be a part of the excitement
and to feel it once. But, because I was a single unmarried officer, I
was asked to go back a day early in order to be ready for the ship's
arrival team in port and didn't get to see or feel any of the homecoming.

> *November 16, 1998*
>
> *Tonight, I sit and look at the wake of a ship . . . at the wake
> of my life. This is my last evening underway and the eve of MY
> homecoming.*
>
> *Unfortunately, I am filled with a lot of different emotions
> and very little of it excitement. I guess it's because I don't know
> exactly what I'm coming home to. I fear that I am coming home
> to nothing.*
>
> *There were many times that I never imagined that this cruise
> would ever be over . . . and now in less than 24 hours, I will be
> at "home." God, I looked forward to coming home for so long,
> but not this way.*
>
> *Everything is moving so damn fast. I don't know how to
> make it stop. Please think good thoughts for me. All of the
> things that I did prior to deployment that felt so "responsible"
> now leave me questioning my judgment: getting out of the lease*

for the Honda Prelude/selling it = no car to drive; sub-leasing apartment made great fiscal sense until she left after six weeks and I wonder if she took any of my stuff with her.

Although I was sad on the eve of our homecoming, I also was in a place where I was ready to just get on with it. Everything turned out OK in the end—I managed to get around without my vehicle for a couple of weeks, all of my personal effects were still intact, and I had saved a tremendous amount of money while on deployment—all good things. I prepared for my move with vigor and began the tedious process of going through twenty-five years' worth of belongings in preparation for the movers to come and box it all up to the Midwest and my ultimate future.

Recruit Training Command, Great Lakes

Build your own dreams, or someone else will hire you to build theirs.

—Farrah Gray

A super cute Force Recon sniper named Trent offered to drive me back to Chicago—he was about to begin his terminal leave from the Marine Corps and finish up college. We had barely talked during the deployment until we were about to offload the Marines. He slipped me his number and asked that we keep in touch. I liked the attention and also welcomed the offer of his company on such a long drive.

Trent drove up from North Carolina and we left Virginia Beach on an overcast morning and began heading west with my bike hastily strapped to the roof of his Volkswagen. I found him to be engaging, super athletic, and surprisingly quite handsome. He was a nice distraction—and he helped to make a stressful move more manageable. We enjoyed each other's company, but weren't meant to ever be more than a short jaunt. But we did get to tromp around Chicago for a few days before he headed back east to begin packing up his life and taking his next steps toward becoming the man that he wanted to be. I remember feeling that there were all these affirmative small signs that I had made the right decision by being back in Chicago. Small subtleties such as a stranger smiling and saying hello as our paths crossed on the street. All those little things helped me to feel better about my more practical decision to come home instead of feed my adventurous spirit in Iceland or Italy.

I reported in to Recruit Training Command, Great Lakes—the Navy's only boot camp—located in a northern suburb of Chicago about forty miles from my parent's home in LaGrange Park, Illinois. I was slated to be the Drill Division Officer and would replace a Civil Engineering Corps LT in running all of the graduation ceremonies. The guy that I was replacing was a lean, tall blonde man who was quite smooth. At the time, over twenty thousand recruits went through RTC Great lakes during the summer surge. The Drill Division had all of the "talented" recruits in it—those recruits that had prior musical backgrounds (instrumental or voice) and/or high ASVAB scores in order to ensure that we could put on a good show for graduation. Our complete turnover was scheduled in two months—after I would have completed the two-month RDC Course (Recruit Drill Commander) which gave me a chance to ease into the very visible role of speaking in front of crowds of up to 4,500 people. Graduation ceremonies were held weekly throughout the year on Friday mornings and two days a week during the summer surge. My job was to emcee the event and I was responsible for the smooth execution and flow.

Right after the holidays, I immediately began my MBA classes at DePaul University. I started by taking only one class the first semester to sort of ease my mind back into the idea of being back in school. My first class met two days a week in the evenings after work. Personally paying for each and every class and book made me really pay a whole lot more attention to what I was doing. I felt a need to completely throw myself into my studies and hung on the words of my professors—many of whom had real-time successful corporate careers with big firms and companies around the United States. Classes began the week of January 11, 1999, and I was excited to finally feel as though I were moving toward something.

Monkey Wrench

With the day off from my day job for Martin Luther King Day, January 18, 1999, and no school, I planned to go with my parents to the hospital where my mom was *supposed* to be in and out for a routine angiogram procedure where they were to shoot dye into her veins in order to identify any possible blockages in her cardiovascular system. We had all planned to go out to dinner and see a movie that evening after the test, but the doctors and surgeons had something else in mind for her. We were not expecting the *monkey wrench* that they threw at us.

We waited for her results the entire day, and finally, close to 9:00 p.m., we were told that they strongly urged Mom to have a triple bypass surgery at 6:00 a.m. the following morning due to the severe degradation of her arteries.

January 19, 1999

I am in a place I never imagined that I would be—the waiting room of the operating room of Rush Presbyterian Hospital where my mother just underwent a triple bypass open heart surgery. Needless to say, my dad and I were dumbfoundedly shocked yesterday as we were matter-of-factly told the news. It was such a shock and something that we weren't prepared for at all. What a rude, sobering awakening.

My mom went in for a stress test in August and was told that they would contact her with the results, but never did. She went back in November for a routine checkup and said "Gee, I must be pretty healthy. I never heard anything about my stress test." NOT SO! They ordered another stress test for her and then an angiogram.

January 20, 1999

She made it through the surgery fine! Mom even talked to us last night as she was coming out of anesthesia and she held my hand. I was so relieved. It wasn't until 8:30 p.m. that we were able to see her. Apparently, her main artery was very diseased— she'll likely need to have angioplasty done sometime in the future due to the severe blockages still in her carotid arteries.

The doctors in the intensive care unit were good, but otherwise, I'm not too impressed. She could have had this whole thing done in August, but she had "slipped through the cracks." I like the way they tap dance around major fuck ups. Apparently, her heart disease has been a slow process that has developed over time (like fifteen-plus years, which shocked me).

When my mom woke up and was finally able to talk to us, she told us that we were with her the entire time and so were her "friends"—the deer, squirrels, and birds that she enjoyed visiting daily during her walks to the nearby forest preserve. I was surprised that she had dreamt of the little animals that she loved so much, but I probably shouldn't have been because they were really important to her. I had accompanied her many times to feed the animals with day-old bread and scrappy apples from the backyard tree. I liked the idea that although her heart stopped for over two minutes, she was in her "safe place" in her head with her friends in the forest . . . and with us. It warmed my heart to know that she never did forget who we were.

As with such a major surgery, it's common for things to not quite seem normal for a while. The doctors told us that it was expected for her to be slower mentally and that it would take time to completely get her back. We also knew that we needed to watch for a stroke, which was common after a surge of blood through arteries that had before been terribly blocked. I watched my mom like a hawk and tried to make things easier for her as best I could.

She was released from the hospital rather quickly and as we got the green light to take her home, I was appalled to realize that they left the anodes stuck to her chest and helped her as she struggled to wipe herself in the bathroom that last time in the hospital. I never imagined wiping my mother's cha-cha. It really felt as though we were coming full circle together and now she needed me in a way that I had once needed her.

Even the simplest of questions would leave her reeling.

"Mom, would you like water, milk, or juice to drink with your dinner?"

She would look at me with panic in her big green eyes as she couldn't answer the question.

It was a very emotional and sobering time for my dad and me as we watched the dynamic woman that we loved forget the key elements of her life—but she never forgot us. I remember that particular Wednesday vividly—in fact, the day before had been a very emotional one for me as I knew that something was *very* wrong with her. She was slow to answer even mundane, easy questions;

couldn't write her own name and could not make simple decisions about anything. My mom, who had always been full of "piss and vinegar," lacked energy and conviction behind her words. The playful spark that had always been in her eyes became dull and she didn't seem like my mother. I was terribly worried. My dad was trying to be strong for all of us and was in denial that there was a problem.

The next day, I went to work and called my mom to check in on her during lunch time and see how she was doing. I was worried and had a bad feeling. When she answered the phone, her words became scrambled and she couldn't really speak to me. She was fumbling over her words and when she tried to say "I love you" it came out "ee jebbba jouuu." The tears that I had been holding back immediately began to roll down my cheeks and fall onto my Service Dress Blues uniform. Somehow my mom managed to understand me and handed the phone to my father and I immediately told him that he had to take her to the hospital ASAP. Something was very wrong with my mother! As I hung up, I knew that I needed to head home immediately and took off on the forty-mile drive.

When I called her, I had just finished PT in the field house and was sitting in the locker room getting ready to go back to work. The Navy and my command was very understanding of the ordeal and allowed me to leave immediately. We went to the emergency room and found out that she had had a mild-to-moderate stroke. It was so scary to see her like that—she couldn't even remember what city she was in! My mom ended up spending the next two weeks in the hospital until she was released to return home again.

One of the things that was most helpful to my dad and me was the help from our dear friends the Hulins—they invited us over for countless dinners on the fly and helped to feed my dad and me in the absence of my mom. More than the food, the warmth and support really helped us to push forward. On a Sunday after my mom's stroke, my dad and I had gone out on a bike ride in order to blow off some steam and relieve stress on the local bike trail. It was on the edge of being warm enough to ride—February in Chicago. There was some remaining snow on the trail and as we came around a bend, and my dad decided that it'd be fun to go ride right through a large snow mound. He didn't count on the snow mound being solid ice and ended up gracefully flying off his handlebars and landing as only an acrobat could.

Since I was just behind him, my only option was to quickly brake. Somehow, I had reached the age of twenty-six without having learned that you never slam on both the right and left brake of a bike—lest you fly off the handlebars. I landed with both arms instinctively (and very stupidly) outstretched and managed to fracture *both* of my elbows. As I tried to get back on my bike and ride the remaining three miles home, shooting pain went up my arms and I knew that I was in big trouble. There was no way, *no way,* that I could even hold onto the handlebars standing, let alone try to ride. Alas, we walked home together—me and my dad with two bikes along the windy trail.

You never realize how much you take certain things for granted until they're all messed up. For me, I quickly developed a new appreciation for how important the elbows are. Life's everyday mundane tasks became a major challenge to me: going to the bathroom became a group effort, as pulling down my pants required an arm bend; getting food into my mouth was a major task; pulling up the covers in the middle of the night was challenging; and holding the phone to my ear nearly impossible. I became quite the story at RTC Great Lakes as my peers and RDC School Classmates found my situation to be quite comical.

The good news is that I got over two weeks of convalescent leave in order to recuperate, which managed to overlap with my mom's return home after her stroke. The free kind of time off is always the best—too bad I had to bust my elbows in order to make that happen. Bilateral elbow fractures are not typically treated with casts, but only rest and time to recuperate and allow the bones to heal. Over time, mine began to heal and soon I was running again and even in the gym lifting weights.

March 2, 1999
 I find myself at this odd juncture in life—trying to find my way, be responsible and yet true to myself. Things are starting to turn around for me (Thank God) . . . my elbows are healing,

my mom is dramatically improving, and I'm starting to do things that I enjoy. And with that, I feel that I'll be able to meet people and make new friends.

Lately, I haven't exactly been very proactive which is OK. Maybe I needed this time alone to sift through things and find my own way. Be with my mom and help her get some of herself back and in doing so, get some of myself back.

Here I am caught somewhere in the middle. There's a big part of me that would like to live downtown "in the middle of it all." But then I'd need some severe loans. If I'm able to finish my goal of graduating/completing my MBA by the time I get out of the Navy, I plan on giving myself a <u>wonderful gift</u>—travel without any strings or rigid destinations. I figure that if I don't do it now, I won't do it for a very long time if ever. I'm single, young, and will be at a juncture in life where I feel it's almost the ideal time to do such a brazen thing. So, I catch myself daydreaming about it sometimes.

Finally Able to Hear My Own Voice

I managed to get into a rhythm of school, work, and working out. I increased my class-load and began taking two or three classes per semester and began training for marathons and triathlons. For the first time in my mom's life, she began working out with me as soon as she was physically able. It was unique for me to be able to share this side of me with her—she had always been in the stands cheering me on or driving me to all those practices, but *never* actively participated. Every evening that I didn't have school, we'd go to the gym together before dinner for an hour. I slowly nursed her back to the closest version of her old self that she could achieve. I took her back to the cemetery to re-teach her how to drive as she had done with me once. Cemeteries are a safe place for driving lessons—there's not much that you can hit and nobody alive that you can run into there! Being home was where I was supposed to be during that time of my life. It was healing for me and a necessity for my mom. I cherished those moments even though my life was running at an awfully fast pace.

I graduated from RDC school in the spring and formally took over the Drill Division (SHIP 4) from LT Liner. My role was one of the most visible in all of RTC Great Lakes and required me to run all of the Command's graduation ceremonies as well as be responsible for one thousand recruits and over fifty Recruit Drill Commanders (RDCs). My first official graduation was quite an event. I wore an ear-bud in my ear much like the Secret Service as I marched out in front of hundreds of people for the first time. I could hear my heart beating in my ears again—this time for a very different reason than when I went in to see Admiral Sinter to fight to stay in the Navy. My palms were sweaty and I was a little scared. I took a deep breath, scanned the crowd, and began to confidently speak.

"Good morning, ladies and gentlemen. On behalf of Rear Admiral Edward E. Hunter, I'd like to welcome you to Recruit Training Command Great Lakes Graduation Ceremony . . ."

I managed to find my rhythm and make it through that very first scary graduation ceremony with a forced smile on my face as I scanned the vast crowd all looking down at me. Although I'd come a long way from being afraid to hear my own voice during my first days on watch on the *Foster*, I was still a little (OK, a lot!) afraid of this many people hearing it at once. I lived by the idea of "faking it 'til I made it" and eventually, I wasn't faking it anymore. My smile wasn't forced and the words smoothly came to me. Oftentimes, the extraordinary becomes ordinary within a short period of time to the person experiencing it—it's all in what we get used to and what becomes our norm.

By the summer, I had many graduation ceremonies under my belt and became much more relaxed in my role. I enjoyed the performance piece and grew into hearing my own voice and developed my stage presence. It also helped that at least once a week I spoke to each and every new division of between 100 and 120 recruits for their on-boarding flag ceremony. My speech was typically about ten minutes long and urged them all to realize the amazing opportunity that lie within their grasp right then. At that very moment, they were a microcosm of America—individuals that had come from *all* different ethnic, social and academic backgrounds across the United States—and would become one division, one unit working toward one common goal. All of a sudden, I began to thrive in that position and looked forward to when I'd be able to work with my staff and with my recruits.

May 28, 1999

Sometimes I sit here and wonder if I'll quietly let the strong current of the military/navy carry me along through twenty years. The only way that I'd stay in this current is if I found something to be passionate about.

And then, there are moments where it all seems worth something—when I feel that I am touching people's lives for the better and maybe even making a difference. And it's on those days that I wonder if I could take command of a vessel or go to dive school. If could do this Navy thing for "reals." If it could be that for me (passionate thing that I yearn for). If I could be like Admiral Sinter who once said to me that he too had made a mistake early in his career. I honestly don't know what's going to happen. This whole life thing has an interesting way of spicing things up!

I sincerely think that someday I would like to begin public speaking/lecturing around the world. I feel so energized when I'm speaking about something that I love.

Right after all of the new ensigns graduated from their college programs around the country, we received about twenty at Great Lakes where they were on "Temporary Duty Assignment" (TAD) throughout the summer waiting for their various school dates. I got to take care of two young junior officers—Ensign Bibi Danko and LTJG Dave Sidewand. Bibi had just graduated from Cornell University and received her commission via their ROTC program. She was a bright young woman who always seemed to have a smile on her face and could be counted on to brighten anyone's mood even on the most stressful of days. Dave had already been to flight school and had suffered a life-changing airplane accident where he had sustained over four Gs and had to eject out the jet. The good news was that he lived to tell the tale, but the bad news was that he was still uncertain about if he would be allowed to continue flying. The summer he spent with me at Great Lakes was a transitional time for him as his future fate in the Navy was still being worked out. He was a welcome addition to my team—very conscientious, tough but fair, and willing to learn and tackle anything that I threw his way. We all became good friends during that unique time in our lives. I tried my best to share all of the information with them that I had wished someone would have shared with me five years beforehand.

My two young JOs shadowed me in everything that I did—we even worked out together on a regular basis. I let them take the reins of a couple of graduation ceremonies as well as the indoctrination of the new recruits. I watched them develop into their new roles and was filled with hope for them as they both embarked on their new careers in the Navy. They weren't cynical and were just filled with the excitement of someone about to embark on a major life adventure.

We had an eventful summer together and even put on a special graduation ceremony at the Daley Center in downtown Chicago in front of many dignitaries, including several members of the Kennedy family. The event was televised on Chicago's Channel 5 news and thankfully, I was completely comfortable by this time with hearing my own voice. Finally! My parents proudly stood in the crowd and I could see my mom's smiling eyes the whole time. Having such a visible role was challenging at first, but eventually became a good fit. I found myself in the unique place of finally being proud of what I was doing and felt that my job mattered to more than just me.

September 7, 1999

I write to you from RTC Great Lakes. A day after I've returned from my five-year reunion from the Naval Academy. This is a day I never thought would come—five years after graduation and the end of my "commitment" to the US Navy for my education from the Academy.

I found myself reflecting this past week on where my life is versus where I wanted it to be. I wondered what I would find when I headed back to my school on the bay—my roots in a sense and the place where I seemingly found myself.

Friday, September 3, 1999, was extremely hectic for me. I RACED out of the graduation review—more accurately snuck out the back door after I escorted the Admiral toward the reception. I sped home at over 80 mph and made it home at 1155. My taxi arrived twenty minutes later and somehow I made it onto my flight.

To my wonderful surprise, I sat next to a beautiful man— "Mr. Dreamy Eyes." We talked for about three hours about everything from our respective pasts to his current dreams and aspirations. He wants to go into the USMC and go to OCS and someday become an FBI agent. Obviously on the opposite end of my experiences—the very beginning of what I was finishing. It was fun to flirt and allow myself to be captivated by him. He carried my bag off the flight as far as he could before our paths diverged and we went our separate ways.

Sante picked me up from the airport—it was so great to see him and to catch up after all this time. Of all my classmates, only eight women showed up. I was kind of saddened by that. I had hoped more women would come. Of those that did show up, three were already out (of the Navy) and two more had already submitted their letters of resignation (me included).

Sometimes I am amazed at where I went to school . . . the opportunity that I had. The ghosts of USNA . . . It was different coming back. I was flooded with memories and the realization that I was now one of the "old ones." Part of that great school's history and would never again be a part of its body. Funny how in retrospect, those were some of the best days of my life. Perhaps that was a little extreme, but true, they still were pretty damn good!

And so it was, four years by the bay, lodged deep in my memory. Probably more a part of me than I'd ever like to admit. We all did the bar crawl up main street—did rounds at Riordan's, Griffin's, McGarvey's, Franny O's, and the Ram's Head. Even though I'm not much of a drinker, it was still fun to see everyone!

I stayed with the Williamses over the weekend. Ben, although he'll always be my "little full of it/ Prince Buttercup," is growing up. He's shaving now and his voice is changing—among other things. His face has changed completely. I can tell that he's getting into that self-conscious stage where you can't give him big hugs anymore.

Shortly after I returned from my five-year reunion, Bibi and Dave prepared to leave me and Great Lakes behind. I was very sad to see them go, but excited for them both to get out there in the fleet. Bibi and I went out to a final special celebration dinner at an exclusive Thai restaurant called Arun's—supposedly the best Thai food this side of Bangkok. It was quite a wonderful experience. The food was superb—oftentimes leaving us sighing in decadent delight. The whole meal cost us $75 *each* . . . quite pricey in 1999. We sort of approached it as a celebration/empowering dinner where we pondered such things as where she would be in five years' time when she's a Lieutenant like me and where I'd be . . . It was exciting for me to think about all of the possibilities. To actually verbalize some of my goals and dreams was exciting and poignant to me.

Something Serious to Reconsider

Despite this, I still resubmitted my letter of resignation on August 29, 1999, and hoped for the best outcome. This particular time, my letter was four pages long and detailed exactly why I was getting out of the Navy. I surmised that things would never get better in the Surface Navy if they didn't know exactly what was broken. It was with that thought that I decided to honestly lay out exactly why I needed to leave. I never imagined that something would happen to make me seriously question my letter of resignation and reconsider my strong positioning.

Every week, as the finale of Command School for new Commanding Officers, they would all spend some time at Great Lakes to see exactly what their new sailors went through before arriving to their ships and duty stations. The new COs' time at Great Lakes culminated with them all attending a Recruit Graduation Ceremony on Friday morning. This particular morning, the graduation ceremonies had become second nature to me and I enjoyed the role that

I got to play emceeing the event. I was confident, smooth, and had become quite polished by then.

At the end of the ceremony, as I was heading to the reception with the Admiral, I was surprised when my very first Executive Officer, CDR Read Brooke, pulled me aside. What he had to say completely blew my socks off! OK, maybe that's a little exaggeration, but I never expected him to say the things that he did to me. I always believed that everyone on that first ship hated me and felt that I was constantly fighting to prove myself.

I was completely taken aback when CDR Brooke approached me with a big smile on his face and said, "LT Sprtel, it's great to see you after all this time. I always marveled at what a great attitude you had and thought that you were a great addition to our wardroom. Do you have a few moments? I'd very much like to talk to you about something."

"Yes, of course, sir! It's great to see you after all this time," I said with a genuine smile on my face.

"I am taking command of a brand new Arleigh Burke destroyer and I can pick whichever department heads that I want. I want you to come and be my CHENG," said CDR Brooke confidently.

My head began spinning as I listened to him. Arleigh Burke destroyers were the crème de la crème during that time in the Navy—they were *hot shit*! I was in shock that:

1. He thought so highly of me that he would offer me this opportunity;
2. That I could maybe, just maybe, have a shot at a really successful career in the Navy despite my "gross lapse in judgment" years ago.

"Sir, I am honored that you would think of me, but I have already submitted my letter of resignation and am finishing up my MBA," I said with disbelief in my voice.

CDR Brooke was incredibly convincing when he said, "I think that you really need to reconsider. The Navy has many programs that I can make sure are available to you. You could finish up your

MBA as a full-time student *on the Navy* and then get the new $50,000 SWO bonus and be my department head on one of the Navy's new premier ships. Just promise me that you'll take this opportunity and me seriously. Think about it over the weekend and let's regroup on Monday."

I shook his hand with a strength and confidence that had been hard-earned and promised to email him my decision at the end of the weekend. I was completely shocked and had some very difficult thinking to do—it was contrary to the direction that my mind had been going for longer than I could remember. I was reeling from the encounter and felt very good about myself. It was nice to be wanted and hand-selected for such an important role. It meant the world to me after everything that I had been through.

> *September 29, 1999*
>
> *I've resubmitted my letter of resignation on the 28th of August. Still, it has yet to leave RTC Great Lakes in spite of the ten-day time limit. To me, I thought it would just be cut and dry. Ironically, it became the direct opposite when I ran into the OLD XO off the* Foster *who is on his way to become the new CO of the USS* Stump. *He's been trying to convince me to stay in. He's written some extremely eloquent emails to me stating that "I'd make a good Department Head" and that the "Navy needs a LT Sprtel in it" and that I "had the potential to be a Commanding Officer if I wanted to."*
>
> *It's really sad that I didn't hear any of this earlier. I'm not sure that it would have altered my course, but it might have. This was the first time that I really took an honest look at Department Head school and all that the Navy had to offer me and what my career path would look like. Congress recently approved the Surface Warfare bonus entitling SWOs in my year group to a $50k bonus paid out as $10k at department head school, $10k upon arrival at first ship and then each year after for a total of $50k. Not bad at all—plus a $40k stipend for grad school. I believe that I would have been able to convince the Captain and Admiral to allow me to take a year's sabbatical to finish my MBA and be a full-time student. I was enticed a bit*

and excited about it, realizing what an amazing opportunity it was. I went on a long run with my dad on the trail (he rode the bike and handed me water) and we talked about the opportunity from all different angles.

Finally, I arrived at the idea that "I am not for sale!" I realized that I would have been locked into three and a half more years and would have found myself at the halfway ten-year mark which would have made staying through retirement that much easier. I wonder, what's the point in climbing the mountain if you get to the top only to realize that you're on the wrong peak? Perhaps that's philosophical. But still, I feel strongly about it. Extremely strongly about it!

I long to be free. It excites me to ponder all of the possibilities to develop a loose framework for my travels after I get out of the Navy. I'd like to visit LT Aspire in Guam and then hop a flight to dive in the South Pacific or the Great Barrier Reef, go see Elise in Nepal and hike to Everest base-camp and then tromp around Europe.

I never imagined that I'd even remotely revisit my decision to get out of the Navy. CDR Brooke threw me a completely unexpected curveball as I reconsidered the decision from an honest, objective place. I was honored that he would think so highly of me to actually hand-select me to be his Chief Engineer and try so hard to retain me in the Navy. That alone made everything that I had gone through worth something and did wonders for my self-esteem. I felt that I had finally come full circle.

November 19, 1999

It's been a month and finally I have a chance to put my thoughts to paper. You guessed it, I'm on a plane to Costa Rica to celebrate Thanksgiving with my parents. A year ago, I was heading home from deployment and getting ready to move cross-country.

I've finally turned over Ship 4 at RTC Great Lakes—the drill division. To be honest, I really missed it when I finally did leave. I was proud of what I did there and really felt as though

I made a difference. I took pride speaking in front of the grad-
uation ceremonies and enjoyed my time with the recruits . . .
as sometimes difficult and political as it was. Here's something
interesting to ponder:

HAPPINESS = REALITY/EXPECTATION

I heard that in one of the many books on tape that I listen
to while driving the forty miles to work. I never thought of hap-
piness before in terms of a mathematical equation, but it does
make sense. I think it's rather a profound thought. I know that
I personally have LARGE dreams and hopes which equates to
very high expectations for myself. But if you don't keep adjusting
your goals to what is realistic and possible, then ultimately you
won't be happy. Still, I know me and I tend to have a high expec-
tation ratio—so, this will be interesting to come to grips with.

In the airport, we ran into the ASU Men's swim team.
They flew into Chicago to swim against Northwestern. I miss
those days and would like to someday train hard again. I still
dream about it and remember four-hour workouts—doubles and
weights and running. I think those moments helped to define me
and make me into who I am.

We had a wonderful vacation together and I was finally able to exhale after juggling my Navy job, training for a marathon, and MBA school. It almost felt odd to have free time to actually read a book, hearing the waves crash beside me. I had never been the kind of girl on vacation who "lays out" by the sea sleeping in the sun—unless I had worked so hard beforehand that I was exhausted. Typically, I am the type of vacationer who needs to relax afterwards! But this trip was a little different for me and for us.

While I still did all of my *normal* athletic adventures such as regular runs along the beach and roads surrounding our hotel complex; canopy tours swinging through the jungle trees in Jaco; surfing in Manuel Antonio and hiking up as far as possible to the Volcano Arenal, I actually allowed myself to sit still for once and enjoy my surroundings. To just breathe and be OK with just that was very different for me. Relaxing didn't mean that I was lazy! Maybe it just meant that I was on a long-overdue vacation with people that I love.

Arenal captivated me and was quite a sight. You could hear the rumbling of the beast within Mother Earth as she spat molten lava down her sides. We watched the lava pick up speed and grow on its flight down the volcano. It was exhilarating and made us feel small all at the same time—to realize the powerful force of nature and all the energy around us. Our hike was very brisk both up and down. My mom waited for us at the bottom and giggled as we stripped down to our undergarments and dove into the mountain lake below to cool off. I liked the fact that I could share that experience with my father and that we had shared so many things together through the years.

On one particular morning, I went for a rather long, hot run along the road. My dad accompanied me on the bike as he often had done back at home. We always managed to have great conversations during these long runs of mine, but this one had a rather funny twist. I learned a big lesson about the risks involved in putting your training bikini through the washing machine—my mom had put my training bikini in the wash prior to our trip. About a mile into our run/ride, after I began to sweat from the heat and humidity, my dad started audibly laughing at me and the drivers in all the cars that passed by kind of looked at me funny. Apparently, the soap never ended up rinsing out of my suit and my bum was exuding many white, foamy bubbles. Once I figured it out, I tried to wipe the bubbles away, but they kept reappearing and regenerating—it almost looked like a Santa Claus beard coming out my rear end. I'll never run my suits through the wash again.

Although we only spent half a day at the white sandy beaches of Manuel Antonio, I loved every moment of my time there. The landscape was so rugged and it reminded me of how Laguna Beach must have appeared a hundred years ago with the rugged cliffs and artist colony. We met some very interesting people—many of them seemed as though they were trying to find themselves somewhere along the windy roads of Costa Rica. Almost as if this place whispers the answers to them somehow. But who really knows if they'll find what they're looking for along the sandy beaches or hidden within the rain forests along the twisty roads? Are they running from themselves or toward something else? Did they really need to go anywhere to look within?

At the end of the day, we all have to run our lives, not let our lives run us!

Those were the thoughts that filled my mind as I headed back to my own reality of taking over my new job at Great Lakes, MBA school, and training for my first marathon.

I felt empowered and energized after that trip and began working hard to focus more on myself and achieving my goals. After over a year of being alone (not dating anyone), I had finally decided that I was ready to get back out there and joined a couple of dating sites—Match.com and Matchmaker.com. A year of celibacy was a good exercise, but also one that I was ready to end. Touch is good.

As I began to do my Christmas shopping that year in early December, I meandered through the outdoor walking mall at Oak Brook on a rare day that I had the time to just stop and look at whatever pleased me. I found myself at an art gallery and was immediately drawn to a blown glass sculpture of two fish kissing. The sculpture was in the shape of a crystal ball and represented, to me, all that I hoped to find someday. I really wanted to buy the sculpture for myself, but couldn't justify spending $550 on it when I didn't really have a special place to put it and didn't need it (not to mention I was an MBA student without much disposable income). That didn't change the fact that I wanted it and *almost* could have justified it as an investment in my dreams. The thought alone—even allowing myself to contemplate such a thing—seemed incredibly decadent to me. I visited *my fish* often and even got to know the sales lady at the gallery. On my second or third visit, she gave me a $50-off coupon in the event that I decided to indulge myself. But as I stopped to eat lunch that day, I left the coupon inside the restaurant and took it as a sign that I wasn't meant to have the kissing fish globe.

About the same time, I began talking to an older man who was around forty, Tobias, from the Matchmaker site. He and I seemed to connect well intellectually and spent many hours on the phone talking the first night before our upcoming date. We were involved in a discussion about how sometimes things happen for a reason and I described the kissing fish globe that I had been wrestling with purchasing. I wistfully told him that I had received my sign that I wasn't meant to have it by losing the generous coupon that the nice lady had given me.

The next day, I anticipated meeting him and couldn't wait to see if there was any chemistry between us in real life as there had been on the phone. I met him at his place early that Sunday evening and we proceeded to head out to dinner at a nice steak restaurant in Oak Brook. It was apparent that he was a regular since the wait staff knew him by name and had a special table reserved for us. I couldn't help but wonder if there had been a revolving door of women seated at that table and wondered how I measured up. The banter from our phone conversation continued through our dinner and I was pleasantly surprised. After dinner, we wove through all the local streets and admired the Christmas light displays. It was easy to be with him and I enjoyed his company—what I knew of it.

We ended up back at his place. As soon as we got inside the doorway, he grabbed me by the hand and led me upstairs. He said, "Don't worry, I'm not taking you up to my bedroom or anything," and he led me to his office. He bent down into his closet and handed me a peach colored box. I was completely shocked by this insanely thoughtful gesture and still had no idea what could be in the box.

When I opened the box and peeled back the delicate tissue paper, I found *my fish sculpture* staring up at me. I was completely speechless and totally blown away by his amazing gesture of warmth and . . . abandon for conventions. I couldn't believe that he allowed himself to chase his emotions and trust them already to do such a thing—find the gallery and sales lady that I had told him of the night before and actually purchase this decadent, beautiful thing for me. No one had ever done anything like that for me before. Ever.

When I finally looked up, I noticed him smiling at me and he said, "It wasn't that you weren't meant to have it. You just weren't meant to buy it."

I was completely overwhelmed by him. It would have been very easy to end my celibacy right then and there. But rationality won out and we waited a little longer.

Tobias was doing a great job of sweeping me off my feet and gave me the royal treatment. We ate at the best restaurants regularly—he never cooked his own meals, worked out at the exclusive East Bank Club, and loosely began to make plans. Tobias was an Italian Internet entrepreneur and had been the CIO of a startup that IPO'd and had the aspiration for even greater endeavors. He had impeccable taste in everything from his clothes to his furniture and Lexus vehicle—quite honestly, Tobias liked and needed the best of everything. I had never been pampered before or treated so well, but I also couldn't shake the feeling that he wasn't real in the most important way that mattered to me. Beneath the glittery designer labels, I feared that he didn't have the substance to completely get me.

We shared the holidays together and painted some nice thought pictures filled with potential and warm feelings. We were like a hot flame that danced and sparked through the darkness for a few moments before burning out. But what a welcome sight that flame was for the short time that I had it—especially after my year of celibacy. It was nice to be pampered and loved for a little while. I left for Steamboat Springs, Colorado, the day after Christmas to meet the Williamses for a week of skiing and snowmobiling to bring in the new millennium together.

December 31, 1999

The eve of the millennium! We've been watching as the world slowly steps into the New Year—this monumental year. The entire world is celebrating—from Egypt and Japan and Korea to Africa, Antarctica and London. The world has yet to rotate enough for the United States to celebrate.

Yesterday, we went snowmobiling on (literally) the Continental Divide for about four hours. It was the first time that I'd ever been snowmobiling. The snow glitters like diamonds as the sun hits it. It's gorgeous! There were several places that I would have liked to stop and take some pictures. It was absolutely spectacular. We ate lunch at the foot of "Rabbit Ears." Ben accidentally hit a tree once—oops. He's growing so nicely—really into a fine young man and I am so proud of him and happy that I get to be a small part of it.

After snowmobiling, we went to the Strawberry Natural Hot Springs. Just getting there was an adventure as we all packed into my new friend Travis's truck and slipped through the windy roads. It was freezing outside when we took our clothes off. Imagine stepping on ice and snow in your bare feet, but once you hit the water all you can feel is needles—literally. The water was over 110 degrees and steam rose up from it. Many people went naked. The best part was the sky . . . with thousands of bright stars on such a dark, serene canvas.

God, I remember imagining what I'd be doing in this monumental year. I would look up to the stars and wonder where I would be in my life. I always imagined that I'd be out of the Navy by now, but I am not. Even though I'm still "in," I like who I am and where I am in my life. I can finally say that I am good.

I always enjoy my time with the Williamses and this was no exception—they are truly part of the family that I choose. We spent our remaining days skiing the champagne powder runs at Steamboat together. Just before we took off for the New Year's event, we watched the Steamboat ski team come down the mountain with lit sparklers and firecrackers above them—it was quite a sight. We went to a restaurant called the Ore House to bring in the millennium and danced through the night. I danced with an older man named Peter a little—we swing danced and he was very good. He gave me a wonderful compliment and told me that with the millennium, I should really do something with my dancing. He said that he could tell that it was in my blood and that he had danced with many women before, but that I had *it*. He made me feel like a million bucks that evening as I finally began to feel as though I were coming into my own. I clung to Nora, Clay, and Ben as the room filled with excitement and everyone began the countdown to 2000.

"10 . . . 9 . . . 8 . . . 7 . . . 6 . . . 5 . . . 4 . . . 3 . . . 2 . . . 1 . . ."

Balloons dropped from the ceiling and all of the couples around me embraced and kissed in the New Year. I took it all in and knew that I was closer than I'd ever been to "becoming her."

When I returned from Steamboat Springs, I was very focused on becoming the best version of myself that I could. I began training for a marathon and Mrs. T's Triathlon, ramped up my course load so that I could get as close to graduation as possible by the time I got out of the Navy, and made some good friends through my MBA program. I began to count down the days until my terminal leave and finally was able to embrace where I was.

My "Pot" Gets Stirred

Spence and I somehow found ourselves back in touch with each other. It had been over three years since our debacle. I received a contemplative message from him in mid-late February and it really opened up a whole can of worms for me—feelings that I had put somewhere else and hidden for a very long time. He was supposed to get out of the Navy in a couple of months and wasn't exactly sure about what he wanted to do.

After we broke up, I sensed that he was trying to make a point by saying that he really didn't need much to be happy in life. He liked to say that he was a simple man who didn't need to make a lot of money or have a prestigious job to be happy (I think making the point that that's who he is—unlike me with the big lofty dreams and goals). His email concluded with asking me, "What's going on in the life of the woman who wants everything?"

He caught me at just the right contemplative moment. I practically verbally puked all over my response and unleashed everything that I had held onto for all that time. And even stirred the pot myself some by asking him if he'd like to see me again . . .

I wondered how we both had evolved and changed and grown these past three years and yet how similar we both still were. I didn't, however, expect the response that I got from him.

He immediately responded with, "What the hell?! Let's do this. And . . . Oh, by the way, I'll be in Santa Barbara in two weeks—you take care of getting yourself there and I'll take care of the rest."

I had wondered what it would feel like to get that response from him after all this time. His closing line was a tongue-in-cheek little nudge that said, "What do you think of that, Miss Spontaneous?"

I would have *loved* to be able to meet him there and then, but there were two big things holding me back: (1) I had a major accounting exam the Monday after I would return home (who am I kidding that I would study at all that weekend!); (2) I knew people on his ship and couldn't afford the heartburn of running into someone I knew while they were in-port. Most importantly, I didn't want to have any distractions when I did finally see him again. I didn't want to feel guilty about not studying enough for my exams or worried about running into anyone in the Navy. I wanted to be able to completely feel that excitement of getting on the plane to see a man that I really loved once and wondering what was still there. I wanted to be excited about exploring the depth of what remained and who we both had become and if there was still room for us to be something together. It had been three years since I fell completely in love and had that same heart broken professionally and financially. Ironically, it was never him as a person that I didn't love or trust—it was all the peripherals and everything that came along with that risk that I thought was worth taking. I still think it was worth it, but God, it was a very difficult, difficult time in my life. It was with that in my mind that I had to put reconnecting with Spence on the back burner.

Unexpected Opportunity

With regards to college, this time around I attacked my courses with a fervor and focus that I lacked while I was at the Academy. Instead of just regurgitating the information, I tried hard to internalize it all and really learn it because I had big plans and expected to need it. I also think that paying for every single class myself (some months, I had to write a check for $10,000 to pay for all of my classes—ugh) made a difference in my appreciation and respect for the process. During that semester, I took a class with an inspirational young entrepreneurship instructor named Dr. Jill Kickul. I looked forward to each of her classes and always walked out to my car after each session motivated to someday become an entrepreneur and have my own success story.

Apparently, Dr. Kickul saw something in me as well and approached me after class one evening just before our final and asked me if I'd be interested in becoming her graduate assistant starting that summer for the upcoming year? I had no idea how in the world I'd juggle it all—my day job as a Navy Lieutenant, practically a full time MBA student, athlete training for a marathon and Olympic distance triathlon—but immediately knew that if there was a way to make it happen, I would find it. This was a *huge* opportunity for me and I was practically giddy with excitement over the prospect. One of the best fringe benefits of becoming a graduate assistant was that you were almost considered part of DePaul's faculty and all classes were free and course books dramatically reduced in price.

I believe that sometimes, opportunity unexpectedly knocks on your door and you had better take notice.

This was certainly a special knock on my door!

I was set to work for Dr. Jill Kickul and Dr. Lisa Gundry in the Business School at DePaul University—both were very well respected in the Entrepreneurship Program and the Business School at large. Jill had been a collegiate runner and was a very accomplished, lean, white-blonde firecracker who always wore signature red lipstick (except during her regular twenty-plus mile runs). She had more energy than virtually anyone that I had ever met and was a publishing machine. Jill was eager to gain tenure at DePaul and wanted to make her mark in the entrepreneurship field—and was *not* limited to the Chicago market. She was a young, inspirational leader and we all hoped to someday be just like her. Lisa rounded out the spectrum by being an award-winning author of several management strategy books, a tenured professor, and wife/mother at the same time. The idea was that two of them would share me.

Even though I had to be very methodical with my time since there wasn't much of it, I still had things that I wanted to accomplish for myself before getting out of the Navy in November:

- Run a marathon
- Do Mrs. T's triathlon
- Fifteen pull-ups
- Have fifteen classes finished by the time I get out and be on track to graduate in June 2001

- Take full advantage of and get as much as possible out of work with Dr. Jill Kickul and Dr. Lisa Gundry
- Travel when I get out of the Navy
- Break six minutes in my last 500m free on my last PRT
- Have a healthy relationship that helps to enrich not only MY life, but his also
  - Be patient with that and careful too while still feeding it and allowing it to grow

I managed to get all of my long runs in on the weekends and trained during the week while at work. I put in over forty miles a week on the road and was on track to check off at least one thing on my list!

MBA School – Graduate Assistant Position

I dug into my new job as Jill and Lisa's graduate assistant and was hungry to make a good impression. I wanted to "hit the deck-plates running" with them both and really wanted to get as much as possible out of the experience. I logged many miles with Jill on the road (training for marathons *and* working at the same time) while we brainstormed our papers and the local entrepreneurship scene that seemed to be exploding. I completed my first twenty-two-mile run with Jill on a very hot and sticky Chicago summer morning. Unfortunately, I didn't eat or hydrate enough and got to experience first-hand exactly what a bonk feels like. As I sat on the floor of her sky-high Chicago condo overlooking Lake Michigan, I could barely move. She laughed at me for the newbie marathoner that I was and helped me to recover. I didn't make that mistake again and was secretly proud of myself for being able to keep up with her and her pace—even if I had bonked.

DePaul had a unique business incubator program where local entrepreneurs could get their ideas off the ground for the first year or two with support from the faculty and student body to help grow their businesses. This was the end of the '90s dot-com boom (and just before the bust) and the entire business landscape was changing right in front of our eyes—it was an exciting time to be in MBA school and especially in the e-business and entrepreneurship program. That was the very reason that I chose DePaul University for my MBA. Businesses straddled the line between the old brick-and-mortar model versus the new dot-com reality. Everyone was jockeying for a position in the space and people began squatting on domain names just to turn around and sell them for major profits. Hundreds of millions of dollars were made (and then lost almost as quickly) during those years as dot-com valuations soared to unheard-of levels until eventually falling back down toward a more business-fundamental-backed reality.

I particularly enjoyed working with Jill's undergraduate students as we brought in Chicago-based companies for them to not only study, but also work on live case studies with the founders and provide them with strategic marketing or business plans. I was able to use my connections to bring in three of the six companies the students worked with and was very proud to watch the students grow from the experience and the companies benefit from the free advice. I enjoyed working with the students as it felt like an extension of what I was doing at Great Lakes with the recruits that I also worked with since they were all around the same age.

I spent my time with Lisa helping her with the book she was in the process of finishing: *Breakthrough Teams for Breakneck Times: Unlocking the Genius of Creative Collaboration*. I came into the project mid-stream and was able to bring in three keynote individuals for her to highlight in the book—I found them, interviewed them, and wrote up their particular chapters. I finally arrived at a place where I recognized and valued my strength of being able to connect the dots and make things happen. Oftentimes, by simply not being afraid to ask for what I wanted. Specifically, I brought in an Olympic gold medalist (who happened to be married to a prominent Illinois swimmer whom I had known years beforehand), Admiral Wilson (my old mentor from the Naval Academy who now happened to be CEO of a Washington DC company), and an inspirational female founder/CEO of a multimillion-dollar scrap metal company in Chicago (who at her own bottom, after a difficult divorce, lived the American Dream and began her business on a shoestring and grew it to its current impressive level).

I also had the opportunity to design the new logo for the Leo J. Ryan Center for Creativity and Innovation and enjoyed the creative process immensely. I felt a source of pride when the new swag (mugs, cups, and other memorabilia) came out with the logo printed front and center. Because most of my other tasks had been so tactical, I embraced the opportunity to be artistically creative in a business capacity.

I finally got into the physical shape that had eluded me while I was onboard the ships. By mid-summer, I was very lean and closing in on the Chicago Marathon and Mrs. T's Triathlon. I ran my last PT test in a blistering (for me) 9:20 for the mile and a half. Frustrated with men and deciding to just focus on me for a bit, I had dropped the Matchmaker.com dating site and was about to drop Match.com when I received a tentative email out of the blue from an interesting man. The email was short, understated, and direct. He piqued my interest and I decided to play along.

That email was the last email on Match that I would end up answering—for a *very* long time.

Summer was coming to an end and I was well into the groove of juggling my full-time job running the physical fitness program at Great Lakes, being an MBA student, working for two professors on the side, and training for a marathon and the upcoming Mrs. T's Triathlon. I barely had a spare moment to carve out, but it's amazing what one can do when properly motivated.

On August 22, I pulled the trigger on the exotic trip I began loosely planning while on deployment and bought an "around the world" ticket from Air Treks where I would go to: Bangkok, Bali, Australia, New Zealand, and Fiji for a forty-day whirlwind trip to kick off the day I got out of the Navy, November 22, 2000. One of my new friends and neighbors, Jeanine, decided to join me and together we began to plan this once-in-a-lifetime adventure.

I was excited that afternoon as I left work early (this was one of the only evenings that I didn't have school, work, or MBA obligations) and headed to the upscale Oak Brook Mall to grab a present for a friend and do a little celebrating for myself too—all sandwiched into the time I had before going on a first date with Mr. Understated Engineer (MUE). I was looking forward to

meeting him and had no idea what to expect. We were scheduled
to meet at the Melting Pot restaurant around 6:30 or 7:00 p.m. I
was happy to be making tangible decisions to start living my own
personal legend. I meandered into some of the upscale shops and
even indulged in a decadent silk handkerchief skirt from Harold's
that felt like it materialized out of one of my classy dreams for the
future. I had started to invest in me because I finally felt that I was
worth it—and it felt good.

I met MUE at the Melting Pot and found him to be attractive
and engaging—not what I perceived the typical engineer to be. We
played Jenga as we waited for our table. I began to peel back the
onion of MUE and was pleasantly surprised to discover how much
more he was than what surfaced at first glance of his emails. We
took our time through the dinner and swapped fun stories of our
respective travels around the world—I was amazed by some of his
experiences at Los Alamos and his trek up Mt. Fuji in Japan. We lost
ourselves in conversation and ended up closing the restaurant—the
waitstaff tactfully tried to get us to leave our table.

MUE walked me to my car and looked at me expectantly. I
extended my right hand out and gave him my very firm handshake
and told him how much I enjoyed our time. He looked at me a little
confused and pulled me into a tight hug—the kind of hug meant
to be a taste of what our bodies might feel like together. He wanted
to kiss me that evening and I knew it. I wanted to kiss him too, but
also wanted this to be different. I didn't want to false start anymore.
My rationale was that *if he wanted to kiss me that night, he'd really want to
kiss me the next time.* I pulled out of the hug and smiled up at him as
I moved my long hair away from my right eye, spun on my heel, and
confidently headed toward my car.

I drove home with a warm smile on my face as I reflected on the
genuinely nice time that we had had. I was happy . . . about the way
things turned out that day—purchased my big plane tickets for the
upcoming trip, invested in myself with the decadent skirt, and had
an unexpectedly pleasant date. As soon as I made my way home and
padded into my room, my mom slipped into bed with me (like old
times) and wanted to hear all about my date. My normal reaction
would have been to call MUE that evening as I was heading to bed

to tell him that I was thinking about him and the nice evening that we had shared together—the odd thing was that he *knew* it too. But, I held back and instead talked to my mom about all of my thoughts and hopes. I allowed myself to go to bed without stirring the pot further and instead trusted this story to play out on its own instead of nudging it along.

It felt good, really good to not only get myself back completely, but to be on the cusp of so many great things in my life. I went to bed that evening at peace and filled with lots of potential.